Creating Digital Exhibits for Cultural Institutions

Creating Digital Exhibits for Cultural Institutions will show you how to create digital exhibits and experiences for your users that will be informative, accessible, and engaging.

Illustrated with real-world examples of digital exhibits from a range of GLAMs, the book addresses the many analytical aspects and practical considerations involved in the creation of such exhibits. It will support you as you go about analyzing content to find hidden themes, applying principles from the museum exhibit literature, placing your content within internal and external information ecosystems, selecting exhibit software, and finding ways to recognize and use your own creativity. Demonstrating that an exhibit provides a useful and creative connecting point where your content, your organization, and your audience can meet, the book also illustrates how such exhibits can provide a way to revisit difficult and painful material in a way that includes frank and enlightened analyses racism, colonialism, sexism, class, and LGBTQI+ issues.

Creating Digital Exhibits for Cultural Institutions is an essential resource for librarians, archivists, and other cultural heritage professionals who want to promote their institution's digital content to the widest possible audience. Academics and students working in the fields of library and information science, museum studies, and digital humanities will also find much to interest them within the pages of this book.

Emily Marsh is Digital Projects Librarian at the National Agricultural Library (USDA). She holds an MLS and doctorate in Library Science and has been trained in principles of user needs assessment, interface design, information architecture principles, and qualitative research methods. She has created multiple digital exhibits and assorted projects in the agricultural digital humanities including those focused on the poet Robert Frost, the agricultural scientist George Washington Carver, the USDA Bureau of Home Economics, and the Local Food movement, among others.

Creating Digital Exhibits for Cultural Institutions

A Guide

Emily Marsh

Routledge
Taylor & Francis Group
LONDON AND NEW YORK

Cover image: Emily Marsh

First published 2023
by Routledge
4 Park Square, Milton Park, Abingdon, Oxon OX14 4RN

and by Routledge
605 Third Avenue, New York, NY 10158

Routledge is an imprint of the Taylor & Francis Group, an informa business

British Library Cataloguing-in-Publication Data
A catalogue record for this book is available from the British Library

Library of Congress Cataloging-in-Publication Data
Names: Marsh, Emily E., author.
Title: Creating digital exhibits for cultural institutions : a practical guide / Emily Marsh.
Description: Abingdon, Oxon ; New York, NY : Routledge, 2023. | Includes bibliographical references and index.
Identifiers: LCCN 2022059059 (print) | LCCN 2022059060 (ebook) | ISBN 9781032294186 (hbk) | ISBN 9781032294162 (pbk) | ISBN 9781003301493 (ebk)
Subjects: LCSH: Cultural property—Digitization. | Digital humanities. | Museum exhibits—Technological innovations. | Museums—Information technology. | Library materials—Digitization. | Library exhibits—Technological innovations. | Libraries—Information technology.
Classification: LCC CC135 .M326 2023 (print) | LCC CC135 (ebook) | DDC 363.690285—dc23/eng/20221220
LC record available at https://lccn.loc.gov/2022059059
LC ebook record available at https://lccn.loc.gov/2022059060

ISBN: 978-1-032-29418-6 (hbk)
ISBN: 978-1-032-29416-2 (pbk)
ISBN: 978-1-003-30149-3 (ebk)

DOI: 10.4324/9781003301493

Typeset in Times New Roman
by Apex CoVantage, LLC

Contents

Figures

Acknowledgments

I need to thank Heidi Lowther of Routledge first, because this work would not exist if she had not seen its potential from my proposal. Her unfailing enthusiasm and support came at a time when I badly needed both, so thank you so much, Heidi. I would like to thank the anonymous reviewers of my proposal. You helped me to make this a better book and I am indebted to you. I am continually surprised by all the creative people who contribute their work to the cultural heritage community and make it available for all of us to use. Thank you.

I also need to thank Scott Hanscom for seeing me and my work clearly and for supporting me when few others did. One of the other supports came from the one and only Vernon Chapman who told me to "find something you love and do it". I thank Sarah Diehl, who asked important questions and gave me room to find myself. Virginia F. Smith, Ph.D., Professor of Chemistry, United States Naval Academy, also provided welcome recognition of and cheerful support for the Robert Frost exhibit. Marilyn Domas White, Ph.D., Professor Emerita of the University of Maryland's iSchool, was and is a source of continual inspiration. Thank you, Betsy Clinton for your friendship. My mother and her sister are not here to read this, but both Pauline and Elizabeth would approve, I think.

This book is dedicated to my wife, Vanessa and our son, Tucker. I could not do anything without you. Both of you believe in me and love me, even when I am convinced that I deserve neither. Thank you for everything. I love you both.

Emily
Web: https://emily-marsh.com/
Email: emily@emily-marsh.com
Twitter: @EmilyMarshPhD

Disclaimer

This book was written by the author in her personal capacity. The views and opinions expressed in this book are the author's own and do not reflect those of the US Department of Agriculture or the US Government.

1 Introduction and Overview

There was a time not that long ago when it might have been challenging for a small cultural heritage organization to demonstrate the need for digital exhibits. The evaluative metrics for many organizations traditionally center physical visits and the activities of physical visitors, with websites and social media being seen as mainly as drivers for those efforts (Northern Ireland Assembly Research and Information Service, 2018). Then COVID-19 and the Great Shutdown of 2020 came along and 90% of GLAMs (galleries, libraries, archives, and museums) worldwide were closed to physical visitors (UNESCO, 2020). Suddenly most everyone in the GLAM community understood why it might be useful to have resources that could be accessed remotely, even if some still wrestled with the digital exhibit concept itself.

The *Getty Art & Architecture Thesaurus* defines exhibitions as "organized, usually named, temporary public displays of works of art, crafts, natural history, science, or other items of cultural interest". Online exhibitions are defined as "exhibitions that are presented online rather than in physical galleries" (Getty Research Institute, 2017). While these definitions are factually correct, they do not give a sense of the potential richness of these projects or offer much assistance to the novice who is tasked with creating an online exhibit for the unnamed "other items of cultural interest" that need interpretation and context for the average user to understand and appreciate.

For this book, a digital exhibit is defined as a web-based exhibit of documents, images, video, and/or audio files, and other materials that have been selected with some rhetorical purpose in mind. This purpose is fulfilled through explanatory and interpretive text, as well as object arrangement, presentation, and organization that is consciously formed by the exhibit creator. The digital exhibit provides a flexible, customizable platform that can serve a variety of organizational and communicative purposes. Organizational goals can include revealing collection contents and demonstrating their cultural significance and relevance to present-day concerns. Goals that are more communicative and user-focused include contextualizing and explaining the significance of a given object or collection of objects in a way that is understandable, accessible, and enjoyable for your targeted audiences. An exhibit provides an engaging and creative connecting point where your content, your organization, and your audience can meet.

DOI:10.4324/9781003301493-1

Given this framework, the value of exhibits for the cultural heritage community seems self-evident, but there is still a fair amount of skepticism among some practitioners. The GLAM exhibit's struggle for legitimacy has not been confined to its nature as physical or digital. Back in the early Internet year of 1993, Bowen and Roberts described the state of library literature as reflecting

> widely held views of [physical] exhibits that equate them with "merely a decorator's task", little more than "displays to dress up the library or add a little color", "an added burden and a necessary evil" that the staff approaches "grudgingly".
>
> (p. 407)

As an update, Lacher-Feldman reports that some archives and special collections library staff describe exhibit work as an "absolute joy" while for others, it is something that "engenders dread, fear, uncertainty, and anxiety" (2013, p. 1). An even more recent review of the library literature found that exhibits are often simply ignored as objects deserving of serious attention or analysis (Fouracre, 2015). I can affirm that these attitudes sometimes carry over into today's library leadership and staff. I would argue that the degree to which an exhibit can be seen as a legitimate work product is a function of what the Knight Foundation describes as an organization's level of "digital readiness and innovation" (2020). Libraries and museums falling into the "untapped" or "emergent" category of readiness and innovation as defined by Knight are more likely to dismiss these kinds of projects as trivial. When organizations fail to see the value of exhibits, they run a risk of missing a relatively low-cost, low-investment opportunity to showcase their collections, employ the creativity and expertise of their staffs, and engage their user communities.

Long before the COVID-19 pandemic, GLAMs (galleries, gardens, libraries, archives, and museums) of all kinds and sizes were already working hard to digitize their holdings. Literally, billions of digital pages and images have been created and cataloged by galleries, libraries, archives, and museums not only for preservation considerations (newspapers crumble; book pages yellow; photographs crack) but also for increased access for users. Physical accessibility to physical collections has long been a barrier for many users for a variety of non-pandemic reasons. Locating materials of interest and then getting the money, time, and physical ability to travel to a remote physical location to view them present barriers that have separated many students, scholars, and hobbyists from our materials. Digital access removes many of those barriers and opens our collections to anyone who can access the web.

In addition to adding new channels for access, how a user can get materials, come new efforts to broaden the subjects of access, what materials we digitize for our users. Now, new initiatives such as the Council on Library and Information Resources' Digitizing Hidden Special Collections and Archives emphasize the need for digitizing "materials that deepen public understanding of the histories of people of color and other communities and populations whose work, experiences, and perspectives have been insufficiently recognized or unattended" (n.d.). Likewise, the University of Oxford contends,

> UK museums have pledged to continue to provide a safe, inclusive, and egalitarian space for all members of the communities they serve. . . . The objects in museum collections, interpreted by skilled staff and volunteers from all walks of life, help people make sense of an increasingly confusing world, providing joy and inspiration as well as a platform for debate. Museums have a key part to play in promoting a tolerant and diverse society and UK museums are committed to continuing this vital role.
>
> (Gardens, Libraries and Museums of the University of Oxford, n.d.)

The United States, United Kingdom, and European Union have become home to many large digital platforms that promise more cultural content than any one person could consume in a lifetime. Smaller institutions of all kinds have become creators and stewards of digital content that they often contribute to large systems such as Europeana, HathiTrust, the Digital Public Library of America (DPLA), or the Internet Archive. In 2016, Europeana reported having 3,703 data partners. HathiTrust currently has 250 large library partners. DPLA has 34 service hubs and 15 content hubs providing access to almost 45 million images, texts, videos, and sounds from across the United States. Internet Archive contains 588 billion archived web pages, 28 million books, 14 million audio recordings, six million videos, and three and a half million images.

These large repositories perform a valuable service in providing a relatively low-cost, stable, and accessible platform for digital content. But the decision to take advantage of these services can sometimes result in becoming overlooked within a vast ocean of material in these massive systems. If your collection is simply one of thousands, how can you stand apart and reveal the importance and value of your content: The very reasons that you decided to digitize it in the first place? This question is equally true if you work in a small library, museum, or other cultural heritage organization and find yourself in charge of a collection of digitized materials such as postcards, academic yearbooks, newspapers, photographs, or oral histories (Caro, 2016; Monson, 2017).

While many organizations have accepted the need to digitize their collections, they sometimes fail to use the resulting materials themselves. But, as argued by the Consortium of Academic and Research Libraries in Illinois (CARLI),

> [P]lanning for digital collections should include thinking about their use and long-term sustainability in addition to production considerations. Simply creating and providing access to the collections is not enough, as users may not serendipitously stumble across them on the library website or by other means. . . . Digital exhibits offer the ability to promote and curate larger amounts of materials and expand the reach of existing physical exhibits.
>
> (2020)

The recent trend toward including visitor engagement measures in evaluations of cultural heritage organizational effectiveness will necessarily include digital projects, especially given the conclusion of Veirum and Christensen's study of museum use from over a decade ago, "If it's not on the Net it doesn't exist" (2011). The empirical truth of that observation was sadly, and inadvertently, demonstrated by the effects of the COVID-19 pandemic on GLAM institutions, particularly those that are small and/or underfunded (Giannini & Bowen, 2022; Pappa & Makropoulos, 2021).

If you want to go deeper and reveal the oftentimes hidden significance of digital objects that might seem trivial or mundane at first glance, then a bigger effort that goes beyond providing mere access is needed. So, you could perhaps feature an image on your organization's website home page or send a tweet or post on Instagram about your newest scanned document. But this is simply a start—more effort is required to serve your content to your users in a meaningful, impactful way. One excellent tool to accomplish such a task is the digital exhibit.

I have been creating digital exhibits for the US Department of Agriculture's (USDA's) National Agricultural Library (NAL) for almost a decade. These exhibits center the many documents produced by USDA over the last century and subsequently digitized by NAL. The NAL repository in the Internet Archive currently contains over 200,000 documents. Many of these documents center agricultural practices of the past and can venture into (now) obscure topics, as illustrated by these titles: "*Shipping Eggs by Parcel Post*, *The Farm Lease Contract*, *The Road Drag and How It Is Used*, and *Coat Making at Home*. When discussing exhibits with others, I have found it difficult at times to explain exactly what they are, both inside and outside the library. When I used to describe my work, I would often see furrowed brows and confused half-smiles as people tried to understand what an exhibit that centered digital documents and was created by a library might be. My conception of exhibits tracks with Miriam Posner's description of many digital humanities (DH) projects. They "do not meet any particular demonstrated need—they are done to find an interesting answer to an interesting question. This can be very difficult to explain to one's supervisors in the library" (2013). The (possibly interesting) questions my exhibits are designed to answer include:

- What is the meaning and ultimate value of historical US Government documents on agriculture?
- What can these documents tell us about past practices in agriculture, the lives of their authors, the nature of American rural life, and the overt and implicit rhetorical messages of the USDA?
- How do these documents sit within a larger context of associated texts, images, and videos?
- What do these documents tell us about how agricultural topics were conceived at various times in the past and present?
- How do these documents illustrate the status of Black, Indigenous, Asian, and Latino people in the United States over time?

It is possible that I am incorrect in thinking that users of libraries and other cultural organizations would be interested in wrestling with these questions within the confines of an exhibit. Perhaps the work required to build an exhibit is a distraction from other, possibly more necessary staff tasks such as building collections and supporting information services. But I would counter those arguments with several observations, albeit ones grounded in personal experience. First, I created an analytic method and digital workflow that allowed one person to complete an exhibit in approximately four months. Second, I completed work duties around collections and reference services while simultaneously creating multiple exhibits. Third, I contend that it is not enough to digitize your organization's materials: You need to put at least some of them to use to demonstrate the inherent value of your collections and the added value that digitization provides if nothing else.

This book aims to help you provide creative access to digital content for your audience, within the context of the exhibit format. My background is that as a librarian and researcher in classification theory and visual information. While these are my intellectual and professional biases, all the issues covered in the book are applicable to almost any cultural heritage organization that has ownership of some digital content.

I came to digital exhibits completely by accident. My job as a librarian was to work on various digital initiatives for NAL. All of these projects were pretty much what you would expect for a library: article databases, book catalogs for our holdings, and digital collections for our digitized reports, monographs, and images, among other similar projects. One day my supervisor called me into a meeting with another librarian who described a call he received from a patron to the library's reference desk. The patron had read a reference to some fictional stories written by the poet Robert Frost for two poultry trade journals in the early 1900s and wanted to know if we held copies. It turned out that the library did indeed hold the journal issues in question. Since they had fallen out of copyright due to age, we had the right to digitize them. My supervisor then smiled and turned to me. "What do you think about creating a digital exhibit for these articles?" I smiled back and said, "Pardon me?" I knew very little about Robert Frost. I certainly never knew anything about Robert Frost's adventures in poultry farming fiction. In addition, I had never worked on any kind of exhibit. I did not even know how a web-based exhibit featuring texts, as opposed to images, should look or function. I knew nothing about Omeka, aside from learning that was the platform I would be using. Using the metric of subject matter expertise, my qualifications for this project were questionable.

But I was a librarian with training in digital interaction design and a doctoral degree in Information Science. Given some time and effort, I could design an interface that would work for an exhibit. I knew how to perform library research. I knew how to find comparable exhibits and learn lessons from what they showed me. I knew how to find the best, most relevant Frost scholarship and apply what I found. So, a certified Frost scholar I was not. But I did have all the tools to create a digital exhibit about Robert Frost and his poultry articles. I just needed to use them in a creative, focused way. After the Frost project was finished and launched,

I went on to create multiple exhibits for the library about a variety of topics. Each subsequent exhibit presented a slightly different challenge and taught me a little more. This book is my attempt to share that knowledge, grounded in research and best practices in exhibit and information design.

Unlike other manuals or how-to guides, this book will not limit the entire exhibit process and resulting product within the structure or architecture of a given exhibit software platform. Instead, the book will support you as you go about understanding and presenting your content guided by thoughtful, integrated theories of presentation and engagement. Working from a foundation of insightful theory and intentional creativity will support the mission of your organization, the interests of your audience, and the nature of your content within the larger landscape of associated documents, images, and ideas. There is a chapter on software, however, but instead of structured tutorials, the book analyzes the underlying argument structures and rhetorical assumptions of popular DH software platforms, focusing most closely on Omeka and Scalar (Drucker & Svensson, 2016).

This book assumes that you are like me when I started down the path of creating exhibits: working in a cultural heritage organization such as a library, museum, archive, or historical society with some type of digital content you would like to share with your patrons. You may have expertise in the subject matter of your content, but you may not. You may know something about museum exhibits, but you may not. You may know something about web design, but you may not. You may have a budget, but you may not. All of these resources and areas of expertise are extremely valid and offer value for digital exhibit building. But based on my experience, there are only a few things that are mandatory for exhibits:

- A willingness to engage with your content on a level deep enough to perceive its meaning and significance, beyond issues of topicality
- The ability to develop a deeper understanding of your content and its relationship with other information artifacts and your audience
- The ability to understand your audiences and what they would find interesting, valuable, or compelling about this content
- If your exhibit is document-based, a clear-eyed acceptance of the likelihood that most visitors are not going to read lengthy original documents and that it is your job to identify the most useful excerpts to include in your project
- The ability to envision your content in a creative way
- The ability to write

This book assumes that all the other aspects of exhibit design and creation can be learned since they are simple extensions of your existing skills as a cultural heritage worker. This book also assumes that you will have limited access to staff and financial support or will be working alone as a "team of one". Since there are many authoritative sources on copyright requirements (Derclaye, 2011; Porsdam, 2016), alternative licensing mechanisms (Creative Commons, 2019), and repositories of digital heritage materials that can be used in exhibit work, these issues will not be addressed directly. The focus of the book is not aimed on ways to find exhibit materials so much as it is on how to analyze them and use them to create an integrated exhibit.

This book is designed to help you learn the basics of digital exhibits in terms of content and audience. The next chapter presents an overarching theory of digital exhibits, including their fundamental nature, their purpose, and how to ground your project in a coherent vision. Chapter 3 provides a pathway for developing your vision in a way that acknowledges and incorporates the needs of your audience and grounds your project within the larger world of relevant resources. Chapter 4 will give you tools that will help you to understand your content, its significance, and ways to explain it to your audience in an engaging and meaningful way. Chapter 5 acts as a series of case studies that will illustrate specific challenges and how they can be addressed and overcome. Chapter 6 sees your project in terms of a lifecycle and provides a vision of the best ways to support it within the context of your organization's priorities. Chapter 7 addresses practical issues of software types, interface design issues, and metadata needs. Finally, the last chapter focuses on your needs as a writer, designer, and creator and provides some sources of support for your creative efforts.

Unlike other works on exhibits that see them as essentially practical efforts, this book sees exhibits as fundamentally works of creativity. All the book's content can be read in any order that fulfills the needs of the reader, with the following recommendation: Chapters 2, 3, and 4 are designed to help you create the foundation of your project and thus should be read, or at the least, reviewed, first. All the other material in the book can be used as the reader sees fit. The goal is not to create a standard "recipe" or step-by-step plan for creating digital exhibits. The goal of the book is to help you as you go about creating a unique project that will honor your material, fulfill the information needs of your audience, and support your work as a cultural heritage worker. It is hoped that the reader will engage with the book using the same level of creativity as that called for when developing the exhibit itself.

This book is built on several assumptions that need to be stated explicitly. Clearly, it is my hope that anyone who is interested in digital exhibits will find this book helpful and thought provoking. The book does have a certain perspective, however, and might be seen as an ancillary source for:

- Professionals who work in well-funded institutions with access to resources such as outside subject matter experts, digital exhibit designers, technological support, and/or enough staff to support specialized teams
- Readers who are more interested in learning about software platform functions, technical considerations, or metadata formation than exhibit content and organization
- Museum staff who have been tasked with creating exhibits for "blockbuster" content
- Digital exhibits that are designed more to be add-ons to physical exhibits than independent creations themselves. This is especially true for virtual walk-throughs of physical exhibits.

This book conceives of digital exhibits as platforms that display, illustrate, and explain the meaning of a set of information objects in a way that fulfills a variety of goals. The exhibit should:

- Be true to the core meanings of the content
- Be attractive and engaging
- Include associated material that will provide additional pathways for your audience to understand, appreciate, and engage with the central exhibit content
- Showcase the content in a way that addresses and fulfills the core mission of your institution

Marini surveyed nine cultural heritage institutions with active physical exhibition programs (2019). The themes voiced by her study participants elucidated these additional purposes:

- Highlight, publicize, and promote collections
- Perform outreach to different communities to increase visitor engagement
- Create context and interpretation for collection materials
- Innovate and engage in "cultural discourse" with external audiences
- Promote research using collection materials

Within this context, an exhibit-ready digital information object can be a text document, an image, or an audio or video file, among other possibilities. Almost any type of digital content could be the focus of a given exhibit. Unless your content is extremely unique or significant in some way, however, this understanding assumes that the core of your exhibit will be a collection of objects instead of a single entity.

Not every project using information objects such as documents and images is constructed in the same way sharing the same communicative goals or rhetorical structure. Figure 1.1 shows these project types organized in a loose network (Marsh, 2022). The network structure and components are informed by the insights from Price on types of digital projects and their similarities and differences (2009).

The projects represented in Figure 1.1 are as follows:

- Thematic Essays: *Subsistence Homesteads*. Stories from the Collection. National Agricultural Library, US Department of Agriculture (Marsh, n.d.)
- Thematic Research Collections and Critical Editions: *Women of the Early Harlem Renaissance: African American Women Writers 1900–1922* (Singh, 2022)
- Digital Exhibits: *Apron Strings and Kitchen Sinks: The USDA Bureau of Home Economics*. National Agricultural Library, US Department of Agriculture (Marsh, n.d.)
- Curated Collections: *Europeana's World War I Collection*
- Search and Discovery Systems: *New York Public Library Digital Collections*

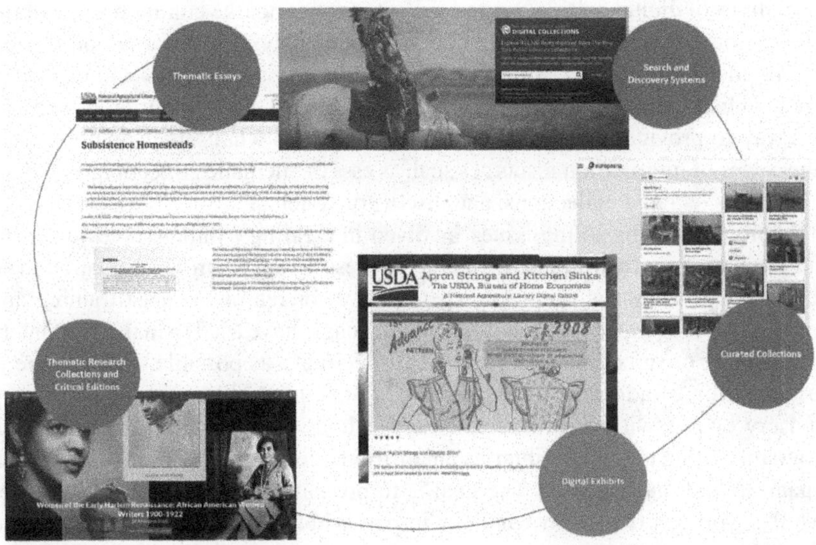

Figure 1.1 Display of different types of information resources, ordered by their degree of interpretation and amount of analytical predetermination: Thematic Essays, Thematic Research Collections and Critical Editions, Digital Exhibits, Curated Collections, and Search and Discovery Systems

These five project types all use digital information objects in various ways, organized by the degree to which they incorporate and display authorial interpretation. At one end of the continuum stand scholarly projects to analyze and understand content for a given set of readers. For thematic essays and thematic research collections, the emphasis is on communicating a given rhetorical program about the objects under study. On the other side stand resources that are designed more to provide direct or mediated access to objects for others to study so they can develop their own rhetorical program.

The digital exhibit strives to stand in balance between these endpoints: It provides access to a curated set of objects in an interactive structure that conveys some sense of meaning and context to the reader. The interpretive structure of an exhibit makes it stand apart from a collection or repository. Likewise, the exhibit's facilitation of object access contrasts it with more thematic and analytical products of scholarly attention.

There is a fundamental recognition that the level of scholarship required by a thematic research collection is different from that of an exhibit. As conceived by Fenlon, the richest types of thematic research collections both support research and embody original scholarship (2017). In essence, they exist as annotated publications. There is no expectation that a digital exhibit contains and expresses original scholarship in this same way. Instead, the focus is on providing digital and intellectual access to objects by including and explaining the scholarship of others. That access may support the research efforts of outside scholars, but that is not the primary goal. Likewise, the kinds of sophisticated search and retrieval capabilities of digital collections and repositories are not the common focus of the information object exhibit. While access to and analysis of information objects are provided by the object exhibit, the goal is to present the objects within a structured context that incorporates the scholarly record. This recognition of exhibits as a way to provide both interpretation and access is what sets them apart from other types of information resources such as essays, thematic collections and critical editions, curated collections, and discovery systems.

Before proceeding to the issues involved in creating exhibits, notes on focus and terminology are warranted. I come to these issues from the background of librarianship, so that is my default perspective for reasons of past training and practice. Although that is my chosen analytic lens, I have tried to make the content as devoid of organizational and technical specificity as possible. Hence there is no discussion of admittedly valuable topics such as dealing with public library advisory boards with sensitive topics or methods for advancing digital exhibit programs within academic libraries, apart from a few general observations about organizational management. The goal is to present a modular, generic perspective that you can deploy in whole or in part within your own specific context. That context could be a gallery, library, archive, museum, association, or other organization or professional working in the broad diffuse area of cultural heritage. I also recognize that I am encroaching on fields that have their own rich traditions and scholarship, specifically museum studies, exhibit curation and exhibit design, and archives and special collections with their constituent subspecialties of practice and study, among others. I have tried to stay within the boundaries of my knowledge, but if I ever stray too far into inaccuracy, the blame lies solely with me. Throughout the remaining chapters, I use several terms synonymously when they are not in fact, true synonyms. I admit to using the terms "curator", "designer", and "creator" almost interchangeably, in spite of my knowledge that all three terms represent distinct areas of practice, especially those of exhibit and digital curation (Barsch, 2020; Dandar et al., 2020; Madrid, 2013). I have tried to aim my description and understanding at the point at which as many disciplines as possible converge, but I may at times miss the mark for a given domain. Please engage with this work in a way that suites your needs.

Digital Exhibits and Associated Resources Discussed in This Chapter

Apron Strings and Kitchen Sinks: The USDA Bureau of Home Economics
Emily Marsh
National Agricultural Library, US Department of Agriculture
www.nal.usda.gov/exhibits/ipd/apronsandkitchens/

Europeana's World War I Collection
Europeana Foundation
www.europeana.eu/en/collections/topic/83-world-war-i

New York Public Library Digital Collections
New York Public Library
https://digitalcollections.nypl.org/

Subsistence Homesteads
Emily Marsh
National Agricultural Library, US Department of Agriculture
www.nal.usda.gov/collections/stories/subsistence-homesteads

Women of the Early Harlem Renaissance: African American Women Writers 1900–1922
Amardeep Singh
https://scalar.lehigh.edu/harlemwomen/index

References

Barsch, P. (2020). Online exhibitions: The curator as director. *OnCurating*, *45*, 59–64. https://on-curating.org/issue-45-reader/online-exhibitions-the-curator-as-director.html#.YnwSF-jMK01.

Bowen, L. G., & Roberts, P. J. (1993). Exhibits: Illegitimate children of academic libraries? *College & Research Libraries*, *54*(5), 407–415. http://hdl.handle.net/2142/41609.

CARLI Created Content Committee. (2020). *Guidelines for the promotion of digital collections: Best practices for promotion and marketing*. Champaign, IL: Consortium of Academic and Research Libraries in Illinois (CARLI). www.carli.illinois.edu/sites/files/digital_collections/documentation/guidelines_for_promotion.pdf.

Caro, S. (2016). *Digitizing your collection: Public library success stories*. Chicago, IL: American Library Association.

Council on Library and Information Resources. (n.d.). *Digitizing hidden special collections and archives: Amplifying unheard voices*. www.clir.org/hiddencollections/.

Creative Commons. (2019). *Creative Commons for educators and librarians*. Chicago: ALA Editions.

Dandar, D., Clifton-Ross, J., Dale, A., & Croft, R. (2020). Showcasing institutional research: Curating library exhibits to support scholarly communication. *Journal of Librarianship and Scholarly Communication*, *8*, eP2335. https://doi.org/10.7710/2162-3309.2335.

Derclaye, E. (Ed.). (2011). *Copyright and cultural heritage: Preservation and access to works in a digital world*. Cheltenham: Edward Elgar Publishing.

Drucker, J., & Svensson, P. B. (2016). The why and how of middleware. *Digital Humanities Quarterly*, *10*(2). www.digitalhumanities.org/dhq/vol/10/2/000248/000248.html.

Fenlon, K. (2017). Thematic research collections: Libraries and the evolution of alternative digital publishing in the humanities. *Library Trends*, *65*(4), 523–539. https://doi.org/10.1353/lib.2017.0016.

Fouracre, D. (2015). Making an exhibition of ourselves? Academic libraries and exhibitions today. *The Journal of Academic Librarianship*, *41*, 377–385. http://dx.doi.org/10.1016/j.acalib.2015.05.008.

Gardens, Libraries and Museums of the University of Oxford. (n.d.). *Statement on inclusion*. www.glam.ox.ac.uk/statement-on-inclusion.

Getty Research Institute. (2017). *Art & Architecture Thesaurus® online*. Los Angeles, CA: The Getty. www.getty.edu/research/tools/vocabularies/aat/index.html.

Giannini, T., & Bowen, J. P. (2022). Museums and digital culture: From reality to digitality in the age of COVID-19. *Heritage, s*, 192–214. https://doi.org/10.3390/heritage5010011.

Knight Foundation. (2020). *Digital readiness and innovation in museums: A baseline national survey*. Miami: Knight Foundation. https://knightfoundation.org/wp-content/uploads/2020/10/Digital-Readiness-and-Innovation-in-Museums-Report.pdf.

Lacher-Feldman, J. L. (2013). *Exhibits in archives and special collections libraries*. Chicago, IL: Society of American Archivists.

Madrid, M. M. (2013). A study of digital curator competences: A survey of experts. *The International Information & Library Review, 45*(3–4), 149–156. https://doi.org/10.1016/j.iilr.2013.09.001.

Marini, F. (2019). Exhibitions in special collections, rare book libraries and archives: Questions to ask ourselves. *Alexandria: The Journal of National and International Library and Information Issues, 29*(1/2), 8–29. https://doi.org/10.1177%2F0955749019876122.

Marsh, E. (2022). *Display of different types of information resources, ordered by their degree of interpretation and amount of analytical predetermination: Thematic essays, thematic research collections and critical editions, digital exhibits, curated collections, and search and discovery systems* [Infographic]. https://emily-marsh.com/Digital_Exhibits_for_Cultural_Institutions/Figure_1.1.jpg.

Marsh, E. (n.d.). *Subsistence homesteads. Stories from the collection*. National Agricultural Library. https://www.nal.usda.gov/collections/stories/subsistence-homesteads.

Monson, J. D. (2017). *Getting started with digital collections: Scaling to fit your organization*. Chicago, IL: American Library Association.

Northern Ireland Assembly Research and Information Service. (2018, September 12). Measuring museum success: How and why? *Research Matters. Northern Ireland Assembly*. www.assemblyresearchmatters.org/2018/09/12/measuring-museum-success-how-and-why/.

Pappa, D., & Makropoulos, C. (2021). Novel ways of discovering, capturing and experiencing cultural heritage: A review of current state-of-the-art, challenges and future directions. In D. Turcanu-Carutiu (Ed.), *Heritage*. London: IntechOpen Limited. https://doi.org/10.5772/intechopen.99170.

Porsdam, H. (Ed.). (2016). *Copyrighting creativity: Creative values, cultural heritage institutions and systems of intellectual property*. London: Routledge.

Posner, M. (2013). No half measures: Overcoming common challenges to doing digital humanities in the library. *Journal of Library Administration, 53*(1), 43–52. https://doi.org/10.1080/01930826.2013.756694.

Price, K. M. (2009). Edition, project, database, archive, thematic research collection: What's in a name? *Digital Humanities Quarterly, 3*(3). www.digitalhumanities.org/dhq/vol/3/3/000053/000053.html.

United Nations Educational, Scientific and Cultural Organization (UNESCO). (2020). *Museums around the world in the face of COVID-19*. Paris: Author. https://unesdoc.unesco.org/ark:/48223/pf0000373530.

Veirum, N. E., & Christensen, M. F. (2011). If it's not on the net it doesn't exist. *Museum Management and Curatorship, 26*(1), 3–9. https://doi.org/10.1080/09647775.2011.540123.

2 The Digital Exhibit

A Creative Meeting Place for Your Content, Your Organization, and Your Audience

This chapter surveys theories of museum exhibit design, qualitative document analysis, and literary analysis in the context of digital exhibits for cultural institutions. The goal of the survey is not to present a comprehensive overview of the museum studies field. Instead, these theories and methods were identified as being the most relevant and useful for digital exhibits, especially when the exhibit staff is small and/or composed of non-curators. The theories were analyzed to identify strategies that could help the exhibit creator to understand, organize, and present their digital materials, especially the type of documents normally associated with libraries, archives, and associated cultural institutions. The analysis of each theory and approach was used to generate a series of recommendations that could inform and guide the exhibit creator. The chapter covers the exhibit theories of Beverly Serrell and Louise Ravelli, an original theory of the author, qualitative research methods for document analysis, the Reader Response theory (RRT) of literary criticism, and theories of narrative within exhibits. The chapter aims to show the relevancy and usefulness of theory within this field and to develop a set of principles and techniques that can be harnessed for immediate use for digital exhibit creators.

Given the human and financial resources required to create even a small collection of digitized materials, it is easy to understand why many librarians, archivists, and museum professionals might assume that this is end of the process. But is it? It might be tempting to trust that a larger aggregator such as Europeana or the Digital Public Library of America will serve as the connecting point for your material and your patrons. This is an excellent solution if all you want to provide is simple access. This access will be limited, however, to those experienced users who are knowledgeable and determined enough to find the content they need from one of these large aggregators. The only remaining task would be to announce the availability of your newly digitized content. So, you could perhaps feature an image on your organization's website home page or send a tweet or post on Instagram about your newest scanned document. For many professionals this would simply be a start—more effort is required to serve your content to your users in a meaningful, impactful way. If you want to go deeper and reveal the oftentimes hidden significance of digital objects that might seem trivial or mundane at first glance, then a larger effort beyond mere provision is needed. Once you have some

DOI:10.4324/9781003301493-2

digital content, how can you present it on the web in a way that honors the source material, the mission of your organization, and the needs and nature of your audience? One excellent tool to accomplish such a task is the digital exhibit.

A web-based exhibit of documents or images with explanatory and interpretive text provides a flexible, customizable platform that serves a variety of purposes. First, it allows organizations the ability to show users attractive views of digital items. But much more important than simple presentation is the ability to contextualize and explain the significance of a given object or collection of objects in a way that is understandable, accessible, and enjoyable for your targeted users. Content never exists in a vacuum. An exhibit provides a useful and creative connecting point where your content, your organization, and your audience can meet. It also provides a way to revisit potentially difficult and painful material in a way that includes frank and enlightened analysis of racism, colonialism, sexism, and LGBTQ+ issues.

Of course, while your content does not exist in isolation, neither does the genre of museum and library exhibits. There is a long and rich history of physical exhibit practice and theory that can guide and inform the creation and implementation of GLAM digital exhibits. This chapter will review a core selection of the most relevant and useful literature from the field of museum studies. While libraries and associated cultural heritage organizations have a long history of physical displays and exhibits, their professional and scholarly literature is, understandably, not as rich as that produced by museum studies' scholars on this particular topic. A recent review by Fouracre of the library literature on exhibits showed that only a small percentage of articles (14%) retrieved from a database of scholarly literature addressed museum or exhibit theory in any meaningful way (2015).

This short dip into museum studies will provide a framework for thinking about your content and the best ways to situate it in an organized and harmonious context of other objects and explanatory text. Specifically, this chapter will briefly cover the work of scholars in museum and visitor studies including:

- Beverly Serrell's theories about exhibit content and "The Big Idea"
- Qualitative Analysis Methods: Reflexive Thematic Analysis and Editing Analysis
- Reader Response Theory
- Storytelling for Exhibits
- Louise Ravelli's Linguistic Communication Theory of Exhibits
- An original model of digital exhibits

It might be tempting to skip the difficult work of analyzing and planning a project in an understandable eagerness to get to the task at hand: building your exhibit. Given the seemingly endless tasks required for a digital exhibit, it is easy to become distracted by procedural issues and questions:

- What software should I use?
- Which items should I feature?

- What metadata standard should I select?
- Who will be responsible for data entry?
- How long will I need to complete this project?
- Do I have a budget?

Some exhibit guides approach these issues as if they comprised elements in a template or storyboard to be checked off one by one in the planning process. Indeed, once the conceptual structure for your exhibit has gotten to a mature state, these issues will take on a true degree of importance and will demand attention. On the other hand, if these procedural issues are privileged above the harder, deeper questions of content and purpose, it is all too possible to develop responses which might help you to develop a linear, straightforward but, all too possibly, forgettable exhibit.

These important questions will be addressed in later chapters. Before getting down to the practical issues of implementation, however, it is necessary to step back and take in a larger view of your project and its constituent objects and ask these richer, more provocative questions:

- Why should I build an exhibit?
- What am I trying to demonstrate or illustrate about these information objects?
- What associated content should be incorporated into the exhibit?
- What will my digital visitors want to see and experience?
- Who am I trying to reach?
- What should they get out of this exhibit?
- Why should they care about this exhibit?
- What intellectual frameworks will my visitors bring to the exhibit?
- What message will they take away from the exhibit?

Even when these types of issues are included within a template framework, they need to be addressed thoughtfully, exclusive of structure. For example, the National Park Service, a US federal agency and part of the Department of the Interior offers a tool for exhibit design and execution. Their *Museum and Visitor Center Exhibit Planning, Design, and Fabrication Process* asserts that the Pre-Design phase "focuses on preparing a solid foundation for all work that follows, insuring [sic] that the project is logically structured, and its goals are understood and realistically attainable" (2011). The only guidance offered for an overall vision of the exhibit is represented by the requirement to develop a "project overview, including updated information and understandings" and "identify interpretive themes and objectives". When conceptual issues about interpretation and purpose are seen as mere items in a list to be checked off, it is easy to underestimate both their difficulty and potential impact. As opposed to a procedural checklist or template, the better way to approach these deeper questions is to see them within a larger context of museum and library theory.

Theory is at times disconnected from informing practice in librarianship for various reasons: Some argue that the "culture of scholarship and the academy works against a more vigorous research practice relationship" (McKechnie et al.,

2008). Some practitioners report they find theoretical literature too time-consuming to read and lacking immediate relevancy to their jobs (Powell et al., 2002). Other writers have pointed out that a "rift" between theory and practice is sometimes experienced as a perceived gap between what is taught in MLS programs and what working librarians feel students actually need to learn to become competent professionals (Myburgh & Tammaro, 2013). For whatever reason, theory in the context of exhibits is sometimes dismissed as an irrelevant luxury by some busy practitioners, who by circumstance or temperament want to engage more with the exhibit material than with making subjective judgments about its essential meaning or placement within a larger cultural context. Given the large number and variety of tasks that exhibits require, it is understandable that some designers, especially those who are under-resourced and/or over-worked, might choose to focus more on issues that can be answered in a straightforward way instead of the ambiguous questions of "interpretation", "themes", and "objectives" that create the framework of exhibit theory, as opposed to practice.

But theory is not an intellectual indulgence or an optional precursor that can be skipped without consequence. The best and most useful theories can act as lenses that allow you to survey the overall landscape, pinpoint your ultimate destination, identify points of interest that might be visited along the way, and recalibrate your journey if you get lost. Instead of thinking of theory as blinders that restrict your vision and limit your creativity, theory allows you to see yourself, your organization, your audience, and, most important, your content, clearly and thoughtfully. This enriched perspective can support and facilitate the creation of exhibits grounded in a context that will both honor the material and reveal a path connecting it to the interests of your audience.

At this point, there is no integrated theory or model of digital exhibits that will help to answer all the questions given earlier. There are several excellent theoretical tools, however, that will support the exhibit creator when used thoughtfully and in combination. The next sections will describe these tools and summarize each of them with recommendations for exhibit creators.

A note of caution is warranted here: Do not think you have to adopt all the ideas offered in this chapter. Aside from developing an overall intellectual program for the exhibit (its "big idea"), none of these suggestions are mandatory. They are offered as tools to be used to help you create your exhibit. Most effective exhibits demonstrate evidence that their creators have successfully grappled with the kinds of questions contained within the following theories. So, while applying all these viewpoints is neither realistic nor necessary, the thoughtful exhibit creator should be prepared to address some of the issues and questions they raise. Specific suggestions that flow out of each theory grouping are offered at the conclusion of each section to help you turn theory into action.

The Big Idea of Beverly Serrell

A core question of exhibit design has been named, appropriately enough, "The Big Idea" by Beverly Serrell. As defined in the second edition of *Exhibit Labels:*

An Interpretive Approach, it is "a sentence—a statement—of what the exhibition is about. It is one complete, noncompound, active sentence that identifies a subject, and action (the verb), and a consequence ('so what?')" (2015, p. 7).

Readers of this definition with a background in library studies might hear the echoes of not one but two core ideas: Topical Relevance: the essential subject of a given information object (Saracevic, 1975) and Pragmatic, or User Relevance: the degree of correspondence between a user's actual information needs and the material offered (i.e., "so what?") (Vickery, 1959). Within Serrell's model, every quality exhibit needs to have a demonstrable grasp on its essential identity—what it is about and why the reader might care to spend time and effort engaging with the material laying within. In other words, demonstrate a relevance relationship between the exhibit and the interests or needs of the visitor. Identifying and demonstrating connections between content and users is a supremely common activity carried out by library and informational professionals daily, whether by catalogers, indexers, or reference staff. When seen through this perspective, librarians are well-situated to act as exhibit builders.

In any event, a final feature of the definition is Serrell's specification of exact linguistic requirements for the form of this big idea identity statement: a subject linked to a verb, and to a "consequence". A well-written big idea can act as the axis of your digital exhibit and help you to re-orient your work if it veers unacceptably off course. While Serrell's directive about the actual structure of your big idea could be termed as overly restrictive, its requirement of cold-eyed clarity is a necessary one. To create a cohesive exhibit possessing a clear identity, you need to be sure and consistent about your focus, what content you will include and what you will not, and how best to present your material. This applies to both the actual items in your exhibit and the themes you will address. As opposed to physical exhibit space, there are virtually no upper limits on the size a digital exhibit can take. Thus, it is up to the creator to make sure that the exhibit is just as large as it needs to be. The best insurance against an exhibit becoming unwieldy or unfocused is a grounded awareness of identity and place within the digital content world. Serrell argues that the best expression of that identity and placement is a big idea statement. She offers several examples from unnamed exhibits including the following: "Most of what we know about the universe comes from messages we read in light" and "A healthy swamp—an example of a threatened ecosystem—provides many surprising benefits to humans" (2015, p. 9).

An example from a current online exhibit can be found from the National Archives of the United States' *Records of Rights: Rights of Native Americans* "Rather than struggle for new liberties, Native Americans fought to preserve rights that they already possessed". A Library of Congress exhibit on the civil rights activist Rosa Parks has this as its functional big idea: "*Rosa Parks: In Her Own Words* showcases rarely seen materials that offer an intimate view of Rosa Parks and documents her life and activism". A Smithsonian Libraries' exhibit states,

> *Doodles, Drafts, and Designs: Industrial Drawings from the Smithsonian* offers a fascinating glimpse into inventors' sketchbooks, engineers'

> mechanical drawings, and architects' renderings from the 1830s to the 1990s, to show the origins of some of the most familiar sites and devices of modern-day life.

The National Archives' exhibit *Abolition of Slavery* states that it will facilitate an understanding of "how slavery shaped the history of Britain, Africa and the former British Empire, and consider its consequences for modern-day British, African and Caribbean societies". Additionally, its exhibit *"All Change!" on Britain's Railways* has this as its central thesis, "Since the 19th century, railways have brought great changes to peoples' lives. Find out how they have changed the environment, standardised time and revolutionised holiday habits". The British Library's exhibit on *Alice in Wonderland* promises a way to "Discover how Lewis Carroll's story has been re-imagined, re-interpreted and re-illustrated over the last 150 years".

The most distinctive feature of all these well-written big ideas is a specific rhetorical argument advanced for each exhibit. These statements demonstrate an engagement with the actual exhibit material beyond issues of description encoded in metadata or digital formatting of content files. Some big ideas take the stance that the fundamental goal of their exhibits is simply providing access to digitized documents or images for the visitor. The argument goes something like this, "This exhibit contains digitized materials related to X. X is an important and fascinating subject/person/place/event, *etc*. We hope you find these materials as unique and interesting as we do". But as Amanda Cox, former editor of the *New York Times* data journalism section, observed, "Nothing really important is headlined, 'Here is some data. Hope you find it interesting. Annotation is critical. Editing is critical'" (2011). You need to give the visitor a distinctive viewpoint into your content that is more specific than simply asserting that you have provided digital equivalents of physical objects. These kinds of general pseudo "big idea" statements are more suited to digital collections where the only essential goal is provision of access to digitized materials.

Digital collection building and maintenance is difficult and essential work. Digital collections are indispensable to digital exhibits because that is where curators often go to get the core building blocks for their projects. But an exhibit is not the same as a collection. Both kinds of resources facilitate access to objects, but an exhibit does so with a clear rhetorical objective. You may think that this kind of statement is not necessary if you are building an exhibit around materials that either are well known or occupy a prominent place in a given culture. But in fact, these kinds of exhibits are in even greater need of unique description since their potential audience will probably think they already know all there is to know about the objects they contain. It is your job to show them that there is something more to see and that is done implicitly with your original exhibit content and explicitly through your big idea.

As these examples illustrate, having a big idea drive the form and content of your exhibit can provide a compact and focused mission statement that can be helpful to visitors when included in exhibit documentation. But the big idea is designed with the needs for the exhibit creator in mind just as much as those of the exhibit reader. For an idea to act as an organizing mechanism, it needs to prioritize directness and linearity over intrigue. Instead, the big idea acts in the same way as a maypole: a central axis around which the exhibit creator works to develop the connective threads or "ribbons" of a unified, focused, and interesting exhibit that is worthy of the reader's time and effort. Stating your big idea explicitly in your exhibit documentation is just as important for yourself as a creator as it is for your visitor. It should be the driver of every key decision as you go about building your project.

The last point to be made about big ideas is how to create them. It has been my experience that the best big ideas are those that arise directly from the exhibit materials. The content that you want to feature in your exhibit acting as the core of your project should suggest your organizing point. Ideas that come from external sources often are more about their own priorities than from the content itself. If you decide to build an exhibit around an external, often arbitrary, assertion, you run the risk of creating a project that either has no authentic identity or one that is constantly being molded and manipulated to conform to an outside force that has little relationship to your content.

As an example, I created an exhibit on local foods for the USDA's National Agricultural Library, "Mailboxes, Mom and Pop Stands, and Markets: Local Foods Then and Now". While the topic was an arbitrary one, assigned by an administrator, it did facilitate the creation of an exhibit that was organized around a big idea that was a total surprise, connected with the construct of "local foods" itself. It turns out that this concept forms a fuzzy category made up of members that Rosch and Mervis describe as having "family resemblances" (1975), after Wittgenstein (1953). The characteristics that can make a food to be perceived as "local" vary and can include its physical point of origin (often, but not always, the closer the customer is to where the food was produced, the more "local" the food is perceived to be), the nature of the producer (generally smaller farms), the nature of the point of purchase (farmers' markets and locally controlled stores are associated with the construct of "local"), sociological factors relating to the nature of the producer and/or retailer, and factors relating to the food in question such as perceptions of freshness and nutrition (Martinez et al., 2010).

All of these factors play varying roles in how a food is judged as local to one degree or another, just like siblings in a family can share nose or mouth shapes but not hair or eye color. There is no magic set of necessary and sufficient conditions for determining if a food will be judged as belonging to the category "local food". A can of sliced peaches manufactured in a small factory in Southern California would likely be judged as less "local" by a Los Angeles consumer than a basket of fresh peaches grown on an industrial farm in Northern California, even though that farm might be hundreds of miles away. This is a good illustration of the way this type of category structure works. While location can be a determinative factor for some category members, for others the freshness factor is what makes a food "local" or not. I did not know the nature of local foods as belonging to the class of family resemblance categories before engaging with this exhibit material. I would never have recognized this concept as the big idea for an exhibit on local foods unless I had been open to what I found in the exhibit's publications. Although not explicitly stated in the exhibit itself, its big idea is actually a provocative one, "There is no stable definition for 'local foods'".

You may be wondering how and when to start work on crafting the big idea statement for your exhibit. This will vary from project to project and from creator to creator. In general, it would be unwise to put other exhibit work off waiting until you have written the perfect big idea statement. While the statement might appear at the top of your documentation in your exhibit's "About" page, it is unrealistic to expect that it be written before the overall project has been started. In general, a mission statement such as big idea should be drafted early in the project, but not too early. Since it should advocate a distinct viewpoint or argument and arise out of your materials, it should be developed after you have had some time to select and read at least some of your most important materials, but before you have finalized your exhibit's structure and information architecture.

Big Idea Recommendations

Develop a compact mission statement for your exhibit that describes both its nature and its significance. This statement can contain two or three "big ideas", but they all need to be clear, interrelated, necessary, and tightly focused. Use your big idea(s) to structure your exhibit.

Qualitative Analysis Methods: Reflexive Thematic Analysis and Editing Analysis

The big idea construct demonstrates the centrality of the exhibit creator's role. This guiding and organizing force is your creation and should arise from your own understanding of the meaning and significance of your exhibit materials. Of course, that understanding must be informed by a thoughtful consideration of the published scholarship relevant to your materials and the subjects on which they touch. The chance of creating a compelling and meaningful exhibit is a direct function of the degree to which you can create and demonstrate an informed understanding of your materials within an exhibit structure.

For example, the core materials of the *Frost on Chickens* exhibit are the 11 articles (ten fiction and one non-fiction) written by Robert Frost for two agricultural trade journals: *The Eastern Poultryman* and *The Farm-Poultry* between 1900 and 1909. The exhibit's entire conceptual structure and information architecture arose directly from the themes of the articles, informed by their significance within the larger world of Frost scholarship and American agriculture. The exhibit is enriched by material from Frost's own poetry, letters, notebooks, and speeches that place the articles in a more literary context. The focus was broadened further to biographical scholarship about the period of Frost's life when he was writing the articles while working as a poultry farmer in Derry, New Hampshire, and the dire circumstances that led him to take up this occupation. Finally, digitized publications published by the US Department of Agriculture were included to illustrate the placement and significance of Frost's observations about chickens and rural life.

Once the core themes of the Frost articles were identified, it became possible to construct an exhibit that would:

- explain and demonstrate their meaning.
- place them in a context understandable to the general visitor unfamiliar with the details of Frost's early life (a tactic of audience analysis discussed in Chapter 3).
- acknowledge and incorporate items from the scholarly record that would further illustrate the significance of the articles for the casual visitor.
- connect the works to the larger world of American agriculture in the early twentieth century.

These curatorial and design decisions arose out of a direct engagement with the core exhibit materials: the articles analyzed within an intellectual context that would connect to an audience interested in this period of Frost's life.

If you are facing your own set of materials and have no ready-made organizing principle or structure for your exhibit, there are tools developed by qualitative researchers in the social sciences that can help you. Qualitative research methodology is a large field with many nuanced techniques resting on theoretical paradigms that can be difficult to grasp in a short time (Denzin & Lincoln, 2017). But in a landmark article Virginia Braun and Victoria Clarke stepped forward to identify a specific approach within this tradition useful for the common document types that are the foundation of digital exhibits for cultural institutions (2006). The method, named thematic analysis, has also the added benefit of being understandable without extensive background reading and training. Finally, it can serve the creator in her effort to distill organizing themes in a "bottom-up" way that can drive the entire organizing process in a way that stays true to the actual materials.

Put simply, thematic analysis is "a method for identifying, analyzing and reporting patterns (themes) within data" (Braun & Clarke, p. 79). While the method was developed for use in research that relies on interview transcripts, it is well-suited to other sorts of documents, including the types in digital exhibits. More specifically, Braun and Clarke encourage the use of what they term "reflexive" thematic analysis which acknowledges and accepts "the importance of the researcher's interpretation of the data. Within reflexive TA, analysis occurs because of, rather than despite, the researcher's subjectivity—their values, backgrounds, decisions, and interests" (Terry & Hayfield, 2021, p. 4). The steps of this approach for document analysis are:

1 Reading the texts
2 Generating some initial large categories
3 Searching for more refined themes, such as Serrell's big ideas
4 Reviewing and refining themes

5 Finalizing themes with names and definitions
6 Organizing the themes to create a coherent and comprehensive view of the texts

Braun and Clarke echo Serrell's requirement that your analysis should result in an integrated picture wherein "all aspects of [each] theme should cohere around a central idea or concept" (Braun & Clarke, p. 94). It should be stressed that the goal is not to create an objectively "true" analysis, but one that represents a rich understanding of the documents. One of the hallmarks of this methodology is its recognition and appreciation of the human interpretive effort that is woven throughout every qualitative research project. The goal is not to strive for objectivity but to engage with the "messy reality" of both data and the effort required to make sense of it (Clarke & Braun, 2013, p. 122). The result of such an effort is a personal understanding of the material under analysis and the ability to describe that personal understanding to the reader in a way that is insightful, supported by evidence, and transparent enough to be interrogated for accuracy and authenticity.

It should be observed that reflexive thematic analysis did not arise spontaneously or in theoretical isolation. It shares much in common with the editing organizing style of qualitative data analysis described by Miller and Crabtree wherein the researcher

> enters the text much like an editor searching for meaningful segments, cutting, pasting, and rearranging until the reduced summary reveals a helpful interpretation. . . . Once identified, these units are stored and organized into categories or codes. It is these categories that are explored for patterns and themes in the connecting phase of analysis.
>
> (1992, 21; 23)

Also, this kind of subjective, interpretive analytic work has a parallel counterpart in the "close reading" method within literary analysis wherein multiple readings of a text are performed to generate a deep understanding of both its meaning and the way in which that meaning is communicated to the reader (Hinchman & Moore, 2013). It stands in stark contrast to the "distant reading" methods used within many digital humanities projects that rely on more quantitative analyses of large text corpora (Underwood, 2017). Finally, it can be seen as relating to the construct of qualitative content analysis described by White and Marsh (2006).

Some thematic analyses will be deeper than others. For example, the "Geppi Gems" exhibit of comic books by the Library of Congress of the United States uses genre as its organizing principle and groups its documents into the following categories: early newspapers, Disney, westerns, superheroes, science fiction, horror, sports, and pop culture (Library of Congress, n.d.). Likewise, an exhibit on women reading in America divides its content into these seven genre-based categories: travel, biographies and memoirs, self-improvement, cookbooks, "Ladies'" magazines and journals, gift books, and fiction (Smith College Libraries, n.d.). The Library of Congress' exhibit about Benjamin Franklin organizes its documents by and about Franklin into broad subject categories based more on their content than form: A Cause for Revolution, Break with Britain, Continental Congress, Treaty of Paris, The New Republic, Scientist and Inventor, and Printer and Writer (2006). The British Library's (n.d.) exhibit, *South Asians in Britain,* is organized around five themes that show some level of analysis of the underlying content and what it reveals about this intersection between cultures: global trade and empire, making home in Britain, activism and politics, culture and intellectual life, and World Wars.

Another, similarly, analytic means of organizing material is used by the Hagley Museum and Library (n.d.) in their exhibit on the *Brandywine Valley Oral History Project.* The approximately 150 interviews of everyday "people who lived and worked in the Brandywine Valley in northern Delaware" were organized and analyzed using the following six categories:

1 Childhood & Mischief
2 Food & Drink
3 Holidays & Traditions
4 Mill Explosions
5 Recreation & Entertainment
6 Working on the Brandywine [River]

This simple list reveals a view of the interviewees' thoughts that are divided between the private, familial concerns of childhood, meals, and holidays, contrasted with their work life centered on the Brandywine River, punctured with memories of over 200 deadly explosions at various local workplaces. This simple contrast between the small joys of private life and the hard, potentially deadly work carried out in the public sphere effectively carries out an insightful rhetorical program about these interviews relying on a thematic-based analysis. This way of coupling the underlying exhibit material with a structure that is created by a thematic analysis demonstrates the value of Braun and Clarke's paradigm for the exhibit creator.

While the value of this method is demonstrated by the kind of thoughtful themes it can help to generate, its essential messiness cannot be overstated. It is much like carrying out an inventory or audit of your documents. While secondary sources and guides are helpful, they cannot substitute for direct examination and analysis. The insights from scholars that are found in secondary sources can act as another data source for triangulation, a method to demonstrate the validity of your insights and categories (Patton, 1999). Chapter 5 will include a detailed account of how I engaged with the messiness of thematic analysis for the *Frost on Chickens* exhibit, using sources from the scholarly record to triangulate my themes and provide a demonstration of their validity and operational utility.

Finally, it should be noted that this method can be used with documents that are not textual. An analysis of visual documents such as photographs can produce the same kind of result. For example, the digital exhibit *Mirrors and Mass: Wayne Thom's Southern California* features photographs of buildings that are organized into four facets: building purpose (civic, educational, commercial, religious, and residential), architectural firm name, date of photograph, and location of building (Bills, 2018). Similarly, the *Safer at Home* exhibit aims to act as an "invitation to examine the many facets of home as well as what safety means and looks like for LGBTQ populations—both past and present" (Johnson, 2020). The bulk of the exhibit is a collection of photographs organized by the following themes: reading, outdoors, pets, costume, AIDS, music, house parties, and protests and marches. Like the *Brandywine Valley Oral History Project*, tragedy and conflict (AIDS; protests and marches) sit side by side with the routine pleasures of domestic life (reading, pets, music). These brief examples show that it is possible to create a thoughtful exhibit of content organized around intuitively appealing themes once the exhibit creator spends some time engaging with its content.

There is a body of literature addressing qualitative methods for visual analysis, although it is not as large as that for textual document analysis (Ball & Smith, 1992; Banks, 2018; Pauwels & Mannay, 2019; Pink, 2012). These analysts can provide more detailed approaches tailored to visual sources, but the essential point remains. In order to create an exhibit about cultural materials, you need to engage with those materials at a level deep and authentic enough to create a thematic structure that remains true to their underlying content.

Thematic Analysis Recommendations

Go deep within your documents to engage in the "messy reality" of understanding their meaning. Let your reading guide you to generate themes that describe the individual content of the documents as well as commonalties that demonstrate relationships between and across documents. Find a way to use those themes as organizing principles that relate to your big idea(s) and will act to create a structure for your exhibit's component parts.

Reader Response Theory

When thinking about the text, organization, and style of your original exhibit content, what is often classed under the umbrella term "exhibit labels" within physical museum studies, it is tempting to see it as essentially a discrete entity—an inert, inanimate thing that is separate from your visitor reader. It is almost like the exhibit becomes an element in a mathematical equation of communication, such as the Shannon–Weaver model (1949). There are (1) cultural professionals who want to promote and provide access to (2) museum object surrogates, which are described within the (3) structure and text of an exhibit which is then (4) consumed by (5) the visitor through the (6) form of a digital exhibit. Creating an effective exhibit is simply a matter of identifying all the individual pieces and linking them all together in a line, much like beads on a string.

Clearly this mechanistic model does not correctly represent the human act of communication encapsulated in either a physical or digital museum exhibit. The exhibit content and structure need to be seen as products of creative endeavors in and of themselves, as well as animated by messages about the exhibit's objects, shaped by a particular perspective for the visitor. Likewise, visitors are also engaging in a work of creation when they engage with the exhibit's content. This act of engagement involves the visitor's act of reading, experiencing, and comprehending the exhibit and should be understood as requiring some creative effort itself.

What does all this mean? You are alive in the physical world and exist in a specific time and place, culture and body, and profession and identity. How you understand and represent your content will be affected by who you are, most strongly by your perceptions and interpretations, which are influenced by all the elements listed and more, in endless variations of degree and tone and expression. There are no Platonic ideals at hand, at least within the confines of a digital exhibit. Creating an abstract truth about your materials should not be pursued as a worthwhile or realistic goal. It is not the exhibit creator's goal to create a static information "product" for a "consumer". A reader does not process content like a sponge absorbing moisture or a gas tank getting filled with fuel. Instead, think of the exhibit as a meeting place where your creative vision of the exhibit's content is stated clearly and explicitly so that your visitors can create their personal understandings which are also informed by their particular reading stances (Rosenblatt, 1978, 2004).

The conventions of Reader Response Theory (RRT) offer one pathway into the thicket of complex processes that make up the activity of writing within the exhibit environment. RRT presumes that meaning is constructed as a reader interacts with a given text. Meaning does not lie in the words so much as it waits to be understood or "activated" by the reader's application of a set of conventional cognitive behaviors that make up the reading process (Iser, 1972, 1978). These behaviors are under the control of the reader but are shaped by the nature of the text, its "schematic framework". Thus, meaning cannot be said to be a sole outgrowth of the text or an arbitrary product of the reader's interpretation. Rather, reading is a socially constructed and situated activity that requires an expressive text, a directed reader, and an awareness of the commonly held cognitive conventions that link one to the other.

To understand the meaning that can arise from this RRT process, it is necessary to identify explicitly those "codes and conventions to which readers refer in making sense of texts" (Regan, 1998, p. 139). For example, the *Safer at Home* exhibit defines "safe" and "home" in the context of being LGBTQ+ in a past age when neither of those concepts existed in a simplistic fashion. Some of the photographs in the exhibit are organized into categories labeled reading, outdoors, pets, costume, music, and house parties—all subjects that are usually fairly mundane home activities. The reader who is activated by the exhibit's schematic framework will recognize these images as portraying people and activities that are anything but mundane, however. It is clear all the people in the photographs are doing these activities while being openly and unapologetically queer when it was not common or safe to do so. The only reason they are able to exist this way and still be *safe* is that they are in a place that they consider *home*.

The photographs categorized as "AIDS" and "Protests and Marches" are a bit more difficult to describe within the RRT paradigm. Given the semantic frame of safe at home, two conclusions make some sense. For many who identify as openly LGBTQ+, the state of being engaged in protest is familiar. It is plausible to think of the concept of "familiar" as analogous to "home". In this way, the category of queer people engaged in seemingly endless protest with their "brothers and sisters" against their oppression fits within the Safer at Home semantic structure. Likewise, the AIDS prevention messages in the exhibit, which feature condoms prominently, evoke the "safe sex" campaign that was created to "enable a generation of gay men . . . to continue celebrating their sexuality without risking their lives or the lives of their partners" (Berkowitz, 2003, cover copy). It is also rhetorically adjacent to the "Silence=Death" poster designed as a message to "to prompt the LGBTQ community to organize politically around AIDS" and to send the message that it was better to "turn anger, fear, grief into action" than to suffer and die in silence (Baumann, 2013). The final connection in the RRT-based analysis is that action is "safer" than silence, especially when carried out in community with others who are sometimes seen as one's chosen family: where you feel at "home". The codes and conventions that create this sort of semantic framework are situated within the larger cultural and historical context of the ways that LGBTQ+ people have existed as oppressed minorities. It seems reasonable that this kind of layered response fits within this cultural exhibit that aims for evocative interpretations of the images pictured which were selected because of their power to "resonate with and reflect on the idea of 'safer at home'" (Johnson, 2020).

Reader Response Theory Recommendations

Exhibit readers are not empty vessels waiting to be filled with your content. If you decide to create an exhibit that contains more evocative messages and concepts, be clear about the way that your targeted audiences will read, understand, and receive these messages and concepts. Paradoxically, this is also true for materials that are more mundane and decidedly unprovocative. You still need to create a rhetorical structure that will hold some interest for the user. You need to demonstrate why the user should spend time with these mundane materials. Also, be clear about your frames of reference, biases, and culturally bound perceptions as an exhibit creator. Acknowledge what you bring to your content and how that influences your design decisions, regardless of the subjects of your exhibit.

Storytelling for Exhibits

Some theorists think exhibits and stories are functionally synonymous, or at the least see exhibits as a type of narrative. For example, Ferguson defines exhibits as "narratives which use art objects as elements in institutionalized stories that are promoted to an audience" (1996, p. 126). Although this assertion was made before digital exhibits as we now know them were even possible, it is echoed in many admonitions to exhibit creators to make sure their physical and digital exhibits "tell a story". Here is how some prominent cultural institutions, theorists, and creators describe the relationship between stories and exhibits, for both physical and digital installations:

> The main business of exhibitions is to tell a story with things (Smithsonian Institution, n.d., p. 5).
>
> The thoughtful, systematic digitization and preservation of your [institution's] assets enables the creative process of sharing your stories to engage and inspire (Starr, 2020).
>
> We often use the term "story" to describe the product of interpretation. This word is the operative device for interpretive exhibits, as it is for most teaching (Toxey & McMillan, 2009, p. 5).
>
> [N]arratives, while used in a range of ways, are a constant presence in museum mediation strategies (Sitzia, 2016, p. 3).
>
> It appears that the vehicle of choice for channeling content in the museum is through narrative (Roppola, 2013, p. 204).
>
> Our perception of ourselves and the world around us is structured around stories, then, and this influence of narrative extends into the museum: as a common language for diverse professionals involved in exhibition making; as a means of creating empathetic links between the subjects and audiences of museum displays; and as a glue which plugs temporal, geographical and cultural gaps within the museum.
>
> (Hanks et al., 2012, p. xxii)

Given this consensus about the nature of exhibits as reliant on a narrative structure, one would think that this advice would go beyond a simple directive to "tell a story" to more actionable guidance and assistance. Clearly, effective, creative storytelling is not a simple thing.

Another viewpoint comes from the world of autobiography and Johnson's observation that,

> [L]ife does not tell stories. Life is chaotic, fluid, random; it leaves myriads of ends untied, untidily. Writers can extract a story from life only by strict, close selection, and this must mean falsification. Telling stories really is telling lies.
>
> (Johnson, 1973, p. 14)

In contrast, Monika Fludernik's text, *An Introduction to Narratology,* states that

> [H]istorians collectively seek to represent one and the same real world in explanatory narrative and from a variety of different perspectives. As readers, we construct the story (characters, setting, events) from the narrative text of a novel, whereas in historical writing it is the historians who produce a story on the basis of their sources and set it down in verbal form.
>
> (2009, p. 4)

Exhibits sit somewhere outside the worlds of fiction, autobiography, and history, although their creators can use the principles and techniques of storytelling that intersect with all these fields. But this is not an easy task. Although compelling, well-told stories can appear straightforward to the exhibit visitor, creating an actual narrative that is factual, interpretively sound, inclusive of alternative viewpoints, based on exhibit materials, and engaging is not simple or straightforward at all. Furthermore, a creator who aims to tell an authentic story based on a rich, thick understanding of the exhibit contents needs to acknowledge and account for their own biases and blind spots. Just as readers are not empty containers waiting to be filled with meaning, exhibit creators are not simple narrators, describing some objective truth with objects. As Fludernik observes about historians,

> [E]very history, moreover, can be traced back to a particular perspective. It betrays the view of the author, his/her nationality and place of origin, the age in which s/he writes (or wrote), and it is tailored to a readership which has certain prejudices, historical convictions, and expectations. History as historiography is never objective, however great its commitment to telling the truth.
>
> (2009, p. 3)

In essence, all histories show evidence of "presentism", whether their authors explicitly label them as such or not (Chang, 2021). So, we need to recognize that within digital exhibit design, truth is not the goal so much as a transparent, nuanced understanding and presentation of objects, informed by a thoughtful and thorough review of the relevant scholarly record. This is what we should mean when we say our exhibits "tell a story".

What is clear is that the drive toward narrative and telling human stories is a complex one that has raised a thicket of difficult questions in museum exhibit creation, as well as journalism and history, among other disciplines (Lepore, 2002). Lisa Roberts has perhaps the best perspective on the question of how and how much exhibits should rely upon storytelling as a rhetorical program,

> [J]ust as literary texts can be written in a way that invites readers' participation in their composition, exhibits can be developed in a way that engages visitors in constructing narratives about what they see. Indeed, such practices as including the social and historical contexts of objects or presenting other cultural perspectives already offer ways of encouraging narrative construction—the first by suggesting that meaning is neither innate nor fixed but exists in reference to a wider set of conditions; and the second by acknowledging that there are multiple ways of interpreting an object.
>
> (1997, p. 143)

We need to resist what exhibit scholars Falk and Dierking describe as a human impulse to "want simple explanations for complex reality" (2004, p. 139). Digital cultural exhibits should offer explanations or stories that are just as rich and interesting as the complex realities which they contain, in the form of digital objects. Finally, stories embedded within exhibit structure and content can be an effective way to create and trigger the pragmatic, or user relevance relationship between reader/visitor and content that can answer the question posed by Sorrell's big idea, "so what?"

Exhibits without stories are a thin gruel: bland, unappetizing, and with little nourishment. But writing accurate, engaging, reality-based stories is challenging, although certainly not impossible. It requires multiple interpretive, research, and creative skills, access to research sources, time, and writing ability. But there is a danger to creating exhibits that rely on stories that are not the products of this type of intellectual work. A cultural institution that aims to document the stories of immigrants—often poor and from marginalized groups—observes that "museums hold power in defining how we understand the past. Who is remembered, and by whom? Whose stories do we hear, and whose stories are erased or forgotten?" (Tenement Museum, n.d.). While not a museum exhibit, the landmark *1619 Project: A New Origin Story*, by Nikole Hannah-Jones and her colleagues at the *New York Times,* is a powerful example of what can happen when different stories are surfaced: In this case the origin story of the United States as one reliant on the enslavement of human beings and the lasting impact of slavery on American life, up to and including the present day (Hannah-Jones et al., 2021). There is a real power in the kind of cultural storytelling that an exhibit can employ and encompass. Thomas and Stornaiuolo term this action as "restorying, of reshaping narratives to better reflect a diversity of perspectives and experiences" after the work of Nigerian author Chimamanda Ngozi Adichie (2016, p. 314).

The following physical exhibits offer striking examples of what can happen when new stories and storytellers are given access to these types of cultural entities. The *Mining the Museum* exhibit created by installation artist Fred Wilson in 1992 for The Contemporary museum and the Maryland Historical Society was a groundbreaking achievement for its use of object selection, display, placement, and juxtaposition to tell a profound "story" about the treatment of non-white Americans, specifically the enslavement of African-Americans and the genocide of Indigenous peoples (Corrin, 2010; Wilson & Halle, 1993). The image in Figure 2.1 shows one of the displays in the exhibit, "a case filled with repoussé silverware cups, ewers and urn alongside a pair of metal slave shackles" used in the exhibit (Maryland Center for History and Culture, 1992–1993).

This juxtaposition of objects was designed by Wilson to engage the viewer in a complex narrative that contained various characters including the people who would use the cups, ewers, and urn, the people who would be imprisoned by the shackles, the relationship between these two sets of people, the physical setting in which all of the objects would appear and be used *simultaneously*, and the larger cultural, social, and economic systems that encompassed the people and objects. In a sense, Wilson was recreating what Pearce described as the "locational relationship" of these objects within a museum exhibit, in a reversal of the work that is done to analyze the artifacts in an archeological site (1994).

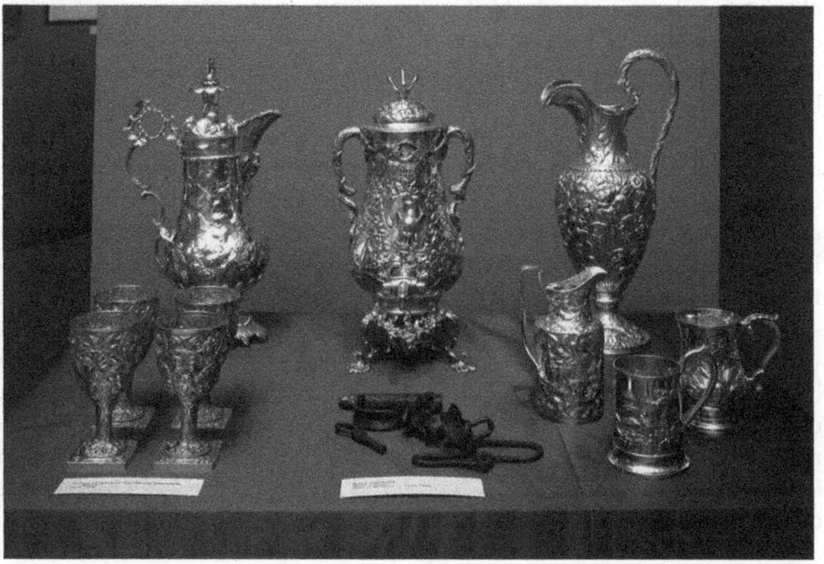

Figure 2.1 "*Mining the Museum: Metalwork 1793–1880*" by Fred Wilson and the Maryland Historical Society used by permission of the Maryland Center for History and Culture

This method of evoking a relationship through object arrangement was also used by Wilson with vintage chairs arranged in a semi-circle around a whipping post and "Cigar Store Indian" statues placed next to photographs of real Indigenous Americans. As described by Corrin, Wilson posted a notice in the museum to direct the exhibit visitors to engage with its constituent objects while thinking about questions such as

- What is it?
- Where is it? Why?
- What is it saying?
- How is it used?
- For whom was it created?

(2010, p. 306)

By engaging with these questions and object displays in such an intensely intimate context, the exhibit visitor would then be able to create a story that would be both personally impactful and historically accurate. It is notable that this visceral story could arise from the simple act of merely placing one object next to another. The lasting power of Wilson's exhibit design is still felt in the museum studies field and shows how clarity of message and creation of a personally activated and felt story can be achieved through exhibits.

The introduction of new, previously oppressed, and marginalized voices telling their stories is continuing, albeit slowly. These important and/or innovative physical exhibits are some examples of what is possible when the doors of cultural heritage organizations are opened to welcome these storytellers:

Two Centuries of Black American Art
Curated by David C. Driskell
Los Angeles County Museum of Art
September 30—November 21, 1976
This massive undertaking is described as the reason Driskell "forever changed art history. His legacy is enduring, impacting generations of artists, curators, scholars, collectors, and more".

(Newkirk, 2020)

The West as America, Reinterpreting Images of the Frontier, 1820–1920
Curated by William Truettner
Smithsonian American Art Museum
March 15—July 20, 1991
Described as a retelling "of America's favorite stories about itself. The premise is that depictions of the westward expansion were propaganda, 'carefully staged fictions' intended to sell Manifest Destiny while concealing or ignoring 'damaging social and environmental change'".

(Masters, 1991)

1993 Whitney Biennial
Curated by Thelma Golden, John G. Hanhardt, Lisa Phillips, and Elisabeth Sussman
Whitney Museum of American Art
March 4—June 20, 1993
Seen as a landmark in its engagement with issues of personal identity, race, class, gender, sexuality, imperialism, poverty and the then-current AIDS crisis.

(Smith, 1993)

In a Different Light: Visual Culture, Sexual Identity, Queer Practice
Curated by Nayland Blake and Lawrence Rinder
UC Berkeley Art Museum and Pacific Film Archive (BAMPFA)
January 11—April 9, 1995
Exhibit which intertwined issues of queer identity and generational affiliation

(Droitcour, 2018)

Phantom Sightings: Art after the Chicano Movement
Curated by Howard N. Fox, Rita Gonzalez, Chon A. Noriega
Los Angeles County Museum of Art
April 6—September 1, 2008

Described as "an exhibition of contemporary conceptually oriented art that redefines notions of ethnic identity and/or community belonging".

(Shaked, 2008, p. 1057)

Soul of a Nation: Art in the Age of Black Power
Curated by Mark Godfrey and Zoe Whitley with Priyesh Mistry
Tate Modern
July 12—October 22, 2017
"Celebrates the work of Black artists working in the United States in the two decades after 1963. During this turbulent time, these artists asked and answered many questions. How should an artist respond to political and cultural changes? Was there a 'Black art' or a 'Black aesthetic'? Should an artist create legible images or make abstract work? Was there a choice to be made between addressing a specifically Black audience or a 'universal' one? The exhibition looks at responses to such questions".

(Tate Modern, 2017)

Posing Modernity: The Black Model from Manet and Matisse to Today
Curated by Denise Murrell
Wallach Gallery, Columbia University
October 24—February 10, 2019
Described as a "taut, riveting exhibition . . . [which] revisits mid-19th-century Paris to examine the significance of black female models in paintings from the earliest years of European modernism".

(Smith, 2018, p. 15)

Guarding the Art
Curated by members of the BMA Security Department
Baltimore Museum of Art
March 27—July 10, 2022
"Guarding the Art will feature works from the BMA's collection, across eras, genres, cultures, and mediums, selected by guest curators from the BMA's Security department. As guest curators, the officers will collaborate with leadership and staff across the museum to select and reinterpret works".

(Baltimore Museum of Art, 2022)

Narratives and Stories Recommendations

The exhibit creator should be able to sit within the dialectic between objects and presentation. Meaning is neither innate nor fixed but exists in reference to a wider set of conditions. Exhibits sometimes need to take a form that is just outside explicit narrative. Provide a context for the objects. Refer to the relevant scholarly record. Beware of relying on familiar tropes or echoing simplistic stories. Invite marginalized voices into the story and center them.

Ravelli's Linguistic Communication Theory of Exhibits

Louise J. Ravelli's *Museum Texts* (2006) reflects the author's background and status as a linguistics scholar. Her model of exhibit structure and content relates to several of the frameworks discussed earlier in this chapter in its recognition that exhibit design and content are products of creative analysis. She differs in her introduction of the associated world of the exhibit's surrounding cultural organization and her analysis of exhibit content as genre texts which each have a specific *purpose* and *structure*. While acknowledging the central role of narrative in exhibits and the existence of marginally relevant genres like procedures, the specific genres Ravelli offers as especially useful for exhibit texts are the following:

- Report: Comprised of factual, essentially descriptive assertions that refer to an entire exhibit or a particular exhibit theme, section, or object; analogous to metadata in narrative form; can be organized from general to specific
- Explanation: If Reports focus on the "what" of an exhibit, explanations look at the "why;" starts with a general assertion, then moves to specific details, sometimes organized within a linear time sequence
- Exposition: Advancing an argument or specific conclusion based on described evidence
- Directive: While expositions aim to influence visitor thoughts, directives aim to sway visitor behaviors
- Discussion: Reviews multiple arguments and may, or may not, offer a conclusion

Ravelli stops short of offering advice to the exhibit creator aside from a general admonition to have a clear understanding of the rhetorical goals of your text, use genre conventions wisely to tap into the common mental schemata that readers of your target audience rely upon, and relate everything back to your exhibit's big idea.

Before looking at these genres in action within some digital exhibits, it should be noted that Ravelli's model of exhibit genres is highly culturally dependent. While she often points to the exhibit's originating institution (e.g., museum, historical society) as the rhetorical culture to which creators need to attend and consider, the larger language culture of the institution is also a driver of a given message's effectiveness at carrying out its genre-bound message. There can be no dispute about the nature of genre as culturally bound rhetorical forms. There is no construct called "Report" or "Explanation" on an abstract plane, away from human beings and the ways that they use language. The ways that genres are defined and used across cultures vary because they are culturally situated. A change in culture will change the kinds of messages deemed appropriate for a given setting and the way in which those messages should be expressed through genre. This rather anodyne observation is seen in language studies that analyzed message genre differences as varied as the business fax (Zhu, 2013), newspaper articles (Rafiee et al., 2018), messages to business stakeholders from corporate leaders (Ngai & Singh, 2017), and social media profile pages (Tobback, 2019), all irrespective of actual language used. Clearly, Ravelli's genres reflect her western cultural background and focus. The previous analysis of the need for alternative voices and modes of thought in the digital exhibit field applies here as well. These genres can be useful, however, when they are understood and applied in culturally sensitive ways.

The following list shows how Ravelli's genres can provide structure and clarity to an online exhibit:

1 Report: *Frost on Chickens*
"Selected USDA Research on Backyard Chickens: The USDA's Agricultural Research Service program of research into poultry farming is highly focused on specific issues such as poultry litter management, disease control and resistance, and nutrition. The most relevant recent USDA research on poultry farming for the non-agricultural professional are confined to the following documents and reports from the USDA's Animal and Plant Health Inspection Service".
2 Explanation: *Apron Strings and Kitchen Sinks*
"The Bureau of Home Economics was a pioneering unit in the US Department of Agriculture for several reasons. It was the first major unit to have been headed by a woman: Louise Stanley, Ph.D. It focused on topics of central concern to women, as defined by the cultural norms of the early 20th century: sewing, kitchen design and features, time spent on housework, children's clothing, and food preparation and preservation. Lastly, it took a then-novel approach to its work: it strove to first understand what its primary audience needed within its broad mandate and then shaped its specific programs around those needs. This exhibit showcases the work of this Bureau, especially the work related to clothing and kitchen design".
3 Exposition: *America During the 1918 Influenza Pandemic*
"Other pandemics and health crises affected early twentieth-century Americans and their predecessors, but this one was different because of its rapid spread, faster progression, and disproportionate effect on the young and healthy. This, combined with the loss of so many young men at the front to disease and injury, led to a population lull in the US that would take several years to rebound to original numbers".
4 Directive: *Baltimore Uprising*
"It is crucial to gather and preserve as many perspectives and experiences of protest and unrest as possible. Too often, history is shaped by official accounts. When the history of the Baltimore Uprising is written, we want to make sure it can include voices from the streets as well as voices from the halls of government. Help us. Share your stories. Upload photographs. Show us what you've seen. Show us the sign you carried. Tell us what you witnessed. When were you there? Where did you stand? Together, we will tell a more complete story".

5 Discussion: *American Empire*
"During his farewell address in 1796 President George Washington warned the young republic to 'steer clear of permanent alliances with . . . the foreign world.' Fast forward to 1823—President James Monroe stood before Congress and issued the Monroe Doctrine which advocated extending the nation's reach through the Americas to safeguard national security. 'We should consider any [foreign] attempt . . . to extend their system to any portion of this hemisphere,' Monroe declared, 'as dangerous to our peace and safety'".

Ravelli's consideration of the larger social and cultural contexts that influence and flavor exhibit language echoes the work of Falk and Dierking on the ways in which visitors learn within the museum exhibit setting (2000; 2004). Their Contextual Model of visitor learning "involves three overlapping contexts: the *personal*, the *sociocultural*, and the *physical*. Learning is the process/product of the interactions between these three contexts" (2000, p. 10). This observation is in close proximity to Ravelli's contention that her model of exhibits is a model of communication, defined as "an active, social process . . . where meaning relates to choice . . . where meaning is complex . . . where meaning relates to context" (5–9).

Linguistic Communication Recommendations

Be sure to consider how your exhibit content relates to other relevant materials, especially materials connected with your home institution, but also the larger cultural and intellectual influences that make up your reader's world of communication. Consider using Ravelli's genres to shape and structure your exhibit content.

An Original Model of Digital Exhibits

The last model to be considered is an original one for digital exhibits first documented in an article about Omeka, an exhibit content management system for cultural institutions and visualized in Figure 2.2 (Marsh, 2017).

Essentially, the model contains specific functions, which can be performed by digital exhibits (identification, display, engagement, interpretation, education, and experience), arranged on a vector illustrating the degree to which each fulfills one of two larger rhetorical orientations (Marsh, 2022). Within the model, exhibits are divided roughly into two groups: those which are focused more on object identification and display, and those that aim not only to fulfill those goals but also to provide a more comprehensive picture through some sort of analytical enrichment. Object-oriented exhibits concern themselves with accurate object modeling, description, and display, much like digital collections, but with a bit more context and specificity to the visitor. In contrast, user-oriented exhibits center digital objects and provide metadata and display functions, while also imparting information about and interpretations of those objects through text, supplemented with associated content, such as images, visualizations, timelines, and maps. The phrase "rhetorical energy" is used to describe this difference in emphasis within an exhibit's purpose. In essence,

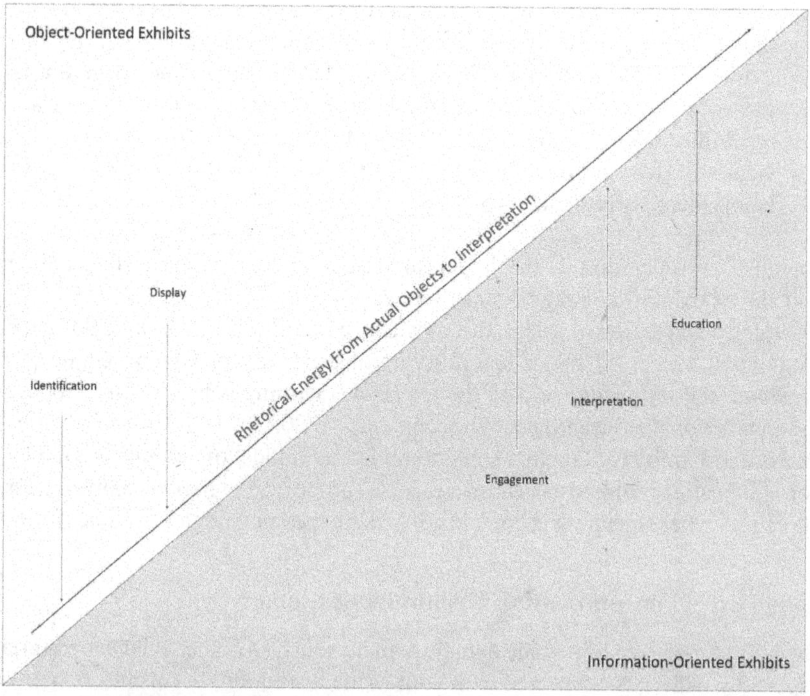

Figure 2.2 Digital exhibit orientation and functions, revised from Marsh (2017)

the use of this model requires the exhibit creator to decide what approach will work better for the objects in question: creating an exhibit that acts essentially as a showcase for information objects or as a multi-part essay illustrated with object views and deeper analysis designed to connect to a user.

Chapter 1 asserted that the basic nature of digital exhibits is to sit at a midpoint between search and discovery object systems and illustrated essays. By this definition, digital exhibits contain objects and surrounding text. While this observation is true, the model presented here adds some further power to tease out distinctions within this range. The degree to which the exhibit features and emphasizes object over text, or *vice versa*, will determine its orientation as either object or user-oriented.

The question arises: What orientation should a given exhibit adopt? Some exhibits focus on objects that are culturally significant, artistically important, previously inaccessible digitally, visually striking, or possessing some other unique characteristic. A straightforward object exhibit might be the best option for this case as a way of simply letting the objects speak for themselves. Other times, object-centered exhibits are preferred by their creators simply because their associated objects have been deemed the sole center of attention and no other content is wanted lest it take attention away from the digital objects themselves. Finally, some institutions might want to launch an exhibit, but do not have the staff, resources, experience, or training to do much beyond creating a collection-like container for their content. This kind of exhibit is common and certainly has an important place in the world of cultural heritage. Object-oriented exhibits exist to provide access to valuable digital content, meaningful description that identifies the items' significance within a given context, attractive means of display for the content, and no more contextualizing information than necessary. Their rhetorical energy is directed toward the tasks of identification and display. While this type of exhibit is somewhat like a digital collection, since both are centered around objects, it is still different because the central user tasks are not search and discovery, but identification, display, and appreciation. Finally, it should be noted that many exhibits of this type can be quite striking and visually engaging.

Some notable examples of object-oriented digital exhibits are:

Signed, Sealed, & Undelivered
Rebekah Ahrendt, Nadine Akkerman, Jana Dambrogio, Daniel Starza Smith, David van der Linden, Sound and Vision The Hague, and the Massachusetts Institute of Technology (M.I.T.)
An exhibit showcasing the contents of a 17th-century trunk of sealed letters that were never delivered

British Library Treasures
British Library
An exhibit of the highlights of the British Library through manuscripts, diaries, stamps, maps and views, scientific reports and illustrations

Benjamin Franklin: In His Own Words
U.S. Library of Congress
Organizes the writings of Franklin into broad themes

The works of Kiersten F. Latham (2013) and Stephen Greenblatt (1991) offer additional insights into this kind of traditional, object-oriented exhibit format. Latham interviewed museum visitors who reported having a "numinous", or deeply meaningful experience with a museum object. A qualitative analysis of the interviews revealed that exhibits focused on simple object display can be the catalyst for profound and intense visitor experience. Likewise, Greenblatt's construct of "wonder" in museum exhibits touches upon this same type of personally intense experience. The object-oriented exhibit tries to tap into a sense of wonder for the visitor, "the power of the displayed object to stop the viewer in his or her tracks, to convey an arresting uniqueness, to evoke an exalted attention" (1991, p. 42). Given that many exhibits comprise materials that are unlikely to stop anyone in their [digital] tracks, creating this type of exhibit in an attempt to evoke wonder or a numinous experience seems like a tall order indeed.

Instead, another type of exhibit seems more likely to succeed and create what Greenblatt calls resonance,

> the power of the displayed object to reach out beyond its formal boundaries to a larger world, to evoke in the viewer the complex, dynamic cultural forces from which it has emerged and for which it may be taken by a viewer to stand. (1991, p. 42)

Of course, these events are not accomplished by objects themselves, but by their placement in an exhibit, along with associated content that aims to provide further context and interpretation: in short, a user-oriented exhibit.

User-oriented exhibits also contain digital objects but aim to reach different communicative goals. For this type of exhibit, the focus is on providing the reader/visitor with an understanding of the essential significance of some aspect(s) of the objects. That understanding may be straightforward, or it may be a multi-faceted exploration, incorporating multiple viewpoints and drawing on multiple sources. The four functions that should be considered by the creator of the user-oriented exhibit are:

1 Engagement: Make the exhibit content engaging to the visitor by offering features such as embedded videos, interactive lightboxes and slideshows for multiple image arrays, or digital page turners for text objects with multiple pages. These features should not be deployed as mere visual frippery or gimmicks but should make a tighter connection between the exhibit's users and its content to achieve a more user-oriented experience, but still embedded in the world of the object.
2 Interpretation: This is a pathway to initiate the reaction of resonance from exhibit visitors that Greenblatt and Ruthven (2021) describe. Providing an interpretive context allows an exhibit to demonstrate the meaning or significance of information objects and provides added value that would not be available through simple identification or display alone. An example of interpretation in a digital exhibit would be to create a single display of objects that reveal a larger network of relationships. Such a display is featured in an exhibit on the history of the US Department of Agriculture's Bureau of Home Economics that contains an embedded video of a digitized documentary about the Bureau from 1949, the film's script, and publications associated with the film's content. All of these objects displayed together provide an enriched context for the visitor to glean a fuller interpretation of the film and its status as a work product of this governmental unit.
3 Education: This is one of the highest goals of the user-oriented exhibit and can be difficult to tease this specific feature out, however, because exhibits fulfilling this higher order goal necessitate the lower order elements of identification, display, engagement, and interpretation. Overall, educational elements build upon, but go beyond the others to affect some change in the viewer. These elements normally take the form of additional materials: objects, documents, images, visualizations, brought into the exhibit to provide a richer

perspective. Attempts at persuasion can also be involved to lead the user to make some conclusion about the entire exhibit or appreciate some insight into one of its constituent parts.

4 Experience: This goal aims to reach into the psychological world of the visitor in ways that are perceived and felt as personal, authentic, and memorable (Pallud & Straub, 2014; Pine & Gilmore, 2007). Clearly this is a very high goal and one that should be pursued with care. At a minimum, the creator of this type of exhibit should have access to the following: deep background knowledge in both the exhibit objects and their nature and status as reflected in the scholarly record, knowledge of and the ability to deploy effective ways to design and represent this knowledge through the channels afforded by the exhibit genre, and insight into the audience for this content and what they would like to see, learn, discover, and experience.

If we return to the earlier examples of the *Safer at Home* and the *Brandywine Valley Oral History Project* exhibits, it is possible to see how it would be possible to modify each to make them more like user-oriented exhibits. The division between images focused on the more quotidian activities of being "at home" and those of AIDS prevention and political protest could be made more explicit instead of being placed within a navigation link labeled "Explore by Category". Next, the intriguing ideas of queer people being "safe at home" could be enriched with a more scholarly discussion of what each concept means in this context. For example, Després surveyed the literature of studies published between 1974 and 1989, which surveyed home residents on their ideas about the question, "what is home", and developed the following categories (1991):

1 Home as Security and Control
2 Home as Reflection of One's Ideas and Values
3 Home as Acting Upon and Modifying One's Dwelling
4 Home as Permanence and Continuity
5 Home as Relationships With Family and Friends
6 Home as Center of Activities
7 Home as Refuge From the Outside World
8 Home as Indicator of Personal Status
9 Home as Material Structure
10 Home as a Place to Own

Després' work could also be combined with that of Easthope (2010) who looked at home as a "place", Mallett's variables of home as "(a) place(s), (a) space(s), feeling(s), practices, and/or an active state of state of being in the world" (2004, p. 62), Fox's characteristics of financial investment, physical structure, territory, identity, and a social and cultural unit (2007), and/or Hohmann's definition of home as offering privacy, identity, and a space (2013). Clearly, many of these concepts would be intriguing to pursue within the context of queer life pictured within the photographs of the exhibit. The analysis of the images would be enriched by this type of reference to associated scholarship on ideas of "home", in addition to that of "safety". It would also shift the exhibit from being one that offered visual imagery of various people engaged in activities (object-oriented) to one that used these images to illustrate the social and cultural forces at work in the larger world, relevant to LGBTQ+ life in the time pictured by these objects (user-oriented).

Some of these aspects of home as a concept could also be explored in the *Brandywine Valley Oral History Project* exhibit, in addition to more factual material about and analysis of the working conditions described by the participants. A separation of material related to the domestic themes of Childhood & Mischief, Food & Drink, Holidays & Traditions, and Recreation & Entertainment from the material on Working on the Brandywine [River] and Mill Explosions would create a stark contrast to the viewer. This contrast could then be extended further by incorporating analyses of the concepts of public–private and work–home life, illustrated by the exhibit's oral histories.

These examples show how a user-oriented exhibit can be created by incorporating relevant scholarship on whatever topics are most applicable and important to the exhibit's objects and, more importantly, how you as the exhibit creator choose to analyze, present, and enrich those objects.

Some notable examples of more thematic, essay-like digital user-oriented exhibits are:

Syrian Refugee Resettlement in Canada
Nergis Canefe, Faida Abu-Ghazaleh, and Robyn Lelacheur
York University Libraries
Strives to offer a documented commentary on the most recent addition to the Canadian resettlement scheme for refugees from Syria

Black Quotidian
Matthew F. Delmont
Stanford University
Drawing on an archive of digitized African-American newspapers, *Black Quotidian* guides readers through a wealth of primary resources that reveal how the Black press popularized African-American history and valued the lives of both famous and ordinary Black people

Women of the Early Harlem Renaissance: African American Women Writers 1900–1922
Amardeep Singh
Lehigh University
This site aims to collect poetry, drama, and fiction by African American women between 1900 and 1922.

Object Versus User-Oriented Exhibits

Consider carefully and clearly the nature of your core object set. If "wonder" or "numinosity" is a likely response, consider how you will create sophisticated views of your objects to create an engaging object-oriented exhibit. If your objects are less evocative and need more context and interpretation, consider how to identify and include associated content to create a user-oriented exhibit. Be sure to investigate the scholarly record for studies that discuss concepts that could organize your objects and provide a framework for a more user-oriented exhibit if that is desired.

Digital Exhibits Discussed in This Chapter

Abolition of Slavery
The National Archives (UK)
www.nationalarchives.gov.uk/slavery/about.htm

Alice in Wonderland
The British Library
www.bl.uk/alice-in-wonderland

"All Change!" on Britain's Railways
The National Archives (UK)
www.nationalarchives.gov.uk/railways/

American Empire
Andrea Ledesma
Digital Public Library of America
https://dp.la/exhibitions/american-empire

America During the 1918 Influenza Pandemic
Bethany Campbell, Michelle John, Samantha Reid-Goldberg, Anne Sexton, and John Weimer
Digital Public Library of America
https://dp.la/exhibitions/1918-influenza

Baltimore Uprising
Denise D. Meringolo and Baltimore community
https://baltimoreuprising2015.org/home

Benjamin Franklin . . . In His Own Words
US Library of Congress
www.loc.gov/exhibits/franklin/index.html

Black Quotidian
Matthew F. Delmont
Stanford University
http://blackquotidian.org/

Brandywine Valley Oral History Project
Angela Schad and Kevin Martin

Hagley Museum and Library
www.hagley.org/research/digital-exhibits/brandywine-valley-oral-history-project

British Library Treasures
British Library
www.bl.uk/british-library-treasures

Doodles, Drafts, and Designs: Industrial Drawings from the Smithsonian
US National Museum of American History. Smithsonian Institution
www.sil.si.edu/exhibitions/doodles/

Frost on Chickens
Emily Marsh
National Agricultural Library, US Department of Agriculture
www.nal.usda.gov/exhibits/ipd/frostonchickens/

George Washington Carver
Emily Marsh
National Agricultural Library, US Department of Agriculture
www.nal.usda.gov/exhibits/ipd/carver/

Geppi Gems
US Library of Congress
www.loc.gov/exhibitions/geppi-gems/about-this-exhibition/

Mailboxes, Mom and Pop Stands, and Markets: Local Foods Then and Now
Emily Marsh
National Agricultural Library, US Department of Agriculture
www.nal.usda.gov/exhibits/ipd/localfoods/

Mirrors and Mass: Wayne Thom's Southern California
Emily Bills and students of The History of Modern Architecture in Southern California, 2018
University of Southern California Libraries
https://scalar.usc.edu/works/wayne-thom/index

Records of Rights: Rights of Native Americans
National Archives and Records Administration (US)
http://recordsofrights.org/themes/4/rights-of-native-americans

Rosa Parks: In Her Own Words
Library of Congress (US)
www.loc.gov/exhibitions/rosa-parks-in-her-own-words/about-this-exhibition/

Safer at Home: Exploring the ONE Archives Collection
Alexis Bard Johnson
University of Southern California Libraries
https://scalar.usc.edu/works/safer-at-home/index

Signed, Sealed, & Undelivered
Rebekah Ahrendt, Nadine Akkerman, Jana Dambrogio, Daniel Starza Smith, David van der Linden, Sound and Vision The Hague, and the Massachusetts Institute of Technology (M.I.T.)
http://brienne.org/

South Asians in Britain
British Library
www.bl.uk/asians-in-britain

Syrian Refugee Resettlement in Canada
Nergis Canefe, Faida Abu-Ghazaleh, and Robyn Lelacheur
York University Libraries
https://scalar.library.yorku.ca/syrian-refugee-settlement-in-canada/index

Women of the Early Harlem Renaissance: African American Women Writers 1900–1922
Amardeep Singh
Lehigh University
https://scalar.lehigh.edu/harlemwomen/index

Women Reading in America
Chloe Collins, Anjana Rao, Mollie Schwam, Erica Zhang, and Martin Antonetti
Smith College Libraries
https://libex.smith.edu/omeka/exhibits/show/reading

References

Ball, M. S., & Smith, G. W. H. (1992). *Analyzing visual data*. Thousand Oaks, CA: SAGE Publishing.

Baltimore Museum of Art. (2022). *Guarding the art: Overview*. https://artbma.org/exhibition/bma-security-officers-take-center-stage-as-guest-curators-of-a-new-exhibition-opening-in-march-2022.

Banks, M. (2018). *Using visual data in qualitative research* (2nd ed.). Thousand Oaks, CA: SAGE Publishing.

Baumann, J. (2013, November 22). The Silence=Death poster. *LGBTQ at NYPL*. New York Public Library. www.nypl.org/blog/2013/11/22/silence-equals-death-poster.

Berkowitz, R. (2003). *Stayin' alive: The invention of safe sex*. Boulder, CO: Westview Press.

Bills, E. (2018). *Mirrors and mass: Wayne Thom's southern California*. University of Southern California. https://scalar.usc.edu/works/wayne-thom/index.

Braun, V., & Clarke, V. (2006) Using thematic analysis in psychology. *Qualitative Research in Psychology*, *3*(2), 77–101. https://doi.org/10.1191/1478088706qp063oa.

British Library. (n.d.). *South Asians in Britain*. https://www.bl.uk/asians-in-britain.

Chang, H. (2021). Presentist history for pluralist science. *Journal for General Philosophy of Science*, *52*. https://doi.org/10.1007/s10838-020-09512-8.

Clarke, V., & Braun, V. (2013). Teaching thematic analysis. *The Psychologist*, *26*, 120–123.

Corrin, L. (2010). Mining the museum: An installation confronting history. *Curator: The Museum Journal*, *36*, 302–313. http://dx.doi.org/10.1111/j.2151-6952.1993.tb00804.x.

Cox, A. (2011). *Visualizing data at the New York Times*. www.slideshare.net/openjournalism/amanda-cox-visualizing-data-at-the-new-york-times.

Denzin, N. K., & Lincoln, Y. S. (Eds.). (2017). *The SAGE handbook of qualitative research* (5th ed.). Thousand Oaks, CA: SAGE Publishing.

Després, C. (1991). The meaning of home: Literature review and directions for future research and theoretical development. *Journal of Architectural and Planning Research*, *8*(2), 96–115. www.jstor.org/stable/43029026.

Droitcour, B. (2018, May 1). Subcultural treasures. *Art in America*. www.artnews.com/art-in-america/features/subcultural-treasures-63510/.

Easthope, H. (2010). A place called home. *Housing, Theory and Society*, *21*(3), 128–138. https://doi.org/10.1080/14036090410021360.

Falk, J. H., & Dierking, L. D. (2000). *Learning from museums: Visitor experiences and the making of meaning*. Lanham, MD: Rowman & Littlefield.

Falk, J. H., & Dierking, L. D. (2004). The contextual model of learning. In G. Anderson (Ed.), *Reinventing the museum: Historical and contemporary perspectives on the paradigm shift* (pp. 139–142). Walnut Creek, CA: AltaMira Press.

Ferguson, B. W. (1996). Exhibition rhetorics: Material speech and utter sense. In R. Greenburg, B. W. Ferguson, & S. Nairine (Eds.), *Thinking about exhibitions* (pp. 126–136). London: Routledge.

Fludernik, M. (2009). *An introduction to narratology*. London: Routledge.

Fouracre, D. (2015). Making an exhibition of ourselves? Academic libraries and exhibitions today. *The Journal of Academic Librarianship*, *41*, 377–385. http://dx.doi.org/10.1016/j.acalib.2015.05.008.

Fox, L. (2007) *Conceptualising home: Theories, laws and policies*. London: Hart.

Greenblatt, S. (1991). Resonance and wonder. In I. Karp & S. D. Lavine (Eds.), *Exhibiting cultures: The poetics and politics of museum display* (pp. 42–56). Washington, DC: Smithsonian Institution.

Hagley Museum and Library. (n.d.). *Brandywine Valley oral history project*. hagley.org/research/digital-exhibits/brandywine-valley-oral-history-project.

Hanks, L. H., Hale, J., & MacLeod, S. (2012). Introduction: Museum making. The place of narrative. In L. H. Hanks, J. Hale, & S. MacLeod (Eds.), *Museum making: Narratives, architectures, exhibitions* (pp. xix–xxiii). London: Routledge.

Hannah-Jones, N., Roper, C., Silverman, I., & Silverstein, J. (Eds.). (2021). *The 1619 project: A new origin story*. New York: One World.

Hinchman, K. A., & Moore, D. W. (2013). Close reading: A cautionary interpretation. *Journal of Adolescent & Adult Literacy*, *56*(6), 441–450. https://doi.org/10.1002/JAAL.163.

Hohmann, J. (2013) *The right to housing: Law, concepts, possibilities*. London: Hart.

Iser, W. (1972). The reading process: A phenomenological approach. *New Literary History*, *3*(2), 279–299. www.jstor.org/stable/468316.

Iser, W. (1978). *The act of reading: A theory of aesthetic response*. Baltimore, MD: Johns Hopkins University Press.

Johnson, A. B. (2020). *Safer at home*. University of Southern California Libraries. https://scalar.usc.edu/works/safer-at-home/index.

Johnson, B. S. (1973). *Aren't you rather young to be writing your memoirs?* London: Hutchinson.

Latham, K. F. (2013). Numinous experiences with museum objects. *Visitor Studies*, *16*(1), 3–20. https://doi.org/10.1080/10645578.2013.767728.

Lepore, J. (2002). Historical writing and the revival of narrative. *Nieman Reports: The Nieman Foundation for Journalism at Harvard University*, *56*(1), 51–53. https://niemanreports.org/wp-content/uploads/2014/04/02spring.pdf.

Library of Congress. (n.d.). *Geppi Gems: A Library of Congress exhibition*. https://www.loc.gov/static/exhibitions/geppi-gems/documents/Geppi-Gems_Exhibition-Brochure.pdf.

Mallett, S. (2004). Understanding home: A critical review of the literature. *The Sociological Review*, *52*(1), 62–89. https://doi.org/10.1111/j.1467-954X.2004.00442.x.

Marsh, E. (2017). Chickens, aprons, markets, and cans: How the National Agricultural Library uses Omeka as its content management system for digital exhibits. *Digital Library Perspectives*, *33*(4), 361–377. https://doi.org/10.1108/DLP-03-2017-0009.

Marsh, E. (2022). *Digital exhibit orientation and functions* [Infographic]. https://emilymarsh.com/Digital_Exhibits_for_Cultural_Institutions/Figure_2.2.jpg.

Martinez, S., Hand, M. S., Da Pra, M., Pollack, S., Ralston, K., Smith, T., Vogel, S., Clark, S., Lohr, L., Low, S., & Newman, C. (2010). *Local food systems: Concepts, impacts, and issues*. Economic Research Report (ERR) Number 97. https://handle.nal.usda.gov/10113/60454.

Maryland Historical Society. (1992–1993). *Mining the museum: 'Metalwork, 1793–1880.'* [Photograph]. Baltimore, MD: Maryland Center for History and Culture. www.mdhistory.org/resources/mining-the-museum-metalwork-1793-1880/.

Masters, K. (1991, June 2). They went that away. *Washington Post*. www.washingtonpost.com/archive/lifestyle/style/1991/06/02/they-went-thataway/842e3f38-cda4-4b2d-811f-bd315b32f3b5/.

McKechnie, L. E. F., Julien, H., & Oliphant, T. (2008). Communicating research findings to library and information science practitioners: A study of ISIC papers from 1996 to 2000. *Information Research*, *13*(4), Paper 375. http://informationr.net/ir/13-4/paper375.html.

Miller, W. L., & Crabtree, B. F. (1992). Primary care research: A multimethod typology and qualitative road map. In B. F. Crabtree & W. L. Miller (Eds.), *Doing qualitative research. Research methods for primary care, volume 3* (pp. 3–30). Newbury Park, CA: SAGE Publications.

Myburgh, S., & Tammaro, A. M. (2013). *Exploring education for digital librarians: Meaning, modes and models*. Oxford: Chandos Publishing.

National Park Service. Harper's Ferry Center. U.S. Department of the Interior. (2011, October 21). *Museum and visitor center exhibit planning, design, and fabrication process: Summary description*. www.nps.gov/subjects/hfc/upload/EX-PD-Prod-Charts-R.pdf.

Newkirk, P. (2020, April 6). How David C. Driskell shaped the story of Black art in America. *ARTnews*. www.artnews.com/art-news/retrospective/david-c-driskell-shaped-black-art-pamela-newkirk-archives-1202683191/.

Ngai, C. S.-B., & Singh, R. G. (2017). Move structure and communication style of leaders' messages in corporate discourse: A cross-cultural perspective. *Discourse & Communication*, *11*(3), 276–295. https://doi.org/10.1177/1750481317697860.

Pallud, J., & Straub, D. W. (2014). Effective website design for experience-influenced environments: The case of high culture museums. *Information & Management, 51*(3), 359–373.

Patton, M. Q. (1999). Enhancing the quality and credibility of qualitative analysis. *HSR: Health Services Research, 34*(5 Pt 2), 1189–1208. www.ncbi.nlm.nih.gov/pmc/articles/PMC1089059/pdf/hsresearch00022-0112.pdf.

Pauwels, L., & Mannay, D. (2019). *The SAGE handbook of visual research methods* (2nd ed.). Thousand Oaks, CA: SAGE Publishing.

Pearce, S. M. (1994). Thinking about things. In S. M. Pearce (Ed.), *Interpreting objects and collections* (pp. 125–132). London: Routledge.

Pine, B. J., & Gilmore, J. H. (2007). Museums & authenticity. *Museum News, 86*(3), 76–80; 92–93.

Pink, S. (2012). *Advances in visual methodology*. Thousand Oaks, CA: SAGE Publishing.

Powell, R. R., Baker, L. M., & Mika, J. J. (2002). Library and information science practitioners and research. *Library & Information Science Research, 24*(1), 49–72. https://doi.org/10.1016/S0740-8188(01)00104-9.

Rafiee, A., Spooren, W., & Sanders, J. (2018). Culture and discourse structure: A comparative study of Dutch and Iranian news texts. *Discourse & Communication, 12*(1), 58–79. https://doi.org/10.1177/1750481317735626.

Ravelli, L. J. (2006). *Museum texts: Communication frameworks*. London: Routledge.

Regan, S. (1998). Reader-response criticism and reception theory. In S. Eliot & W. R. Owens (Eds.), *A handbook to literary research* (pp. 139–149). London: Routledge.

Roberts, L. C. (1997). *From knowledge to narrative: Educators and the changing museum*. Washington, DC: Smithsonian Institution Press.

Roppola, T. (2013). *Designing for the museum visitor experience*. London: Routledge.

Rosch, E., & Mervis, C. G. (1975). Family resemblances: Studies in the internal structure of categories. *Cognitive Psychology, 7*(4), 573–605. https://doi.org/10.1016/0010-0285(75)90024-9.

Rosenblatt, L. M. (1978). *The reader, the text, the poem: The transactional theory of the literary work*. Carbondale, IL: Southern Illinois University Press.

Rosenblatt, L. M. (2004). The transactional theory of reading and writing. In Ruddell, R. B. & Unrau, N. J. (Eds.), *Theoretical models and processes of reading* (5th ed., pp. 1363–1398). Newark, DE: International Reading Association.

Ruthven, I. (2021). Resonance and the experience of relevance. *Journal of the American Society of Information Science and Technology, 72*(5), 554–569. https://doi.org/10.1002/asi.24424.

Saracevic, T. (1975). Relevance: A review of and a framework for the thinking on the notion in information science. *Journal of the American Society for Information Science, 26*(6), 321–343. https://doi.org/10.1002/asi.4630260604.

Serrell, B. (2015). *Exhibit labels: An interpretive approach* (2nd ed.). Lanham, MD: Rowman & Littlefield.

Shaked, N. (2008). Phantom sightings: Art after the Chicano movement. *American Quarterly, 60*(4), 1057–1072. www.jstor.org/stable/40068561.

Shannon, C. E., & Weaver, W. (1949). *The mathematical theory of communication*. Champaign, IL: University of Illinois Press.

Sitzia, E. (2016). Narrative theories and learning in contemporary art museums: A theoretical exploration. *Stedelijk Studies, 4*(Spring). https://stedelijkstudies.com/journal/narrative-theories-learning-contemporary-art-museums-theoretical-exploration/.

Smith, B. (1993, March 5). At the Whitney, a biennial with a social conscience. *New York Times*, Section C, Page 1. www.nytimes.com/1993/03/05/arts/at-the-whitney-a-biennial-with-a-social-conscience.html.

Smith, R. (2018, November 1). A long overdue light on Black models of early modernism. *New York Times*, Section C, Page 15. www.nytimes.com/2018/11/01/arts/design/black-models-olympia-columbia-university.html.

Smith College Libraries. (n.d.). *Women reading in America*. https://libex.smith.edu/omeka/exhibits/show/reading.

Smithsonian Institution. (n.d.). *Museum on main street: Exhibition planning guide*. Washington, DC: Smithsonian Institution. https://museumonmainstreet.org/sites/default/files/exhibition_planning_guide_sk_final.pdf.

Starr, L. (2020, September 24). Laying the foundation for storytelling: Tips for digital transformation & sustainability. *Pass It Down Blog*. www.passitdown.com/blog-posts/laying-the-foundation-for-storytelling-tips-for-digital-transformation-sustainability.

Tate Modern. (2017). *Exhibition guide: The sound of a nation*. London: Tate Modern. www.tate.org.uk/art/sound-of-a-nation.

Tenement Museum. (n.d.). *Reclaiming black spaces*. New York: Tenement Museum. www.tenement.org/reclaiming-black-spaces/.

Terry, G., & Hayfield, N. (2021). *Essentials of thematic analysis*. Washington, DC: American Psychological Association.

Tobback, E. (2019). Telling the world how skillful you are: Self-praise strategies on LinkedIn. *Discourse & Communication*, *13*(6), 647–668. https://doi.org/10.1177/1750481319868854.

Toxey, A. P., & McMillan, P. C. (2009). *Exhibit design and development workbook*. Austin, TX: Texas Historical Commission. www.thc.texas.gov/public/upload/publications/2015%20LR%20Museum%20Services%20Exhibit%20Development%20Workbook%20with%20Introduction.pdf.

Underwood, T. (2017). A genealogy of distant reading. *Digital Humanities Quarterly*, *11*(2). www.digitalhumanities.org/dhq/vol/11/2/000317/000317.html.

Vickery, B. (1959). Subject analysis for information retrieval systems. In National Research Council (Ed.), *Proceedings of the international conference on scientific information: Two volumes* (pp. 855–865). Washington, DC: The National Academies Press. https://doi.org/10.17226/10866.

White, M. D., & Marsh, E. E. (2006). Content analysis: A flexible methodology. *Library Trends*, *55*(1), 22–45. https://doi.org/10.1353/lib.2006.0053.

Wilson, F., & Halle, H. (1993). Mining the museum. *Grand Street*, *44*, 151–172. https://doi.org/10.2307/25007622.

Wittgenstein, L. (1953). *Philosophical investigations* (G. E. M. Anscombe, Trans.). Oxford: Basil Blackwell.

Zhu, Y. (2013). A cross-cultural analysis of English and Chinese business faxes: A genre perspective. *Ibérica*, *26*, 35–54. https://revistaiberica.org/index.php/iberica/article/view/272.

3 Connecting Your Exhibit to Your Audience and the Larger Information Ecosystem

It might seem counter-intuitive, but before you engage deeply with your exhibit material, you should spend some time looking outward at your audience and the larger information ecosystem, including other work within your organization to understand how these elements might work together to their mutual benefit.

While it might be tempting to focus on your exhibit content to the exclusion of everything else, this would be a mistake. Unless you are lucky enough to work on projects associated with iconic items such as Charles Dickens' manuscripts or Thomas Edison's patents, you will need to expend some energy and effort in determining the best way to explain your material to your audience. Why should they spend their time and attention looking at your exhibit? What is unique and compelling about the story you want to tell with your materials? Why should your users care? How can you incorporate and elevate diverse perspectives on your content and engage multiple audiences with your exhibit? How will this exhibit fit into the larger content strategy for your organization?

To answer these hard questions, it is tempting to look for a ready-made set of categories to help you slice and dice your potential audiences into this or that type. This can result in decisions like "We know that our users are 'casual browsers,' so let's have a timeline or an image carousel they can click through" or "We want to appeal to academic researchers so let's make sure all the content is text-heavy and written by a subject matter expert". These decisions are not necessarily bad, but trying to find simple prescriptive solutions, "if this, then do that" to what are essentially complex problems will probably not result in a meaningful, carefully designed exhibit. Users of cultural heritage content are not simple and one-dimensional. We need to think about our users in ways that foster inclusivity, diversity, intellectual flexibility, and deep understanding, just as we strive to uphold the same values in the ways we think about the mission of our organizations and the value and meaning of our content holdings.

This need becomes even more important when you realize that user behavior in a digital exhibit can be radically different than that in a physical exhibit. Whereas exhibit curators can direct visitors through a physical space and can, to varying degrees, guide them along pre-determined paths (Bitgood, 2010; Carliner, 2003; Tzortzi, 2014), in the digital world, any exhibit data point or content page can

DOI:10.4324/9781003301493-3

function as a landing point for the user. You cannot assume that all users will dutifully click through the sensible linear paths you may want to lay out for them. While some users will move through your exhibit this way, many, if not most, will not. To a greater or lesser degree, they will pick and choose whatever content they find interesting or useful in your exhibit and leave the rest behind. Exactly what content they pick and choose can be shaped by your exhibit structure, but not ultimately determined. The essentially discrete, compartmentalized nature of digital content (documents, images, video, exhibit text) compels the exhibit creator to develop multiple entry points, paths, and functions for the greatest number of users' needs that is feasible.

While you work to support realistic and legitimate information needs, you also need to attend to the aesthetic and experiential aspects of your exhibit, at a level that is not the same as typical information resources. Generally, especially in libraries and archives, information professionals are tasked with creating tools that are meant to be used to achieve some concrete purpose. Pathfinders, finding aids, bibliographic databases, document repositories, reference services, indexing, and cataloging terms are all designed with a purposeful user in mind. The overarching goal always is to link the right resources to the right person in a way that is efficient and effective, and honors the essential integrity of both parties. Cultural heritage exhibits operate within a slightly different conceptual space. The primary goal is not the provision of either an information entity or an information service, like those held and offered by Europeana's or the Digital Public Library of America's (DPLA's) digital collections. The primary goal of an exhibit is to showcase information artifacts in ways that are appealing, engaging, and informative. As Allen observes, "to be effective as teaching tools, exhibits need to be highly intrinsically motivating at every step of an interaction in order to sustain involvement by an audience who views their visit primarily as a leisure activity" (Allen, 2004, p. S17).

The best way to simultaneously honor the nature of our content and the diverse needs of our users is to create a digital space where the greatest number of needs can be fulfilled in ways that are not only intellectually sound and rigorous but also intuitive and flexible. This more nuanced way of thinking about users in terms of interests they may have or actions they might perform versus types to which they belong will help to liberate your creativity. This will in turn help you to understand and represent your content in multiple ways that will serve the greatest variety of user needs possible. The foundation you build while working with the materials will also help your efforts to analyze your audience and create an exhibit that will compliment and address their needs, preferences, and interests. (This drive overlaps with Chapter 8's discussion of creativity and "inside the box" thinking in digital exhibit design.)

The remaining sections of this chapter will:

- Address exhibits as resources for people and not just about objects
- Briefly review models of exhibit audience types and user personas

- Look at other methods of audience research and evaluation
- See your exhibit as an element of an information ecosystem, using the techniques of digital content strategy and competitive analysis

Digital Exhibits: "From Being About Something, to Being for Somebody"

There has been a profound shift in how cultural heritage exhibits are conceived: from being fundamentally about collections acknowledging a single, one-dimensional view of the audience to a more inclusive view that acknowledges exhibits as a resource that is ultimately for users. Hooper-Greenhill's review of visitor studies for museums makes the following broad observations:

1 In the 21st century the museum studies field has deepened its understanding of visitors from a simplistic, one-dimensional construct to a richer, more humanistic conception of visitors as active learners and interpreters of exhibit and collection content.
2 Arising from this change in viewpoint is an associated recognition that exhibit content needs to incorporate and reflect "a cultural view of communication involving the negotiation of meaning" between visitor and museum content.
3 Museums have broadened their evaluation efforts and research from internally-focused inquiries centered around collections and organizational workflows to include more outward looking efforts to "policy-related work and deep studies based on a drive to understand and explain rather than (or as well as) to manage" visitors and the visitor experience.

(2006, p. 362)

Stephen E. Weil sums up the new emphasis of museum visitor studies on people when he observes "In the emerging museum, responsiveness to the community . . . consistent with the museum's public-service obligations and with the professional standards of its field must be understood not as a surrender but, quite literally, as a fulfillment" (1999, pp. 254–255). In other words, cultural heritage institutions like museums and the resources they offer (like exhibits) should not only be "about something, but for somebody". Douglas Zweizig's oft-quoted observation that information professionals should spend more time looking at "the library in the life of the user" instead of "the user in the life of the library" provides an interesting parallel for exhibit studies (1973).

If we look at the model of digital exhibits in Figure 2.2 from Chapter 2 with its two orientations (object vs. user), and its functions of identification, display, engagement, interpretation, education, and experience, we can see that the main determinant of an exhibit is the degree to which its energy is focused on being about things or being for people. This continuum of focus starting with information objects shifting to people's information needs is mirrored in the traditional division in libraries between technical and reference services. The technical services field is defined traditionally as encompassing tasks related to information objects including acquisitions, collection development, management, and preservation, and metadata management (cataloging and indexing). In contrast, traditional reference was seen as the "people" side of the house and was focused on addressing and fulfilling the needs of library users through direct consultation, instruction, and provision of services such as pathfinders and systematic literature reviews. More modern views of reference services see them as natural relatives of aspects of digital user experience such as interface and interaction design, information architecture, usability, and user task analysis, among others (MacDonald, 2016). Conversely there have long been calls for more technical library services such as indexing to be oriented toward users and their needs (Fidel, 1994; Soergel, 1994). The degree to which an exhibit's purpose is conceived as being about its objects or its users will determine its placement in the model as being more or less oriented toward object representation and presentation or user engagement and experience.

Digital exhibits that focus on objects to the exclusion of almost anything else, including an audience, can be easy to recognize. Often, new users of exhibit software spend much time and effort on object selection and description and fail to take a larger view that would encompass the actual users of their exhibit. For example, Omeka is a tool used often in schools of library science and cultural heritage studies (Cuenca & Kowaleski, 2018; Earhart & Taylor, 2016; Kilroy-Ewbank, 2018). Instructors use Omeka to introduce the concepts of metadata and digital object representation while providing training in the work involved in creating digital collections and exhibits. One teacher was frank in her assessment of her students' work using Omeka. "So far the results of the online exhibits have been mostly disastrous. As a whole, the exhibits are terrible. . . . They have clunky navigation, lack any elegance in design and often are just plain boring". This instructor's assessment of the central problem with her students' work is "(1) students need more training on basic digital tools and (2) students need more training on effective narration/curation/storytelling in an online exhibit" (Marsh, 2013, p. 280). Alas, it is not enough to learn the basics of metadata and exhibit software to build an engaging exhibit. It requires a deeper understanding of content that is connected to a specific model or conception of user engagement. This last element is what turns an organized, curated collection of objects with accompanying text into a working exhibit for users.

The USDA *Frost on Chickens* digital exhibit is offered as an example of such an attempt to couple a model of audience needs with an exhibit's content and structure. The core materials of the exhibit are the 11 articles published by the American poet Robert Frost for two agricultural trade journals between 1900 and 1909. To be frank, these articles are of minimal interest to scholars of Frost's poetry for two reasons. First, they do not address the themes that are commonly associated with Frost's poetry. Second, their genre, format, and subject matter align with their nature as trade journal pieces targeted to working poultry farmers of early twentieth-century America and not the typical publication type in Frost's oeuvre (Poirier & Richardson, 1995; Richardson, 2014). Any possible appeal these texts could offer a potential audience lie in the degree to which they relate to Frost's personal life at the time he wrote them and, to a lesser extent, their reflection of the state of poultry farming in New England of the time. When I created this exhibit, I wanted to bring the interests of current audiences into the project and (with the permissions of the creators involved) included photographs of chickens used in competitive poultry shows and the chickens raised in the backyard coops of an author and illustrator. All three of these strands of audience interest: Frost's life, historic poultry farming, and present-day chicken showing and raising were explicitly addressed in the structure and content of the exhibit in a way that placed them in the forefront for maximum audience engagement.

This simple example shows how it is not enough to have a deep understanding of your materials from an information management perspective (i.e., metadata creation). You also need to have a good understanding of the true significance of your materials, how they relate to your organization's mission, and their possible relevance to other institutional resources. You also need to have a realistic understanding of the potential audiences for your exhibit and how your materials should be presented to them to achieve maximum approachability and usefulness while also demonstrating intellectual rigor.

Audience Types for Digital Exhibits and User Personas

There are infinite ways of imagining the types of people who would visit a digital exhibit and the ways in which they would use it. To introduce some order into this effort, it makes sense to look at the literature on visitors of physical museum exhibits to begin to understand the kinds of variables and parameters central to this question. John H. Falk represents a key contribution to this effort, with his books written with his collaborator Lynn D. Dierking (1992; 2000). Falk (2013) observes,

> The lens of identity-related museum motivations provides a unique window through which we can understand how best to accommodate museum visitor needs; it allows us to better understand the nature of the museum experience and potentially improve it. . . . My hope is that this model will provide a usable and practical tool that enables museum professionals to design ever more attractive, satisfying and memorable experiences for visitors.
>
> (p. 124)

Falk's model of museum visitor identity includes five main categories (2009):

1. Explorers: driven by curiosity and a desire to learn
2. Facilitators: motivated by needs for socialization with other museum-goers
3. Professional/Hobbyists: searching for information that will fulfill some need connected to a long-standing personal interest
4. Experience Seekers: want to visit a museum simply because it is important, interesting, and/or available
5. Rechargers: in search of a spiritual or emotional experience

Falk's model is especially useful because he argues that these categories are fluid and can be used in multiple ways, even by a single visitor. Thus, in a single museum visit to the Phillips Collection in Washington, DC, a person could fulfill the "Professional/Hobbyist" role when entering an exhibit on a favorite topic such as Picasso's Blue Period and then switch to being a "Recharger" in the Rothko Room, "a small, silent space with Mark Rothko's big, dark, glowing canvasses on all four walls", designed by the museum, with input from the artist himself, for just this kind of emotional engagement (Stamburg, 2021). This model must be seen as limited, however, for its reliance on data gathered primarily from participant interviews from a single source: the California Science Center. Emily Dawson has been in the forefront of scholars challenging the conclusions of Falk's model in particular for its reliance on an overly restricted dataset of users (2014a, 2014b, 2019).

While Falk's work is grounded in interviews carried out at the California Science Center, the Morris Hargreaves McIntyre (n.d.a, n.d.b) consultant firm's Culture Segments model relies on the Audience Atlas UK, a much larger dataset of results from 4,500 online surveys conducted with adults from the United Kingdom on their needs and interests in cultural heritage activities and institutions. This model is closer to traditional business market research because it focuses more on demographical characteristics such as age, income, family composition, and education. The eight Culture Segments are described as searching for:

1 Enrichment: older adults who like spending their leisure time close to the home
2 Entertainment: younger adults for whom the arts are on the periphery of their lives
3 Expression: fun-loving, self-aware people who accommodate a wide range of interests
4 Perspective: settled, fulfilled, and home-oriented people who see some forms of culture as providing the opportunity to pursue an interest or broaden their horizons
5 Stimulation: an active, independent group looking for new experiences and challenges
6 Affirmation: young adults who see the arts as one of many leisure choices
7 Release: younger, busy adults who used to enjoy arts and culture, who have limited time and resources to enjoy them now, although they would like to do more
8 Essence: well-educated professionals who are highly active cultural consumers and creators

One other value of this taxonomy is its inclusion of data from survey respondents who had not visited a cultural heritage organization in two years or more. It is crucial to address how your exhibit conceives of the "non-user", and how it can be both built and marketed to this potential audience (Augustin et al., 2020). Morris Hargreaves McIntyre describes how the firm used these audience types to shape an exhibit on the works of Grayson Perry for the British Museum and to create specific, targeted marketing plans for the three motivations identified as most relevant for this situation: essence, expression, and stimulation (n.d.a).

The parallel of this approach in the library and information science community is the creation and application of personas for the broad groups of people who use (and ideally, who do not use) its information services and resources. Personas are idealized stand-ins for audience segments of a given resource (Cooper, 2004; Goodwin, 2009; Priestner & Borg, 2016). They take the form of a fictitious person who is given a label, background characteristics, and specific, detailed descriptions of whatever relevant behaviors, needs, and attributes they bring to the targeted resource. Every audience segment identified as important for the given project, both major, minor, and aspirational, is given its own persona. The fundamental purpose of user personas is to foster understanding and empathy among the members of whatever internal teams work on a given project. It also helps to re-ground efforts that may go too far afield from task at hand. It gives staff a structured way of asking and addressing the question, "who is our audience?"

An essential point that often gets overlooked in discussions of personas is their need to be grounded in actual data about actual people. If the personas are either a bundle of stereotyped assumptions about your audience or a wish list of groups you would like to attract someday, in some way, then they will not be authentic enough to drive the kind of radical empathy that would make them worthwhile to create in the first place. It would almost be better to implement no personas at all, than to rely on truly fictitious ones that are either misleading or inauthentic. That is the bad news: You need real data about real people to create personas. The good news is that you do not have to collect this data yourself. It is possible to create an effective set of personas using the research of others documented in the literature of user information needs and behavior studies. These studies, which can use various methodological approaches such as surveys, interviews, and ethnographic observation, engage people to identify the essential characteristics of their "information lives" in various areas (Case & Given, 2016). User studies relevant to audiences of digital culture can be found in various sources and have been carried out with user groups broadly interested in digital cultural heritage (Dorner et al., 2007; Kelly, 2018; Skov, 2013; Skov & Ingwersen, 2008).

Reviewing some background literature on your targeted user groups and then creating three or more user personas for your imagined exhibit would be a good start before you pursue any other exhibit work. Additionally, it would be helpful to also consult any studies you can find that investigate the information worlds (Chatman 1987, 1996, 1999) or information horizons (Sonnenwald, 1999; Sonnenwald et al., 2001) of your intended audience to better understand the information sources they consult. An example of a user persona created for a data system based on user studies of actual data repositories is shown in Figure 3.1.

The literature on visitor studies and arts' audience analysis is large and describes many other ways to think about the characteristics, motivations, and interests of cultural heritage consumers (Anderson, 2019; Audience Agency, 2020; Bourdieu & Darbel, 1991; Cerquetti, 2011, 2016, 2018; Dawson & Jensen, 2011; Everett &

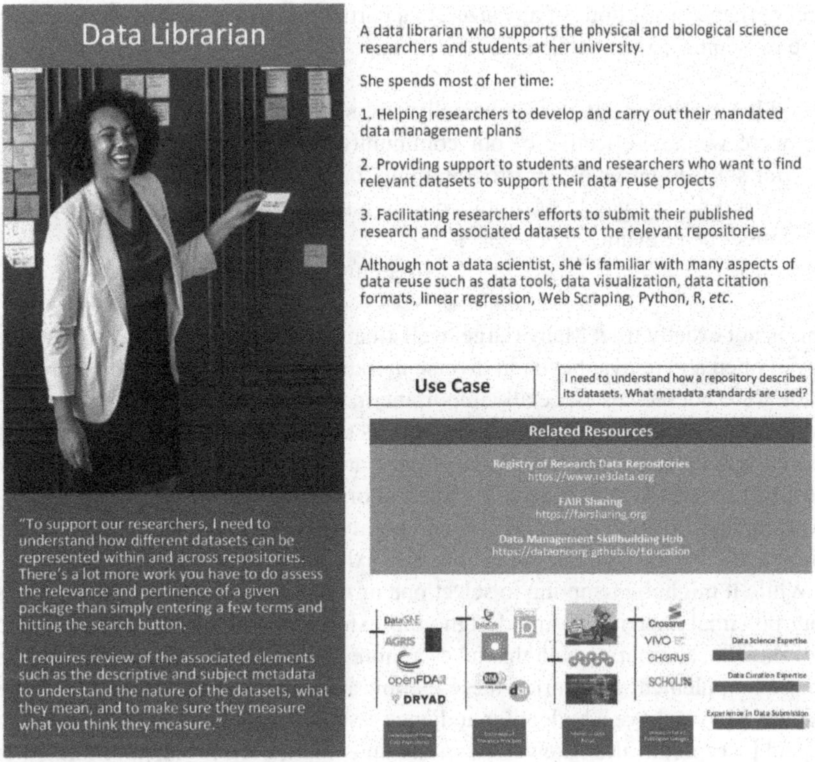

Figure 3.1 Data librarian persona for a scientific data repository

Barrett, 2009; Kirchberg & Tröndle, 2012; Peacock & Brownbill, 2007; Rounds, 2006; Smithsonian Institution Office of Policy and Analysis, 2002; Stylianou-Lambert, 2010; Walsh et al., 2018). These detailed models are the products of extensive academic research and work sponsored by large, well-funded, and staffed organizations such as the Smithsonian Institution and the British Museum. It should be noted that these museums also have significant built-in audiences for their physical exhibits and digital content. It can be challenging for the staffs of small organizations to even think about this question, much less incorporate a model of user engagement into an exhibit structure and/or content management plan.

But simply ignoring questions of audience and asserting that "if you build it, they will come", as an incantation is not a strategy and carries significant risk. While Pallud and Straub observe correctly that an online presence is mandatory for high culture museums to attract visitors to their physical buildings and exhibits, this relationship is not reciprocal (2014). While we need users to engage with our digital content (including digital exhibits), users, for the most part, do not need us in quite the same way. Yes, we may "build it", but there is no guarantee that "they will come". Overt, demonstrable efforts at ensuring diverse audience representation and engagement are no longer seen as an optional activity for cultural heritage institutions of any size. As a participant in a study of American science museums and centers put it,

> [T]he market itself is so ethnically and socio-economically diverse that if were we not reflective of our community both in terms of the board and our staff, in terms of our programming, our language capacity, the list goes on and on, we would have folded up a long time ago because we would no longer be relevant.
>
> (Feinstein & Meshoulam, 2014, p. 376)

This is not exactly true: Many (large, well-financed, admired) cultural institutions stayed open and relevant even in diverse markets because diversity and representation were not seen as especially important or, in some cases, even desired. Ash's work on reculturating museums describes this supposed neutrality as "norms, settled expectations or 'the way we do things around here'" and argues that they must be confronted and changed by internal organizational staff if we are to promote change, advance social justice and equity, and hence become relevant to a larger audience through our collections and exhibits (2022, p. 8).

While it might be tempting to select one or more of these abstract identities as your potential audience(s) and design your exhibit around them, the next section will show an alternative path that takes a more "bottom-up" approach that can be used to supplement and enrich these exhibit audience models. Also, it does not assume that you have a budget for audience research. It is a way to identify, listen to, and incorporate alternate voices within an exhibit, even if you have limited or no resources for explicit outreach. Lastly, it has the added benefit of providing sources for your outreach and evaluation efforts after your project is launched.

Other Methods of Audience Research: Discourse Communities and Communities of Practice

Another path into a richer understanding of your audience lies in learning about any social networks that might be actively working in topic fields relevant to your exhibit content. An understanding of these networks will be useful when it comes time to market your exhibit, but this type of audience research is not geared specifically to marketing. This work is designed to make you as an exhibit creator more aware of and sensitive to the lives of your audience members, especially in the ways they think about and describe the subject of concern, what information sources they use (and do not use) and why, information trends, and many other potential variables. Understanding how your audience thinks, talks, and potentially feels about your topic will help to enrich your own understanding and can lead you to create an exhibit that will not only be original but also connected to the lived experience of your audience. As observed by Visser, "reaching tastemakers, engaging active communities, and offering generous, unexpected content are three ingredients or projects that will reach and engage people" (2014, p. 79).

There are several constructs that will be useful to explain the power of this approach. Diana Crane is credited with developing the "Invisible College" social network model (1972). Crane's sociological study of science analyzed the professional relationships of academic scientists and related them to patterns of work outputs, scientific advances, and, most important in this context, their shared information artifacts. Crane, along with many others, laid the groundwork for perspectives of individual information behaviors to be studied, analyzed, and, eventually, explained by a perspective that incorporated other relevant actors, all existing within an inter-connected network.

The more linguistically oriented Discourse Community (DC) construct of networked behavior was outlined by John Swale's and his six defining characteristics (1988). As re-cast by Prior (2003) a DC has:

1 Common public goals
2 Mechanisms for intercommunication
3 Participatory mechanisms to provide members with feedback and information
4 Discourse expectations reflected in genres
5 Specialized terminology
6 Critical mass of experts

Clearly identifying the common goals, genres, and terminology of a potential DC that could act as an audience network will be most important for potential exhibit creators.

Finally, the idea of a Community of Practice (COP) has taken hold recently across many fields including library and information science studies. A COP was developed as a learning theory and is described by the Wenger-Trainers as a group of people "who share a concern or a passion for something they do and learn how to do it better as they interact regularly" (2015). The three central features of the construct are:

1 Its focus on a specific subject domain
2 Its nature as a social network
3 Its emphasis on practice

Prior argues in favor of the DC construct over the COP because the former centers questions of personal and social identity (e.g., gender, race, sexual orientation, class) while the latter puts questions of more impersonal, less emotional identity (e.g., education, profession) at the top level of concern (2003). While this argument is debatable, it is important to see that each domain of concern needs to be accounted for: the personal, the social, the professional, and the political, among others. All these perspectives can offer valuable theoretical insights and frameworks for analyzing and understanding any relevant communities and potential audiences who might be interested in your exhibit.

The last theory to be covered is that of Serious Leisure created by Robert A. Stebbins (2015). He defines leisure as "un-coerced, contextually framed activity engaged in during free time, which people want to do and, using their abilities and resources, actually do in either a satisfying or a fulfilling way (or both)" (Elkington & Stebbins, 2014, p. 12). The "serious" part of the definition refers to the hobbyist's or practitioner's experience of the activity as "substantial, interesting and fulfilling", as well as its nature as systematic and pursued over a period of time (p. 4). Serious hobbyists working in domains relevant to your proposed exhibit can also provide an entry point into potential audiences and their attendant areas of concern, ways of expression, and information sources.

It can enrich your exhibit to look at the available digital landscape to identify the kinds of language codes and conventions of the various logical constituencies of your exhibit content. While the theories developed to model these communities can be quite complex, it is much easier to see the potential of them in action, along with inherent reasons for engaging with them for exhibit enrichment purposes.

One final point needs to be made: You need to be careful once you identify relevant language communities and start to engage with their content, especially if you are not entitled to claim membership with them. It is important to stay within the bounds of cultural appreciation and not cross over into cultural appropriation. Gertner defines cultural appropriation as "the unsuitable, unauthorized, or objectionable use of cultural elements in a context other than that of the culture by outsiders who might lack understanding and/or respect for the culture in question" (2019, p. 873). Arya adds this important point,

> [I]ntegral to the definition of cultural appropriation is an asymmetry of power between two cultures that involves the majority/dominant culture taking from the marginalised culture. . . . Many definitions emphasize the taking from a culture that is not one's own. This is incomplete when the investigation is delimited to cultural appropriation (and not simply appropriation) because what is essential is the power imbalance, and critically the taking from the culture that has relatively less power.
>
> (2021, p. 3)

At a minimum, you need to respect the conventions of copyright and give credit to the creators of whatever outside content you incorporate into your exhibit. A higher goal would be to ensure that any content you use or perspective you include represents its community of origin in a way that centers their authentic voices and experiences. That might require you to make personal contact with a member of the community under consideration for a "member check" to make sure that your purpose for content use is legitimate and will not result in any harm (Frey, 2018). This is especially important for traditionally marginalized and oppressed communities.

Here are some examples of exhibits with their relevant discourse and/or and practice communities, along with their areas of interest and external materials that were incorporated into each exhibit:

1 Frost on Chickens
www.nal.usda.gov/exhibits/ipd/frostonchickens/

The poet Robert Frost lived and worked as a poultry farmer in Derry, New Hampshire from 1900 to 1909. During that period, he published a dozen articles for two trade journals: *The Eastern Poultryman* and *The Farm-Poultry*. This exhibit contains digital copies of all these articles, along with associated materials on nine topical areas that relate directly to the subjects contained in Frost's pieces.

Relevant Communities and Interests

- Robert Frost scholars: relationships between exhibit articles and Frost's personal life
- Backyard chicken hobbyists: chicken housing, health, and feeding
- Poultry show competitors: standards of poultry breeds and nature of competitive shows

External Materials Incorporated into Exhibit

- Illustrations of backyard chickens contributed by Lauren Scheuer
- Photographs of chickens contributed by Tamara Staples
- Images from the USDA Pomological Watercolor Collection
- Images from the Derry New Hampshire Public Library Historic Postcard collection on Flickr

2 Apron Strings and Kitchen Sinks: The USDA Bureau of Home Economics
www.nal.usda.gov/exhibits/ipd/apronsandkitchens/
The Bureau of Home Economics was a pioneering unit in the US Department of Agriculture (USDA). It focused on topics of central concern to women, as defined by the cultural norms of the early 20th century: sewing, kitchen design and features, time spent on housework, children's clothing, and food preparation and preservation. Lastly, it took a then-novel approach to its work: It strove to first understand what its primary audience needed within its broad mandate and then shaped its specific programs around those needs. This exhibit showcases the work of this Bureau, especially the work related to clothing and kitchen design.

Relevant Communities and Interests

- Historians of Home Economics discipline: all exhibit features and content
- Vintage sewing pattern collectors: patterns for aprons and work clothes developed by this USDA bureau
- Historians of interior and mid-century design: designs for efficient kitchens developed by USDA

External Materials Incorporated into Exhibit

- Images of vintage USDA-developed clothing patterns contributed by Flickr user Little Black Car
- Photographs from The Library of Congress Prints and Photographs Division, The Smithsonian Institution, and the University of Chicago Library

3 Small Agriculture
www.nal.usda.gov/exhibits/ipd/small/
The USDA has supported small-scale farming and niche agricultural initiatives throughout its lifespan. This exhibit showcases three of these initiatives: school gardens, the Subsistence Homestead project, and Victory Gardens and farms.

Relevant Communities and Interests

- World War II Historians: Victory Garden and Subsistence Homestead project exhibit materials, especially USDA publications
- Garden Educators and Extension Agents: historical content on the educational value of school gardens

External Materials Incorporated Into Exhibit

- Photographs from the Library of Congress Prints and Photographs Division, Montana State University Historical Photographs Collection, National Archives and Records Administration, Wikimedia
- Embedded video from Internet Archive

4 Mailboxes, Mom and Pop Stands, and Markets: Local Foods Then and Now
www.nal.usda.gov/exhibits/ipd/localfoods/
The current interest in local foods is reflected in a long-standing focus of the USDA on the best ways to get food from producers to consumers. This exhibit showcases these resources, placed within a larger context of agricultural marketing and purchasing. The exhibit is divided into three main sections: a review of the "Farm-To-Table" Movement of the early 1900s, a survey of Roadside Stands and Farmers' Markets, and a list of current USDA local food initiatives.

Relevant Communities and Interests

- Food Studies scholars: materials on the history of the "Farm-To-Table" movement and farmers' markets

External Materials Incorporated Into Exhibit

- Images from the Library of Congress Prints and Photographs Division, University of North Texas Libraries, Wikimedia, Smithsonian Institution's National Postal Museum
- Embedded video from the National Postal Museum

5 George Washington Carver
www.nal.usda.gov/exhibits/ipd/carver/
George Washington Carver was an agricultural scientist whose importance lies in his practical work supporting African-American farmers and his advocacy for specific crops such as peanuts and sweet potatoes. This exhibit showcases the 38 *Tuskegee Institute Experiment Station Bulletins* written by Carver during his tenure as Director. The exhibit also includes a selection of US Department of Agriculture historical publications relevant to Carver's Bulletins.

Relevant Communities and Interests

- Scholars of Black American agricultural science and farming practices: *Tuskegee Institute Experiment Station Bulletins* and associated USDA publications

External Materials Incorporated Into Exhibit

- Images from the Library of Congress Prints and Photographs Division, National Park Service, Iowa State University Library Special Collections and University Archives, *The Encyclopedia of Alabama*, Wikimedia

6 How Did We Can? The Evolution of Home Canning
www.nal.usda.gov/exhibits/ipd/canning/
This exhibit covers the following aspects of this home food preservation method: canning techniques, consequences of improper canning, evolution of canning equipment, canning through the world wars, and home canning: post-World War II to the present.

Relevant Communities and Interests

- Community: Food Studies scholars
- Interests: content on the history of canning in America, as supported by the USDA
- Home canning hobbyists: instructional content
- World War II Historians: food-related war conservation content, especially USDA posters

External Materials Incorporated Into Exhibit

- Images and illustrations from the Centers for Disease Control and Prevention, United States Patent and Trademark Office, Internet Archive, personal blogs of Jessica Zafra and Patrice Miller, personal site of "Granny Miller", The New York Public Library, the National Safety Council, *The Walsh County Record*

Information Ecosystems for Exhibits

Even if you work as a "team of one" to create a digital exhibit, it is always crucial to see and place your work within a larger context, much as the actual living ecosystem pictured by Hartwich (2016). Although the construct of an information ecosystem has come under criticism for its vagueness and, ironically enough, artificiality (Norris & Suomela, 2017), it remains a useful metaphor for a complex and dynamic network of information sources. I find the metaphor useful for its acknowledgment that information resources can co-exist in chaotic, messy, unpredictable, and indistinct relationship to one another. These relationships can seem organic because they often appear and disappear unexpectedly; exhibits, collections, repositories, and digital objects can come and go with little or no warning. Also, the ecosystem metaphor can seem apt because the internal relationships between resources within an exhibit's originating organization can be straightforward, dysfunctional, hidden, or non-existent, just like a complex biological system. It all depends on the degree to which the human actors involved invest themselves to create and maintain them, much like a gardener tends to a patch of earth. While an information ecosystem can never be truly "alive", its nature as a richly complex and dynamic system makes the metaphor useful.

There are two central practices that are helpful for assessing and managing the status of your exhibit as existing within a larger information ecosystem: content strategy and competitive analysis. Having a larger content strategy can model and guide an exhibit as an entity existing within your internal organization. To appraise your exhibit as an entity in the context of other outside organizations,

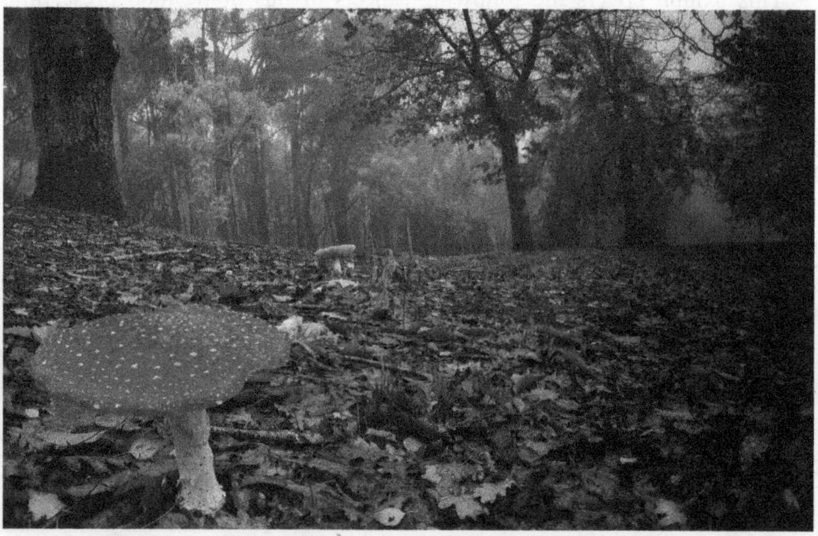

Figure 3.2 Mushroom in the Hills of Adelaide by Michael Hartwich is used under the Creative Commons Attribution-Share Alike 4.0 International License (CC BY-SA 4.0)

the technique of competitive analysis is helpful. These two approaches will be described briefly in the context of digital exhibits.

Content Strategy

There are shifting definitions for the practice of web-based content strategy, but one of the most comprehensive is provided by Halvorson (2011).

> Content strategy plans for the creation, publication and governance of useful, usable content. Necessarily, the content strategist must work to define not only which content will be published, but why publish it in the first place. Otherwise, content strategy isn't strategy at all: It's just a glorified production line for content nobody really needs or wants.
>
> (p. 23)

This is a complex mission since it touches on all aspects of an information organization, including:

- The content objects themselves
- Themes, topics, and messages contained within the content
- Methods for content presentation and delivery
- Staff roles for the people who will create, select, and present the content
- Audience needs and delivery preferences for the content
- Metadata for representing the content to make it findable by people and machines
- Mechanisms for enhancing the findability of content through search engine optimization (SEO)
- Collection management policies and practices for content acquisition, preservation, and maintenance

A common artifact of an organization with no clear content strategy is the information silo. If a content type is not seen having a relationship with the entire organization, then it is likely it will be claimed and controlled within a single department or other management unit. Libraries have a particular problem with siloed content. As Kowalski observes,

> [L]ibrary work has historically been organized into different silos: public services, technical services, and administration. . . . Silos are workplace constructs and mindsets that isolate departments from one another through bureaucracy or rigid hierarchies. They are characterized by a lack of communication, information sharing, and collaboration that inhibit efficiency and productivity, reduce morale, and constrict positive workplace culture. The silo mentality splits the library into distinct groups that compete against one another instead of working towards common goals as a holistic organization.
>
> (2017, p. 1)

This observation points out the obvious challenge to creating and implementing an integrated, connected content strategy. It is not the content that needs to be reimagined and reorganized so much as it is the organization's collective understanding of its meaning that needs to be reimagined and reorganized.

Creating and implementing an organizational content strategy is clearly beyond the bounds of this book. Information workers who are interested in taking up this task should start with *Content Strategy for the Web* by Kristina Halvorson and Melissa Rach (2012) and then consult some recent books such as those by Casey (2015) and Hane and Atherton (2017). For those of us who work in organizations who struggle with this kind of difficult work and who do not have a clear roadmap or mandate will need to find a way to create a mini-content strategy for our exhibits. The risk of not working strategically is having digital exhibits be placed in a silo of their own. The silo sometimes carries the label "special projects" and is created for exhibits that are not created and deployed in service of an authorized, ongoing strategy, but merely as tactical responses. Some of the responses could be to recognize organizational events and commemorations, hence the label of "special", or to fulfill the personal agendas of leaders who have the power to command creation of an exhibit for their own reasons, on subjects of their choice. While it is inevitable that this kind of thing will happen from time to time in almost every organization, it will be problematic if your exhibit program is driven by this type of motivation to the exclusion of others. If exhibits are seen as boutique projects tied to the personal agendas of either their creators or leaders, there will be little to no organizational motivation to maintain them once these staff move on, as they inevitably do. This kind of silo is also a problematic place for the exhibit creator. If staff members see exhibits as work performed in isolation by one or two people, then marginalization and ostracization become more likely. This not only is difficult on the exhibit creator(s), but also increases the likelihood that their work will not be supported and sustained by the organization as a whole.

The better way to create an exhibit that will be both meaningful and sustainable on an organizational level is through a strategy that places content within a holistic context. I developed a vision for an organizational ecosystem that could support and platform exhibits and illustrated essays in addition to providing an "evergreen" content source for social media platforms and internal and external information needs (Marsh, 2016). There are several other methods to achieve this goal, all conditional on seeing the exhibit as part of a larger information ecosystem. Some ways to ground digital exhibits in a way that will make them more likely to take root in an organization's mission and larger environment are:

- Recognize exhibit creators as part of the organization's permanent structure and grant them with authority, resources, and managerial support
- Avoid labeling digital exhibits as special, exotic, or a luxury
- Connect exhibits topically and form to specific, documentable audience interests
- Connect both the work of exhibit making and the exhibit's content to staff and information resources within the organization

- Identify and connect with relevant external audience groups and other resources such as institutional repositories and collections, as well as material posted on social media platforms such as Flickr, Instagram, YouTube, and TikTok
- Finally, tie each exhibit to a clear strategy that connects to the needs of your organization and its various audiences.

Some notable examples of large cultural heritage organizations with demonstrable robust content strategies and suites of digital resources include:

Biodiversity Heritage Library (BHL)

- Strategic plan
- Digital collection
- Digital exhibits
- Blog
- Newsletter
- Digital tools and services
- Volunteer projects
- Social media accounts: Flickr, Instagram, TikTok, Twitter, YouTube

British Library

- Strategic plan: "Living Knowledge"
- Digital collections
- Digital exhibits
- Learning resources
- Online courses
- Social media accounts: Flickr, Instagram, TikTok, Twitter, YouTube

Europeana and Europeana Pro

- Strategic plan
- Digital collections
- Digital storytelling
- Annual Conference
- Online events and webinars
- Events toolkit
- Social media accounts: Flickr, Instagram, Twitter, YouTube

Digital Public Library of America (DPLA)

- Strategic roadmap
- Digital collections
- Digital exhibits

- Primary source sets
- Social media accounts: Flickr, Instagram, Twitter, YouTube

JSTOR

- Digital collections
- Thematic collections
- Text-mining support
- Stories: *JSTOR Daily*
- JSTOR Labs
- Blog
- Social media accounts: Flickr, Instagram, TikTok, Twitter, YouTube

Smithsonian Institution

- Strategic plan
- Digital collections
- Digital exhibits
- Blogs
- Podcast
- Magazine
- Social media accounts: Flickr, Instagram, TikTok, Twitter, YouTube

Competitive Analysis

In addition to getting a comprehensive, clear-eyed understanding of your potential audience, you also need to complete an informal competitive analysis of other relevant information exhibits and resources to find out where your project would sit in a larger landscape. It would be ideal if your project contained some exclusive content and had a correspondingly singular analytical perspective. But often you will need to address topics that are not startingly unique, but nonetheless are still valuable and of interest to a significant audience, if not a massively large one.

Brown provides a helpful description of the digital competitive analysis from a user experience (UX) perspective (2007).

> A web design competitive analysis shows the differences between the site you're working on and comparable sites. . . . Most often, the competitive analysis helps the design team . . . position their product in the landscape of offerings. It helps determine what customers are used to and best practices in everything from interface design to features offered. Though not the best driver of design decisions, the competitive analysis can provide a baseline understanding of what works and what doesn't.
>
> (pp. 107, 109)

Even if your project would occupy a unique niche among comparable resources, you can still learn a great deal from this kind of background research. It can tell you if your exhibit will face an over-saturated landscape of similar projects or if it promises to be a unique addition. It can give you an indication of the current state of the art in digital project information architecture and user interface design for exhibits. It can also provide inspiration for your project that might guide you to incorporate features you like in the work of others and advice to avoid things you do not think work as well as they could.

In short, this kind of preliminary review and analysis acts as an empirical reality test of your project ideas before you have committed to any one path or strategy. It will help to guide and support your creativity in a way that will ensure maximum chances of completion and ultimate success for you, your organization, and your users.

Practice Recommendations

1 Before you start building the structure of your exhibit, spend some time thinking about its orientation. Would you like to create a structure that emphasizes the exhibit objects themselves, or would you prefer to introduce elements of engagement, interpretation, education, or providing a unique experience for visitors? There are legitimate reasons for creating both object- and user-oriented exhibits. But your chance of success will increase if you consciously choose one path over another instead of letting circumstances or convenience make the decision for you.

2 Questions of audience types and information needs are even more difficult and require advance research and planning as well. It helps to broaden your view beyond your exhibit content and your internal organization to consider external audience groups. Who will be likely to be drawn to your exhibit? What will these visitors want to see, do, and experience? What pre-existing knowledge will they bring? Consider creating one to three user personas to focus your thinking and apply your research findings into a distilled representation of your audience targets. Consider the models of visitor types by scholars such as Falk, Dierking, and Stebbins to enrich your thinking.

3 Published studies of information user communities offer an ideal way to access vital information about your users. This, along with investigations of actual user communities on social network platforms like Flickr, Instagram, and YouTube, offers a way to develop a model of specific user engagement with your specific topic area. The time you spend getting to know active external groups will greatly enhance your understanding and help you to create a fully realized, 360-degree view of your audience in all its naturalistic richness.

4 Work to place your exhibit within a larger information ecosystem that encompasses both your institution and other external entities. Incorporate material

from other sources to bring life to your content, especially images, photographs, and embedded video for a document-based exhibit. Introducing other content streams into your exhibit is one small way to start an individual effort to place your work into a digital content strategy that will increase the odds that your exhibit will be seen by others as part of a larger picture and not just a "special" project of limited worth.

Digital and Physical Exhibits Discussed in This Chapter

Apron Strings and Kitchen Sinks: The USDA Bureau of Home Economics
Emily Marsh
National Agricultural Library, US Department of Agriculture
www.nal.usda.gov/exhibits/ipd/apronsandkitchens/

Frost on Chickens
Emily Marsh
National Agricultural Library, US Department of Agriculture
www.nal.usda.gov/exhibits/ipd/frostonchickens/

George Washington Carver
Emily Marsh
National Agricultural Library, US Department of Agriculture
www.nal.usda.gov/exhibits/ipd/carver/

How Did We Can? The Evolution of Home Canning
Emily Marsh and Taira Sullivan
National Agricultural Library, US Department of Agriculture
www.nal.usda.gov/exhibits/ipd/canning/

Mailboxes, Mom and Pop Stands, and Markets: Local Foods Then and Now
Emily Marsh
National Agricultural Library, US Department of Agriculture
www.nal.usda.gov/exhibits/ipd/localfoods/

Small Agriculture
Emily Marsh
National Agricultural Library, US Department of Agriculture
www.nal.usda.gov/exhibits/ipd/small/

References

Allen, S. (2004). Designs for learning: Studying science museum exhibits that do more than entertain. *Science Education*, *8*(S1), S17–S33. https://doi.org/10.1002/sce.20016.

Anderson, S. (2019). Visitor and audience research in museums. In K. Drotner, V. Dziekan, R. Parry, & K. C. Schrøder (Eds.), *The Routledge handbook of museums, media, and communication* (pp. 80–95). London: Routledge.

Ash, D. B. (2022). *Reculturing museums: Embrace conflict, create change*. London: Routledge.

Audience Agency. (2020). *The Audience Agency digital audience survey*. London: Author. www.theaudienceagency.org/asset/2547.

Augustin, L., Kokoschko, B., Wiesner, M., & Schabacker, M. (2020). Toward a comprehensive definition of the non-user. In *Proceedings of the design society: DESIGN conference* (Vol. 1, pp. 1853–1862). Cambridge: Cambridge University Press. https://doi.org/10.1017/dsd.2020.124.

Arya, R. (2021). Cultural appropriation: What it is and why it matters? *Sociology Compass*, *15*(10), e12923. https://doi.org/10.1111/soc4.12923.

Bitgood, S. (2010). An analysis of visitor circulation: Movement patterns and the general value principle. *Curator*, *49*(4), 463–475. https://doi.org/10.1111/j.2151-6952.2006.tb00237.x.

Bourdieu, P., & Darbel, A. (1991). *The love of art: European art museums and their public*. Cambridge: Polity Press.

Brown, D. M. (2007). *Communicating design: Developing web site documentation for design and planning*. Indianapolis, IN: New Riders Publishing.

Carliner, S. (2003). Modeling information for three dimensional space: Lessons learned from museum exhibit design. *Technical Communication*, *50*(4), 554–570.

Case, D. O., & Given, L. M. (2016). *Looking for information: A survey of research on information seeking, needs, and behavior* (4th ed.). Bingley: Emerald Publishing Limited.

Casey, M. (2015). *Content strategy toolkit: The methods, guidelines, and templates for getting content right*. Indianapolis, IN: New Riders Publishing.

Cerquetti, M. (2011). Local art museums and visitors: Audience and attendance development. Theoretical requirements and empirical evidence. *ENCATC: Journal of Cultural Management and Policy*, *1*(1), 20–27.

Cerquetti, M. (2016). More is better! Current issues and challenges for museum audience development: A literature review. *ENCATC: Journal of Cultural Management and Policy*, *6*(1), 30–43.

Cerquetti, M., & Ferrara, C. (2018). Marketing research for cultural heritage conservation and sustainability: Lessons from the field. *Sustainability*, *10*(3), 774. https://doi.org/10.3390/su10030774.

Chatman, E. A. (1987). The information world of low-skilled workers. *Library and Information Science Research*, *9*(4), 265–283.

Chatman, E. A. (1996). The impoverished life-world of outsiders. *Journal of the American Society for Information Science*, *47*(3), 193–206. https://doi.org/10.1002/(SICI)1097-4571(199603)47:3%3C193::AID-ASI3%3E3.0.CO;2-T.

Chatman, E. A. (1999). A theory of life in the round. *Journal of the American Society for Information Science*, *50*(3), 207–217. https://doi.org/10.1002/(SICI)1097-4571(1999)50:3%3C207::AID-ASI3%3E3.0.CO;2-8.

Cooper, A. (2004). *The inmates are running the asylum: Why high tech products drive us crazy and how to restore the sanity*. Indianapolis, IN: Sams.

Crane, D. (1972). *Invisible colleges: Diffusion of knowledge in scientific communities*. Chicago, IL: University of Chicago Press.

Cuenca, E. L., & Kowaleski, M. (2018). Omeka and other digital platforms for undergraduate research projects on the Middle Ages. *Digital Medievalist*, *11*(1), 1–21. http://doi.org/10.16995/dm.69.

Dawson, E. (2014a) Equity in informal science education: Developing an access and equity framework for science museums and science centres. *Studies in Science Education*, *50*(2), 209–247. https://doi.org/10.1080/03057267.2014.957558.

Dawson, E. (2014b). "Not designed for us": How science museums and science centers socially exclude low-income, minority ethnic groups. *Science Education*, *98*(6), 981–1008. https://doi.org/10.1002/sce.21133.

Dawson, E. (2019). *Equity, exclusion and everyday science learning: The experiences of minoritized groups*. London: Routledge.

Dawson, E., & Jensen, E. (2011). Towards a 'contextual turn' in visitor studies: Evaluating visitor segmentation and identity-related motivations. *Visitor Studies*, *14*(2), 127–140. http://dx.doi.org/10.1080/10645578.2011.608001.

Dorner, D. G., Li Liew, C., & Ping Yeo, Y. (2007). A textured sculpture: The information needs of users of digitised New Zealand cultural heritage resources. *Online Information Review*, *31*(2), 166–184. https://doi.org/10.1108/14684520710747211.

Earhart, A. E., & Taylor, T. L. (2016). Pedagogies of race: Digital humanities in the age of Ferguson. In M. K. Gold & L. F. Klein (Eds.), *Debates in the digital humanities 2016* (pp. 251–264). Minneapolis, MN: University of Minnesota Press. https://doi.org/10.5749/j.cttlcn6thb.24.

Elkington, S., & Stebbins, R. A. (2014). *The serious leisure perspective: An introduction*. London: Routledge.

Everett, M., & Barrett, M. S. (2009) Investigating sustained visitor/museum relationships: Employing narrative research in the field of museum visitor studies. *Visitor Studies*, *12*(1), 2–15. https://doi.org/10.1080/10645570902769084.

Falk, J. H. (2009). *Identity and the museum visitor experience*. London: Routledge.

Falk, J. H. (2013). Understanding museum visitors' motivations and learning. In I. E. Lundgaard & J. T. Jensen (Eds.), *Museums: Social learning spaces and knowledge producing processes* (pp. 106–127). København V and Hovedstaden: Kulturstyrelsen.

Falk, J. H., & Dierking, L. D. (1992). *The museum experience*. Washington, DC: Howells House.

Falk, J. H., & Dierking, L. D. (2000). *Learning from museums: Visitor experiences and the making of meaning*. Lanham, MD: Rowman & Littlefield.

Feinstein, N. W., & Meshoulam, D. (2014). Science for what public? Addressing equity in American science museums and science centers. *Journal of Research in Science Teaching*, *51*(3), 368–394. https://doi.org/10.1002/tea.21130.

Fidel, R. (1994). User-centered indexing. *Journal of the American Society for Information Science*, *45*(8), 572–576. https://doi.org/10.1002/(SICI)1097-4571(199409)45:8%3C572::AID-ASI11%3E3.0.CO;2-X.

Frey, B. B. (2018). Member check. In *The SAGE encyclopedia of educational research, measurement, and evaluation*. Thousand Oaks, CA: SAGE Publications. https://dx.doi.org/10.4135/9781506326139.n426.

Gertner, R. K. (2019). The impact of cultural appropriation on destination image, tourism, and hospitality. *Thunderbird International Business Review*, *61*(6), 873–877. https://doi.org/10.1002/tie.22068.

Goodwin, K. (2009). *Designing for the digital age: How to create human-centered products and services*. Hoboken, NJ: Wiley.

Halvorson, K. (2011). Understanding the discipline of web content strategy. *Bulletin of the American Society for Information Science and Technology*, *37*(2), 23–25. https://doi.org/10.1002/bult.2011.1720370208.

Halvorson, K., & Rach, M. (2012). *Content strategy for the web* (2nd ed.). Indianapolis, IN: New Riders Publishing.

Hane, C., & Atherton, M. (2017). *Designing connected content: Plan and model digital products for today and tomorrow*. Indianapolis, IN: New Riders Publishing.

Hartwich, M. (2016). *Mushroom in the Hills of Adelaide* [Photograph]. https://commons.wikimedia.org/wiki/File:Mushroom_in_the_Hills_of_Adelaide.jpg.

Hooper-Greenhill, E. (2006). Studying visitors. In S. McDonald (Ed.), *A companion to museum studies* (pp. 362–376). Malden, MA: Blackwell Publishing.

Kelly, E. J. (2018). Use of Louisiana's digital cultural heritage by wikipedians. *Journal of Web Librarianship*, *12*(2), 85–106. https://doi.org/10.1080/19322909.2017.1391733.

Kilroy-Ewbank, L. G. (2018). Doing digital art history in a pre-Columbian art survey class: Creating an Omeka exhibition around the Mixtec Codex Zouche-Nuttall. *The Journal of Interactive Technology and Pedagogy*, *12*. https://jitp.commons.gc.cuny.edu/doing-digital-art-history-in-a-pre-columbian-art-survey-class-creating-an-omeka-exhibition-around-the-mixtec-codex-zouche-nuttall/.

Kirchberg, V., & Tröndle, M. (2012). Experiencing exhibitions: A review of studies on visitor experiences in museums. *Curator: The Museum Journal*, *55*(4), 435–452. https://doi.org/10.1111/j.2151-6952.2012.00167.x.

Kowalski, M. (2017). Breaking down silo walls: Successful collaboration across library departments. *Library Leadership & Management*, *31*(2), 1–15.

MacDonald, C. M. (2016). User experience librarians: User advocates, user researchers, usability evaluators, or all of the above? *Proceedings of the Association for Information Science and Technology*, *52*(1), 1–10. https://doi.org/10.1002/pra2.2015.145052010055.

Marsh, A. C. (2013). Omeka in the classroom: The challenges of teaching material culture in a digital world. *Literary and Linguistic Computing*, *28*(2), 279–282. https://doi.org/10.1093/llc/fqs068.

Marsh, E. (2016, April 15). *If a pdf falls in the forest will anyone see it? Building a library ecosystem for digital materials* [Conference presentation]. Washington, DC: Digital Public Library of America's DPLAFest. https://youtu.be/YQ2TniMc0Dg?t=1551.

Marsh, E. (2017). Chickens, aprons, markets, and cans: How the National Agricultural Library uses Omeka as its content management system for digital exhibits. *Digital Library Perspectives*, *33*(4), 361–377. https://doi.org/10.1108/DLP-03-2017-0009.

Morris Hargreaves McIntyre. (n.d.a). *Culture segments*. www.culturehive.co.uk/wp-content/uploads/2013/05/CultureSegments2.pdf.

Morris Hargreaves McIntyre. (n.d.b). *Culture segments in action: Grayson Perry at the British Museum*. www.culturehive.co.uk/wp-content/uploads/2020/10/GraysonPerry-case-study-FINAL1-1.pdf.

Norris, T. B., & Suomela, T. (2017). Information in the ecosystem: Against the "information ecosystem." *First Monday*, *22*(9). https://firstmonday.org/ojs/index.php/fm/article/download/6847/6530.

Pallud, J., & Straub, D. W. (2014). Effective website design for experience-influenced environments: The case of high culture museums. *Information & Management*, *51*(3), 359–373. https://doi.org/10.1016/j.im.2014.02.010.

Peacock, D., & Brownbill, J. (2007). Audiences, visitors, users: Reconceptualising users of museum on-line content and services. In J. Trant & D. Bearman (Eds.), *Museums and The web 2007: Selected papers from an international conference* (pp. 223–240). Toronto, ON: Archives & Museum Informatics. www.archimuse.com/mw2007/papers/peacock/peacock.html.

Poirier, R., & Richardson, M. (Eds.). (1995). *Robert Frost: Collected poems, prose, and plays*. New York: The Library of America.

Priestner, A., & Borg, M. (Eds.). (2016). *User experience in libraries: Applying ethnography and human-center design*. London: Routledge.

Prior, P. (2003, March). *Are communities of practice really an alternative to discourse communities?* [Conference presentation]. Meeting of the American Association of Applied Linguistics (AAAL): The Diversity of Applied Linguistics, Arlington, VA.

Richardson, M. (Ed.). (2014). *Robert Frost in context*. Oxford: Oxford University Press.

Rounds, J. (2006). Doing identity work in museums. *Curator: The Museum Journal*, *49*(2), 133–150. https://doi.org/10.1111/j.2151-6952.2006.tb00208.x.

Skov, M. (2013). Hobby-related information-seeking behaviour of highly dedicated online museum visitors. *Information Research*, *18*(4). http://informationr.net/ir/18-4/paper597.html#.YnMUTdrMK00.

Skov, M., & Ingwersen, P. (2008). Exploring information seeking behaviour in a digital museum context. In P. Borlund & J. W. Schneider (Eds.), *IIiX'08: Proceedings of the second international symposium on information interaction in context* (pp. 110–115). New York: Association for Computing Machinery. https://doi.org/10.1145/1414694.1414719.

Smithsonian Institution Office of Policy and Analysis. (2002). *Exhibitions and their audiences: Actual and potential*. Washington, DC: Smithsonian Institution. www.si.edu/content/opanda/docs/rpts2002/02.09.exhibitaudience.final.pdf.

Soergel, D. (1994). Indexing and retrieval performance: The logical evidence. *Journal of the American Society for Information Science*, *45*(8), 589–599. https://doi.org/10.1002/(SICI)1097-4571(199409)45:8%3C589::AID-ASI14%3E3.0.CO;2-E.

Sonnenwald, D. H. (1999). Evolving perspectives of human information behavior: Contexts, situations, social networks and information horizons. In T. Wilson & D. Allen (Eds.), *Exploring the contexts of information behavior: Proceedings of the second international conference in information needs* (pp. 176–190). London: Taylor Graham.

Sonnenwald, D. H., Wildemuth, B. S., & Harmon, G. L. (2001). A research method to investigate information seeking using the concept of information horizons: An example from a study of lower socio-economic students' information seeking behavior. *The New Review of Information Behavior Research*, *2*, 65–86. http://hdl.handle.net/10150/105932.

Stamburg, S. (2021, February 22). Happy birthday to the Phillips Collection, America's first museum of modern art. *NPR*. www.npr.org/2021/02/22/965371115/happy-birthday-to-the-phillips-collection-americas-first-museum-of-modern-art.

Stebbins, R. A. (2015). *Serious leisure: A perspective for our time* (2nd ed.). London: Routledge.

Stylianou-Lambert, T. (2010). Re-conceptualizing museum audiences: Power, activity, responsibility. *Visitor Studies*, *13*(2), 130–144. https://doi.org/10.1080/10645578.2010.509693.

Swales, J. (1988). Discourse communities, genres and English as an international language. *World Englishes*, *7*(2), 211–220. https://doi.org/10.1111/j.1467-971X.1988.tb00232.x.

Tzortzi, K. (2014) Movement in museums: Mediating between museum intent and visitor experience. *Museum Management and Curatorship*, *29*(4), 327–348. https://doi.org/10.1080/09647775.2014.939844.

Visser, J. (2014). Strategies for a heritage revival in the digital age. In L. Egberts & K. Bosma (Eds.), *Companion to European heritage revivals*. New York: Springer.

Walsh, D., Hall, M. M., Clough, P., & Foster, J. (2018). Characterising online museum users: A study of the National Museums Liverpool museum website. *International Journal of Digital Libraries*, *21*, 75–87. https://doi.org/10.1007/s00799-018-0248-8.

Weill, S. E. (1999). From being about something to being for somebody: The ongoing transformation of the American museum. *Daedalus*, *128*(3), 229–258. www.jstor.org/stable/20027573.

Wenger-Trainer, E., & Wenger-Trainer, B. (2015). *Communities of practice a brief introduction*. https://wenger-trayner.com/wp-content/uploads/2015/04/07-Brief-introduction-to-communities-of-practice.pdf.

Zweizig, D. (1973). *Predicting the amount of library use: An empirical study of the role of the public library in the life of the adult public*. Unpublished doctoral dissertation. Syracuse, NY: Syracuse University.

4 Big Ideas, Small Themes, and Everything In-Between

Many of the tasks required by exhibit work can be open-ended and indeterminate. A useful theoretical stance that can guide you through many of these processes is that of qualitative inquiry. This methodological orientation assumes that your understanding of your exhibit topic and the best way to create an exhibit structure arise from intense engagement with your material. Thus, your exhibit structure and content become actual extensions of your understanding of its primary materials, along with secondary materials that will ground your exhibit within a larger scholarly framework. The issues of exhibit building that are addressed in this chapter are the value of direct engagement with exhibit materials, how to address feelings of anxiety and insecurity, how to start writing original text, conceptual modeling for your exhibit, including creating its big idea and component themes, and decisions about object placement. This chapter will use an extended example to show how to apply the ideas and strategies of exhibit building, including a list of primary and secondary resources, a sample proposal, and an interface wireframe and final mockup.

Here is where we will engage with some essential tasks with the help of an extended example to help you:

- Develop an organizing conceptual model for your exhibit
- Create the "big idea" of your exhibit, including identification of smaller themes
- Organize stories and content thematically into subexhibits
- Identify the crucial excerpts within your documents you would like to highlight
- Decide if you would like to build an object or user-oriented exhibit
- Bring in associated images and text from other organizations or contributors
- Analyze documents taking on your audience's perspective, especially when they relate to historically oppressed and ignored communities
- Use authoritative material that will help in content interpretation and writing
- Write short thematic essays to contextualize your content
- Decide how objects will be arranged into integrated displays including interface elements such as timelines, image light boxes, and slideshows

DOI:10.4324/9781003301493-4

This is the point at which you will start engaging with your exhibit material in earnest. At this stage, you should begin to see the meaning and value of your documents and associated resources. Your reading will be driven by the need to create the "big idea" that will shape and drive the exhibit, coupled with your knowledge of your organization's mission and your audience's needs and interests. On the basis of the material in earlier chapters, you should also have a sense of potential audiences, comparable exhibits and collections, and the larger information ecosystem your creation will occupy.

Addressing Anxiety and the Challenge of Building an Original Exhibit

This is also the stage of the project that can be the most uncertain and anxiety-producing. For those exhibits where you do not have a pre-set curatorial direction from a subject matter expert or other source, it can be daunting to start the selection and reading process without a clear roadmap. This open path can offer a sense of creative liberation to some exhibit creators, while for others, the lack of direction and parameters can be a source of apprehension. In essence, exhibit creators need to build their structures inductively and iteratively, from the ground up using their content as the raw material and their analytic and interpretive powers as the driving creative force. Engaging in close reading of textual and pictorial materials to create a structured analysis for presentation, in other words, an exhibit, can be compared to the kind of intellectual work performed by the qualitative researcher who builds a "grounded theory" of human behavior. This is a research method to create "theory that is grounded in data systematically gathered and analysed. Theory evolves during actual research, and it does this through continuous interplay between analysis and data collection" (Strauss & Corbin, 1994, p. 273). But instead of building a theory of behavior grounded in data, you will be building the structure and content of a digital exhibit, based on a qualitative reading of data through thematic analysis, covered in detail in the previous chapter.

While many authors describe the processes of qualitative research methods from the data analysis perspective, there have been far fewer inquiries that center the researcher herself, aside from the study data. In an editorial, Clark and Sousa point out some of the challenges,

> [Q]ualitative research is not only challenging paradigmatically but is intellectually and interpersonally demanding too. Historically, those doing qualitative work—either by itself or in mixed method research—have not necessarily felt readily understood or as respected by funders, mainstream journals, or even colleagues. Attaining funding, publications, and respect is challenging enough for everyone—harder still when your work and its epistemological and ontological foundations are not well known or recognized.
>
> (2018, p. 1)

While these observations reflect a general cultural prejudice against qualitative method itself and not the problems encountered by the people using the method, their description of an "area of risk" for the process of qualitative data analysis is telling. "Very high volumes of data are generated that are required to be analyzed [by the researcher]. These data are usually also highly complex and 'messy,' thus presenting potential challenges to the analyst, beyond the normal difficulties of research itself" (p. 2). This messiness can be challenging for those with a low tolerance for ambiguity. As John and Lyn Lofland observe, engaging in inductive, open-ended data identification and analysis "can produce frustration and anxiety—as well as exhilaration. That is, the openness of the situation calls on the researcher to construct social science order and, for some, that circumstance is fearsome" (1995, p. 185).

If you can engage fully and openly with this "fearsome" process of discovery, it becomes possible to create an exhibit that explicitly models and displays the richness of cultural heritage and moves beyond the status of a simple collection. Thus engaged, you also create an opportunity to open yourself to the kinds of discovery to which the Loflands allude by revealing unexpected aspects of your content that can add interest to your exhibit. For example, Figure 4.1 shows items that were discovered while I was reading the materials for four exhibits: a charmingly illustrated book cover in an exhibit on small agricultural initiatives by the US Federal government, a drawing by the agricultural scientist George Washington Carver of roots from the cow pea plant, a detailed illustration of a basket packed for delivery in a local foods exhibit, and a data collection and display tool created to capture the "daily time record of the homemaker" as part of an exhibit on the US Department of Agriculture's (USDA's) Bureau of Home Economics (Marsh, 2022a). These elements were all highlighted in their respective exhibits.

Aside from finding these types of unexpected artifacts, reading candidates for your exhibit content allows you to simultaneously carry out several complex agendas:

- First and foremost, it provides a way to learn about your exhibit topic directly, without outside filters or judgments

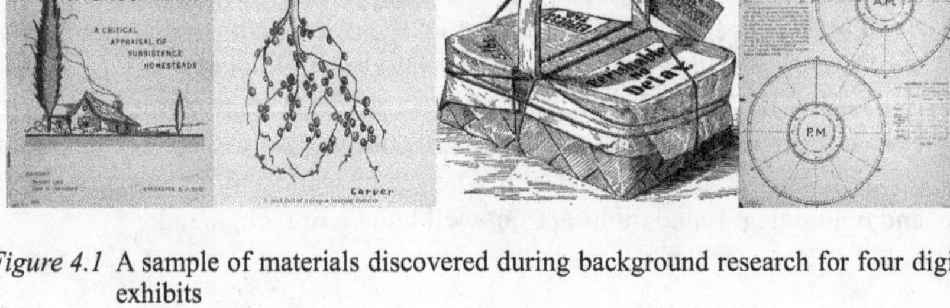

Figure 4.1 A sample of materials discovered during background research for four digital exhibits

- It allows you to assess what content will be useful for your exhibit and in what fashion: as items to be highlighted, as basis for an organizing structure, as background material, or in some other way
- It will also allow you to form a basis to reject materials that may be unsuitable for exhibit display due to a lack of visual interest, irrelevancy, or other features
- It will point out the main contours of your exhibit structure including suggestions of organizing themes (the "big idea") subtopics (small themes), aspects of side interest, possible timelines for process illustrations, and slideshows for multiple image presentation
- It will often reveal hidden content that or facts that perhaps did not make it to the scholarly record but will nonetheless enrich your exhibit
- As you review content sources, it can encourage empathy for your audience and imagine what they would (and would not) like to see within the confines of an exhibit

Frankly, this is the most difficult stage of your project because you must build a conceptual structure for your content that will then be enriched with original text. This new exhibit text needs to fulfill many requirements simultaneously with creativity, rigor, and polish. Your original exhibit text needs to:

- Capture and express some meaning about your items that remains true to their content
- Say something meaningful about the content that is not readily apparent or obvious
- Incorporate a clear-eyed analysis of the present existence and past legacy of racism, colonialism, sexism, heteronormativity, and social and economic class
- Acknowledge any controversy about the exhibit content
- Meet users where they are and encourage them to engage with the content in a reflective way
- Fulfill requirements of accessibility and plain language, when necessary

Having to consider and address these questions within a single project can seem "fearsomely" overwhelming, and they certainly present challenges. But by creating a strong conceptual foundation including your big idea and your smaller themes and always striving to remain true to your original content, you can create a unique and engaging exhibit that will enrich the lives of your users, advance the mission of your organization, and fulfill your creativity.

As discussed in previous chapters, it can be helpful to make a conscious decision to place your exhibit at a specific point in the continuum of rhetorical energy: more toward object identification or user engagement achieved through accompanying text, images, and interactive features. Sometimes it is clear from the outset which side you will lean toward, especially when you have an assortment of culturally significant or well-known materials that will form your base.

But if you do not have a clear preference at the start of your review, you should be able to make a choice after you engage with your materials within this deep analytic process.

Exhibit Text: Too Little, Too Much, or Just Right?

At this stage of your process, you should use the materials you are gathering in your background research to form the basis of your original exhibit content. This refers to all the text that is going to appear in your exhibit, excluding items like metadata object descriptions. In my experience, I have found that people starting out with their first exhibit tend to lean too far in one direction or another. Either they assume that their objects' inherent meaning and significance speaks for itself, and little explanation is necessary, or they think their audience will want to read an extensive essay on their focal topic or topics. Of course, the best answer usually lies somewhere closer to the middle of this continuum, but the nature of your exhibit content cannot be predetermined.

While studies exist of how visitors read exhibit text, they are often confined to physical displays in museums (Reitstätter et al., 2022; Kirchberg & Tröndle, 2012) or are focused on museum websites with more explicit instructional aims (Chong & Smith, 2017; Gazi, 2017; Lin et al., 2012). It is tempting to want to find a source that will direct the form your exhibit should take. But rigid rules based on facile prescriptions or dubious conclusions such as "write in the active voice", "users don't know how to scroll", or "the public can't understand anything above a certain grade level" will not help you create a meaningful exhibit. This kind of project occupies a unique, liminal place in the information landscape. Both physical and digital exhibits offer experiential interactions that can support what Falk and Dierking term "free-choice learning" (2002) or the activities within the "serious leisure" construct of Stebbins (2015). While the very nature of these unstructured contexts can be liberating, their lack of structure can present challenges to the writer.

Ultimately, your original text needs to balance the nature of your exhibit's objects, the needs of your audience, and the talents and availability of the exhibit team, all within a digital context. Since this will vary across exhibits and organizations, any static recommendation will necessarily devolve into a formula. Gazi puts this issue in very clear terms,

> Museum text is perhaps the most demanding category of text . . . one that resists ordinary rules of style and defies any attempt at conventional writing. Writing for museums and exhibitions is a challenging, time consuming, and at times painful process that requires familiarity with a significant range of knowledge from modalities of learning and basic tenets of gnostic psychology to principles of conceptual orientation to modes of reading in the museum space. . . . Nevertheless, museum text is one of the most powerful media of museum communication and an essential part of an exhibition's overall narrative.
>
> (2017, p. 57)

These observations were written with physical exhibits in mind, but their truth is equally applicable to digital exhibits. Just as the initial process of engaging with exhibit content can be anxiety-inducing, this later task of writing effective text can also present clear challenges.

Given these knotty issues, there are no ready instructions for writing exhibit text. Unless you are working with a project such as an annotated academic dissertation or book, or a pseudo collection requiring minimal content aside from object descriptions, you will have to engage with the writing process. Several discussions in this book are designed to prepare you for this work, including the recommendation to perform a competitive analysis, engage in audience research, and grapple with theories of exhibit design and structure.

Without question, the best framework that has helped me to both engage with exhibit material and writing the text that will bind it all together in an organized, engaging structure is that of qualitative research analysis, specifically content analysis. White and Marsh lay out the general rationale and procedures for this kind of data engagement (2006). Specifically, the editing style of qualitative document analysis has been of great support to create exhibit structure and content, as well as helping in reviewing document candidates to include in exhibits. As described in Chapter 2, Miller and Crabtree describe this type of analytic technique when they write,

> This style is termed editing because the interpreter enters the text much like an editor searching for meaningful segments, cutting, pasting, and rearranging until the produced summary reveals the interpretive truth in the text. . . . The researcher attempts to identify and separate from preconceptions prior to reading the data. . . . Once identified, these units are stored and organized into categories or codes. It is these categories that are explored for patterns and themes in the connecting phase of analysis.
>
> (1992, pp. 21, 23)

Following in the tradition of editing style analysis, here are some suggestions to help you with several exhibit tasks:

- If you are working with document-based exhibits, skim through candidates looking for main themes and quotations you can use both in the original content as pull quotes or as extended descriptions of the objects themselves.
- Within your time constraints, review as much scholarly literature as you can to better understand the central ideas of your exhibit topic and any areas of controversy or disagreement you might need to consider and address.
- Keep an open mind as you go through all this primary and secondary material and record any novel or unexpected content that you might be able to use.
- Use your identified pull quotes to structure and focus your writing.

Working Through Exhibit Questions With an Extended Example: The Negro Extension Service

This chapter will rely upon an extended example of an exhibit about an American agricultural education program that was racially segregated. This initiative, known as "Negro Extension", was a federally funded program that sent Black professional educators from the agricultural programs of universities to train local Black farmers and their families in a variety of activities including farming, food preservation and preparation, sewing, and home maintenance. An informal program of cooperative extension had been started in 1862 with the *Morrill Act* "which provided for a university in each state to provide education to citizens in agricultural and mechanical fields. These colleges are known as 'land-grant universities'" (The Ohio State University, 2022). After a 1905 "conference between a representative of the United States Department of Agriculture and Booker T. Washington, then principal of Tuskegee Institute, it was decided to appoint the first Negro demonstration agent to work exclusively with Negro farmers" (Mercier, 1921, p. 3).

As described by the USDA,

> [T]he Smith Lever Act formalized extension in 1914, establishing USDA's partnership with land-grant universities to apply research and provide education in agriculture. Congress created the extension system to address exclusively rural, agricultural issues. At that time, more than 50 percent of the U.S. population lived in rural areas, and 30 percent of the workforce was engaged in farming. Extension's engagement with rural America helped make possible the American agricultural revolution, which dramatically increased farm productivity, allowing fewer farmers to produce more food.
>
> (National Institute of Food and Agriculture. USDA, n.d.)

It is notable that the program's nature as racially segregated is omitted from this official history.

While the federal government became racially integrated during the Reconstruction period after the Civil War, it was re-segregated in 1913 by President Woodrow Wilson. As described by the Woodrow Wilson House, the US Federal government

> had been integrated in the early days of Reconstruction and continued to be so up to Wilson's arrival at the White House. Making up at least 10% of the federal workforce, African Americans federal workers had the professional opportunities and resources to build a network of thriving, though segregated, educational and communal institutions in Washington, D.C. With the new Wilson administration, all that changed. As the first Southerner to ascend to the Presidency since before the Civil War, Wilson brought with him a segregationist ideology and sympathy for the 'Lost Cause' narrative. With segregation laws becoming more entrenched across the South—and segregation in northern states bolstered by redlining—Wilson gave his newly appointed cabinet the permission to segregate their departments. As historian Eric Yellin explains, segregation did not simply separate Black and white workers in the federal government, it halted Black professional advancement and restricted

> hiring in the desirable positions for which these men and women were qualified having passed the requisite civil service exams.
>
> (n.d.)

Given the racist perspective of the Wilson administration, it was unsurprising that the newly sanctioned USDA Cooperative Extension Service was segregated into units with white employees who served white citizens and those with Black employees serving Black citizens. Following the practice of naming institutions of the dominant culture as the default and minority cultural institutions as "other", the Black extension service was given the qualifying label, "Negro" and was placed into a lessor role described as "supplementing the activities of the white county agricultural and home demonstration agents" (Mercier, 1921, p. 2). The explicitly segregated Negro Extension Service did not end officially until the Civil Rights Act of 1964 was passed (Crosby, 1983).

Developing an Exhibit Conceptual Model: What Is Black? What Is History?

Given this background, the first questions to arise are ones of nomenclature and historical viewpoint. Clearly the word "Negro" needs to be included when it appears in documents that would be included in the exhibit such as the 1925 publication, *Extension Work Among Negros Conducted by Negro Agents* by Albert J. Evans and *Developments in Negro Extension Work* by C.B. Smith from 1927. But what terms should appear in the item metadata and the exhibit text to describe the people involved in this work? Several candidates come to mind: African-American, black, and Black.

The broader terms person of color and BIPOC (Black, Indigenous, and People of Color) are not as accurate since they include categories of racial and ethnic identity that are not centrally relevant to the program in question. The recent Black Lives Matter (BLM) protests in the United States about race-based inequality in policing specifically and life generally have led to some changes in how non-white people are calling for representation. There are some arguments in favor of black spelled with a lower-case letter and some in favor of the uppercase spelling (Coleman, 2020). The writer Adam Serwer includes a Note to the Reader in his 2021 book and writes,

> [T]hroughout this book, I use lowercase when referring to racial terms such as "black" or "white". This is against the prevailing trend in letters, but I do it because I fear that capitalization reinforces the notion that race is a biological reality rather than a social reality. Racism and bigotry are very real, but race itself is a biological fiction.
>
> (p. xi)

Although some see African-American as a problematic phrase that is not accurate for many people who identify as black or Black, it still appears frequently in text and as library descriptors. For example, the Library of Congress Subject Heading (LCSH) that is most relevant to this topic is "African American county agricultural agents".

While there are no clear answers for this question, this brief discussion should demonstrate the need to address nomenclature for this topic and to use language in a way that is respectful, clear, and consistent, and that centers the black/Black/African-American experience. This decision might be informed by reaching out to a relevant Community of Practice (Wenger-Trainer & Wenger-Trainer, 2015) such as Black scholars of history, or Black farmers for their perspective. (Note: this chapter will use the capitalized version of Black.)

A related question is one of viewpoint: Should the exhibit take the perspective that Black history is American history or is not American history? The simplicity of the question conceals a difficult choice. There is a rhetorical program behind the assertion that "Black history is American history". The goal is to move Black American history out of a perceived attentional ghetto of Black History Month to a more central and sustained place in both the academy, K-12 education, and the popular culture. As argued by Gaston,

> The fact of the matter is—Black history is American history. The African American impact on history is far-reaching and is deeply etched in the social fabric of America. We cannot talk about American history without talking about African American history. These two stories are intrinsically intertwined. (2015)

King argues to the contrary when he writes, "we will have to reconcile that Black history has its own historical entry points, its own historical timelines, historical perspectives, and historical people" (2020, p. 340). This effort will require a new consciousness to understand Black historical experiences outside of a white, Western European perspective.

Choosing one of these conceptual models over the other would impact the entire nature of an exhibit on Black agricultural extension. Should "Negro Extension" be analyzed from the perspective of USDA and the larger world of institutionalized, capitalistic white American agriculture? Or should it be seen through a perspective of Black historical consciousness that centers the Black extension agents themselves and the Black people they served? The first choice would accept Crosby's description of Negro extension (1983) as achieving "limited success against long odds", whereas the second supports Paley's contention that the program was an effort to bring "healthful ways of living to the rural Negro home" (1941) and Jones-Branch's more recent argument that the Arkansas Home Demonstration agents of Negro extension were in effect "Black women activists who uplifted their communities while subverting the formidable structures of white supremacy" (2021). A "big idea" candidate could be the Black agents of the USDA extension program operated under a system of officially sanctioned and enforced racial segregation and had an outsized impact on the lives of the Black farm families they served. This lands more on the second foundational concept and centers the extension agents and their clients, instead of the white-controlled system of the segregated

USDA. Following from this idea, the exhibit title could be "Negro Extension: Empowerment Through Connection", with the themes of empowerment and connection both arising from the actions of the agents themselves, working in relationship with their clients, all under the same system of racial segregation.

This extended example illustrates several principles:

1. It is possible to get a limited sense of the scholarship of a specific topic fairly quickly within limits. Spending some time reading secondary sources should help to refine your topic and your understanding of some of its more nuanced aspects. Of course, if you have access to someone with true expertise in a field related to your proposed exhibit, they would be a good source of verification for any conclusions you may reach.
2. Sometimes making seemingly small decisions like a simple word choice ("Black" vs. "black" vs. "African-American") can have a large impact on the direction and nature of your exhibit.
3. While potentially difficult, this type of initial background research will help you to focus your thinking and will make other later decisions much easier. Such decisions include topics for your exhibit, types of images to include to illustrate key points, and the quotes to pull from either exhibit items or secondary sources. Finally, it will help you to create the big idea and small themes for your exhibit. An excellent example of this idea in action is the big idea for an exhibit of photographs from the Travis County, Texas Negro Extension Service Collection. The title "Clearing Stones, Sowing Seeds" expresses an elegant balance between the oppression these Black educators faced (the stones) and the effects of their work (the seeds) (Austin History Center & Austin Public Library, n.d.).
4. Finally, as Beverly Serrell observes, your big idea need not even appear explicitly in your exhibit. "Having a big idea does not mean that the exhibition has to insist on communicating it overtly [to visitors]. But it provides a thread of meaning, coherence, and weight. Exhibit developers use the big idea to delineate what will and will not be included in the exhibit. It is primarily a tool for the team, not an actual label for visitors, so although it must be clear, it can use a complex vocabulary. The big idea guides the development of exhibit elements and their labels. . . . This means that each element must have a clearly defined objective that supports, exemplifies, or illustrates aspects of the big idea. For each exhibit component, the question, 'What's this got to do with the big idea?' should have a clear and positive answer" (2015, p. 12).

Building Upon Your Big Idea and Developing Smaller Themes: "Negro Extension: Empowerment Through Connection"

Once you have adopted your big idea ("Negro Extension: Empowerment Through Connection"), you should apply it as a viewing lens and conceptual organizing system to help you develop the smaller themes of your exhibit. This step needs to be carried out by identifying relevant exhibit objects and useful secondary literature that will flesh out your "big idea" skeleton. In this case of the Black extension exhibit some obvious candidates appear for small themes:

- Relationships between and among Black extension agents and their Black clients
- The gendered [female] home demonstration agent versus [male] cooperative extension agent
- Relationships with white USDA and university staff
- Actual impact of programs on local Black citizens' lives
- Timeline of program, along with legislative references, prominent agents, and innovations such as the Tuskegee Movable School (aka, the "Jesup Wagon"), and the annual Tuskegee Negro Farmers' Conference, 1892–1915

This is the point at which the exhibit really begins to come together. It becomes much easier to identify useful secondary sources once you have delineated your big idea and smaller themes and have organized them into a structure. As you identify your component themes, be sure to stay alert and gather useful quotations that will illustrate your themes, as well as to identify how your objects will be used within the exhibit. For example, to show how gender was used as a general organizing principle to justify segregated services within extension, this quote would be useful and could introduce this section of the exhibit:

> All the extension agents in a county work cooperatively with the entire rural family, although the county agricultural agent's responsibility is primarily to the men and boys, the home demonstration agent's to the women and girls. . . . This publication tells chiefly about the county home demonstration agent's work. . . . In addition to the 580 counties that do not have home demonstration agents, approximately 30 counties, mostly in the Southern States, have large enough Negro farm populations to justify the employment of a Negro home demonstration agent, but do not now have them. In all, 388 Negro home demonstration agents are now employed in the Southern States, West Virginia, and Maryland.
>
> (U.S. Department of Agriculture, 1951, pp. 1–2)

It is also important to always consider exhibit materials within the framework of your big idea. When you distill themes or narratives that are compelling but are only indirectly relevant to your exhibit's main idea, you can keep them in reserve to be used in future ancillary projects. Thus, the big idea becomes a tool that acts both to identify what is of central concern for your exhibit and your audience, and to keep peripheral materials on the margins.

In this case, the core theme is the relationship between the Black agricultural extension agents and the Black citizens they served, within a segregated governmental agency and a culture driven by Jim Crow laws and culture (Gates, 2020). If a given candidate for the exhibit does not touch upon this conceptual organizing

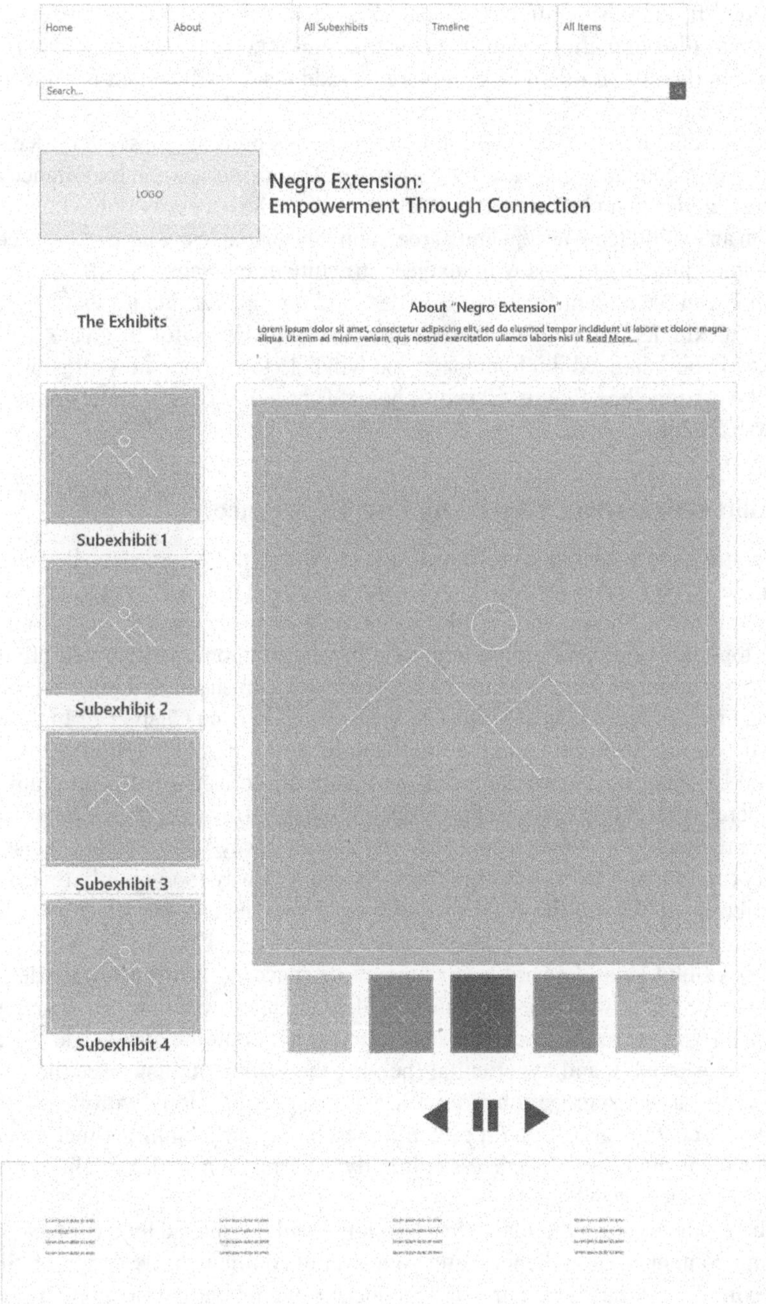

Figure 4.2 Wireframe of home page for proposed exhibit on Negro Extension with slideshow of featured items and list of topic areas

axis, and relates only indirectly to USDA extension, then it should probably be excluded from consideration. Conversely, if a candidate is found that relates to the racial discrimination of the time within agriculture, but is not about Black extension directly, it might be considered to add detail and context to the central idea of the exhibit.

Alas, there are no rules to be found to guide this process; most every decision will need to be made on a case-by-case basis. This illustrates the importance of a strong big idea that can drive your work, as well as the necessity of having everyone on an exhibit team accept and agree upon this vision, lest your exhibit become a muddled jumble of items with no clear structure or message.

Once you have identified your big idea, and the smaller themes that can form the "subexhibits" of your main structure, it would be useful to create a wireframe of your main exhibit homepage that will help to envision how all your ideas could work together. Figure 4.2 shows how this proposal could appear on the web (Marsh, 2022b).

Exhibit Orientation: Objects or User Experience?

Once you have your big idea formed and at least some of your smaller themes identified, you need to step back and make a decision that will affect the entirety of your project. Should your exhibit focus more on the documents that comprise your topic area or should more emphasis be placed upon an integrated program of interpretation of those documents for your users? In short, will your exhibit be object or user-focused, as described by the continuum from Chapter 2? In the case of our Negro Extension example, the balance of the exhibit's rhetorical energy should be spent on interpretation of the nature and effects of this program and not merely presenting historical government reports. However, this interpretative program should not be seen as a way to "explain away" the inherent racism of this corner of American agricultural history but as a way to explicitly reveal and describe its effects on the lives of Black rural citizens and the Black extension agents.

This exhibit should spend a fair amount of space on fulfilling goals that are interpretive (what were the mechanisms of segregation within extension?), educational (what were the effects of segregated services on the agents and the citizens they served?), and experiential (helping the exhibit audience see the nature of racially driven segregation from a Black perspective, along with illustrations of the effects of segregation on past and present-day agriculture). Other types of exhibits that showcase objects less culturally determined than this might be recast better as object-oriented.

There is no easy way to make this decision. It will be shaped by the intersection of your content, your audiences, and your overall communicative program. Since my exhibit work has centered mass-produced government publications from the twentieth century, it has incorporated a fair number of outside images, videos, and secondary sources to make these materials interesting and relevant to a modern audience. Exhibits featuring content more exciting than obsolete century-old agricultural reports might be more suitable for an object-oriented structure and approach. Two excellent examples are Amardeep Singh's *Women of the Early Harlem Renaissance: African American Women Writers 1900–1922* and *Digital Paxton: Digital Collection, Critical Edition, and Teaching Platform*, edited by Will Fenton.

Exhibit Objects: Selection

Once the preliminary research is done, it is time to start selecting the objects that will form the core of your exhibit, secondary sources that will serve as useful interpretive lenses, and useful quotes that can introduce exhibit sections. In our Negro Extension exhibit, here are some sample resources that would offer images and documents that could be showcased. This is not an exhaustive list, however, and should be considered as initial suggestions.

Prominent Original Serials

Service Bulletin: A Monthly Statement of the Negro Extension Work (1928–1930)
Georgia State College of Agriculture Extension Division

Negro Extension News and *Negro Extension Supervisors*
Extension Service, Office of Cooperative Extension Work, United States Department of Agriculture
National Agricultural Library

Extension Service Circular
US Department of Agriculture
https://archive.org/details/usda-extensionservicecircular

Annual Report of Negro Agricultural Extension Work in Louisiana
Louisiana. University and Agricultural and Mechanical College. Division of Agricultural Extension

Prominent Original Monographs and Reports

Mercier, W. B. (1921). *Extension work among Negroes 1920* (United States Department of Agriculture Department Circular, Number 190). Washington, DC: U.S. Department of Agriculture. https://archive.org/details/extensionworkamo190merc.

Campbell, T. M. (1936). The movable school goes to the Negro farmer. Tuskegee, AL: Tuskegee Institute Press.

Evans, J. A. (1925). Extension work among Negros conducted by Negro agents. U.S. Department of Agriculture. Department Circular, Number 355. https://archive.org/details/extensionworkamo355evan.

Martin, O. B. (1926). A decade of Negro extension work, 1914-1924. U.S. Department of Agriculture. Miscellaneous Circular, Number 72. https://archive.org/details/decadeofnegroext72mart.

Paley, L. M. (1941). The education and responsibilities of Negro home demonstration agents in Texas. Unpublished Master's Thesis. Kansas State College of Agriculture and Applied Science. https://core.ac.uk/download/pdf/10653109.pdf.

Shinn, E. H. (1934). Agencies used and methods of procedure followed by Negro agricultural agents (1) in carrying out their extension programs and (2) in measuring the results of their work. Cooperative Extension Work in Agriculture and Home Economics. Extension Service Circular, Number 196. https://archive.org/details/agenciesusedmeth19shin.

Smith, C. B. (1927). Developments in Negro extension work. Cooperative Extension Work in Agriculture and Home Economics. Extension Service Circular, Number 38. https://archive.org/details/developmentsinne38smit.

United States Extension Service. (1937). *Minutes [of the] regional conference for Negro district agents, Petersburg, Virginia*. U.S. Department of Agriculture. https://archive.org/details/CAT10678126.

Prominent Secondary Sources

Crosby, E. W. (1983). Limited success against long odds: The Black county agent. *Agricultural History*, *57*(3), 277–288. www.jstor.org/stable/3742454/.

Harris, C. V. (2008). "The Extension Service is not an integration agency": The idea of race in the Cooperative Extension Service. Agricultural History, 82(2), 193–219. www.jstor.org/stable/20454817.

Jones, A. W. (1979). Thomas M. Campbell: Black agricultural leader of the new south. Agricultural History, 53(1), 42–59. www.jstor.org/stable/3742858.

Jones-Branch, C. (2021). Better living by their own bootstraps: Black women's activism in rural Arkansas, 1914–1965. Fayetteville, AR: The University of Arkansas Press.

Mayberry, B. (1991). The Tuskegee Movable School: A unique contribution to national and international agriculture and rural development. Agricultural History, 65(2), 85-104. www.jstor.org/stable/3743710.

Schor, J. (1986). The Black presence in the U.S. Cooperative Extension Service since 1945: An American quest for service and equity. Agricultural History, 60(2), 137–153. www.jstor.org/stable/3743436.

US Department of Agriculture. (1951). The home demonstration agent. Agriculture Information Bulletin, 38. https://handle.nal.usda.gov/10113/CAT87791369.

Winn, J. E. (2008). Documenting racism in an agricultural extension film. Film & History: An Interdisciplinary Journal of Film and Television Studies, 38(1), 33–43. http://doi.org/10.1353/flm.0.0023.

Winn, J. E. (2012). Helping Negroes to become better farmers and homemakers. *Documenting racism: African Americans in US Department of Agriculture documentaries, 1921–42* (pp. 13–35). New York: Continuum. http://dx.doi.org/10.5040/9781628928679.ch-002.

On the basis of the nature and extent of your smaller themes, it would be helpful to include relevant images and to embed out-of-copyright video from these sources, among others.

Digital Collections Relevant to American Agricultural Extension

Auburn University's Alabama Cooperative Extension Service (ACES) Photographs
https://content.lib.auburn.edu/digital/collection/autest/search

Clemson University Libraries' Cooperative Extension Service Photographs 1880–1979
https://digitalcollections.clemson.edu/explore/collections/cu-coop-photos/

Cornell University Library: HEARTH—Home Economics Archive: Research, Tradition, History
https://digital.library.cornell.edu/collections/hearth

Library of Congress Catalog
https://catalog.loc.gov/

National Agricultural Library's Internet Archive Collection
https://archive.org/details/usdanationalagriculturallibrary

National Archives and Records Administration Catalog
https://catalog.archives.gov/

The New York Public Library Digital Collections
https://digitalcollections.nypl.org/

Oklahoma State University Library: Ag Cooperative Extension Collection
https://library.okstate.edu/search-and-find/collections/digital-collections/ag-cooperative-extension-collection

University of North Texas Libraries' Travis County Negro Extension Service Program Photograph Collection
https://texashistory.unt.edu/explore/collections/TNESPC/

Original Films

Helping Negroes to Become Better Farmers and Homemakers, 1921
US Department of Agriculture
National Archives and Records Administration
https://catalog.archives.gov/catalogmedia/lz/mopix/033/GENERAL/33-156-r1.mp4

The Negro Farmer: Extension Work for Better Farming and Better Living. 1938
US Department of Agriculture
National Archives and Records Administration Video Collection on YouTube
www.youtube.com/watch?v=Y9xnfqKtI2A

Once your preliminary research has identified a critical mass of materials, you can start to make a conceptual structure and information architecture for your exhibit. It is also possible that if you fail to identify enough useful sources you might have to re-consider your exhibit idea. If this happens, you may decide to adapt your idea into a smaller project such as an illustrated essay that would fit better into your organizational content strategy and information ecosystem.

This would be a good point to pull your ideas and a sample of your materials into a short proposal that could serve two purposes: (1) to offer an overview for anyone who might need to approve or review your idea and (2) to help you to organize your sources and thoughts into an initial structure that would guide future work, assuming you decide to pursue your project idea. The next two figures illustrate a proposal for the imaginary Negro Extension exhibit and a mockup of what the home page of your exhibit might look like, based on your preliminary ideas (Marsh, 2022c, 2022d). The proposal includes:

- Pull quote from a prominent scholar of extension for setting the project's framework
- List of tentative topics for the exhibit sections
- List of secondary sources
- Sample images
- Twitter suggestions
- Relevant events
- Scholars who would be good candidates for consultation and/or presentation requests

The mockup is a version of the wireframes shown earlier with overlaid sample content. This brings richness and authenticity to the original proposed design.

This background work might seem potentially tedious to anyone more interested in simply diving into a pile of images or documents to start the exhibit-building process. But much like your big idea, these design and content artifacts will be extremely useful in several ways: They will help to frame and initiate your

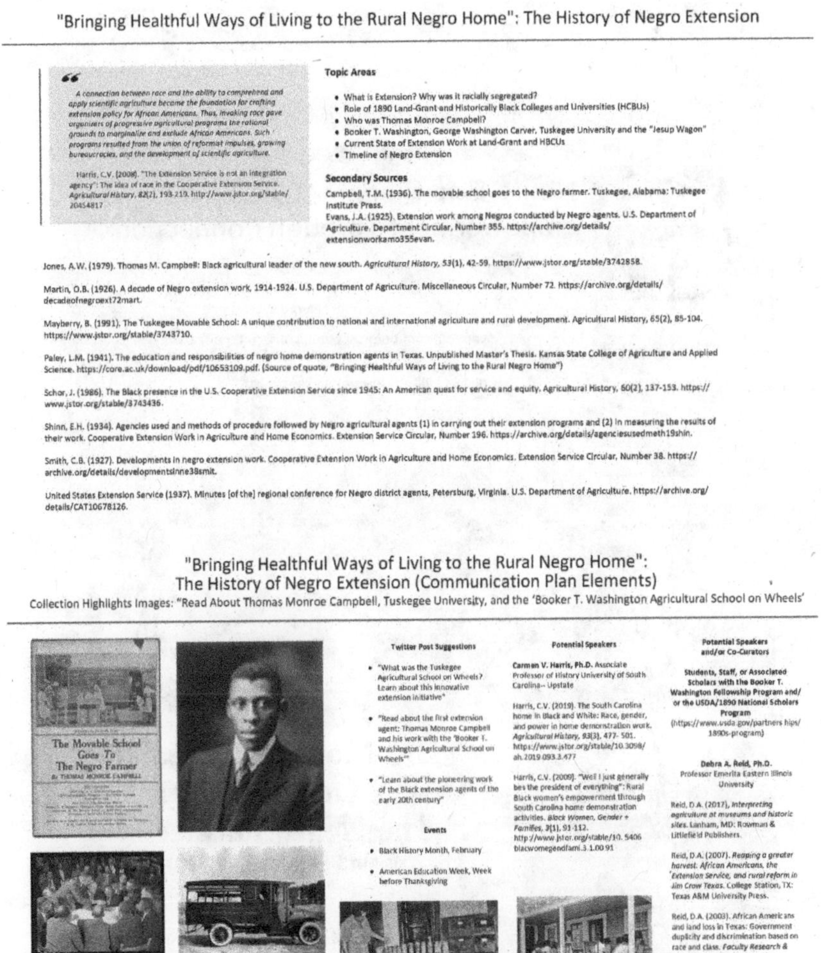

"Bringing Healthful Ways of Living to the Rural Negro Home": The History of Negro Extension

> A connection between race and the ability to comprehend and apply scientific agriculture became the foundation for crafting extension policy for African Americans. Thus, invoking race gave organizers of progressive agricultural programs the rational grounds to marginalize and exclude African Americans. Such programs resulted from the union of reformist impulses, growing bureaucracies, and the development of scientific agriculture.
>
> Harris, C.V. (2008). "The Extension Service is not an integration agency": The idea of race in the Cooperative Extension Service. *Agricultural History, 82*(2), 193-219. http://www.jstor.org/stable/20454817

Topic Areas

- What is Extension? Why was it racially segregated?
- Role of 1890 Land-Grant and Historically Black Colleges and Universities (HCBUs)
- Who was Thomas Monroe Campbell?
- Booker T. Washington, George Washington Carver, Tuskegee University and the "Jesup Wagon"
- Current State of Extension Work at Land-Grant and HBCUs
- Timeline of Negro Extension

Secondary Sources

Campbell, T.M. (1936). The movable school goes to the Negro farmer. Tuskegee, Alabama: Tuskegee Institute Press.

Evans, J.A. (1925). Extension work among Negros conducted by Negro agents. U.S. Department of Agriculture. Department Circular, Number 355. https://archive.org/details/extensionworkamo355evan.

Jones, A.W. (1979). Thomas M. Campbell: Black agricultural leader of the new south. *Agricultural History, 53*(1), 42-59. https://www.jstor.org/stable/3742858.

Martin, O.B. (1926). A decade of Negro extension work, 1914-1924. U.S. Department of Agriculture. Miscellaneous Circular, Number 72. https://archive.org/details/decadeofnegroext72mart.

Mayberry, B. (1991). The Tuskegee Movable School: A unique contribution to national and international agriculture and rural development. Agricultural History, 65(2), 85-104. https://www.jstor.org/stable/3743710.

Paley, L.M. (1941). The education and responsibilities of negro home demonstration agents in Texas. Unpublished Master's Thesis. Kansas State College of Agriculture and Applied Science. https://core.ac.uk/download/pdf/10653109.pdf. (Source of quote, "Bringing Healthful Ways of Living to the Rural Negro Home")

Schor, J. (1986). The Black presence in the U.S. Cooperative Extension Service since 1945: An American quest for service and equity. Agricultural History, 60(2), 137-153. https://www.jstor.org/stable/3743436.

Shinn, E.H. (1934). Agencies used and methods of procedure followed by Negro agricultural agents (1) in carrying out their extension programs and (2) in measuring the results of their work. Cooperative Extension Work in Agriculture and Home Economics. Extension Service Circular, Number 196. https://archive.org/details/agenciesusedmeth19shin.

Smith, C.B. (1927). Developments in negro extension work. Cooperative Extension Work in Agriculture and Home Economics. Extension Service Circular, Number 38. https://archive.org/details/developmentsinne38smit.

United States Extension Service (1937). Minutes [of the] regional conference for Negro district agents, Petersburg, Virginia. U.S. Department of Agriculture. https://archive.org/details/CAT10678126.

"Bringing Healthful Ways of Living to the Rural Negro Home":
The History of Negro Extension (Communication Plan Elements)

Collection Highlights Images: "Read About Thomas Monroe Campbell, Tuskegee University, and the 'Booker T. Washington Agricultural School on Wheels'

Twitter Post Suggestions

- "What was the Tuskegee Agricultural School on Wheels? Learn about this innovative extension initiative"
- "Read about the first extension agent: Thomas Monroe Campbell and his work with the 'Booker T. Washington Agricultural School on Wheels'"
- "Learn about the pioneering work of the Black extension agents of the early 20th century"

Events

- Black History Month, February
- American Education Week, Week before Thanksgiving

Potential Speakers

Carmen V. Harris, Ph.D. Associate Professor of History University of South Carolina-- Upstate

Harris, C.V. (2019). The South Carolina home in Black and White: Race, gender, and power in home demonstration work. *Agricultural History, 93*(3), 477- 501. https://www.jstor.org/stable/10.3098/ah.2019.093.3.477

Harris, C.V. (2009). "Well I just generally bes the president of everything": Rural Black women's empowerment through South Carolina home demonstration activities. *Black Women, Gender + Families, 3*(1), 91-112. http://www.jstor.org/stable/10.5406/blacwomegendfami.3.1.0091

Potential Speakers and/or Co-Curators

Students, Staff, or Associated Scholars with the Booker T. Washington Fellowship Program and/or the USDA/1890 National Scholars Program
(https://www.usda.gov/partners hips/1890s-program)

Debra A. Reid, Ph.D.
Professor Emerita Eastern Illinois University

Reid, D.A. (2017), *Interpreting agriculture at museums and historic sites*. Lanham, MD: Rowman & Littlefield Publishers.

Reid, D.A. (2007). *Reaping a greater harvest: African Americans, the Extension Service, and rural reform in Jim Crow Texas*. College Station, TX: Texas A&M University Press.

Reid, D.A. (2003). African Americans and land loss in Texas: Government duplicity and discrimination based on race and class. *Faculty Research & Creative Activity*, 72. http://thekeep.eiu.edu/history_fac/72.

Figure 4.3 Exhibit proposal with communication plan

research, they will help you to course-correct if you find yourself lost in minutia or irrelevancy, and they will serve as the basis of your communication plan to help you explain your project to leadership, to your colleagues, to your patrons, and future outlets such as professional conference presentations.

Going through this process also forces you to engage with the digital documentation you plan to use in your exhibit. This gets you much closer to a deep understanding of the material and consequently, a better sense of how it should be presented. Also, it bears repeating that you might conclude that materials you thought might make a compelling exhibit are simply not suitable for one reason

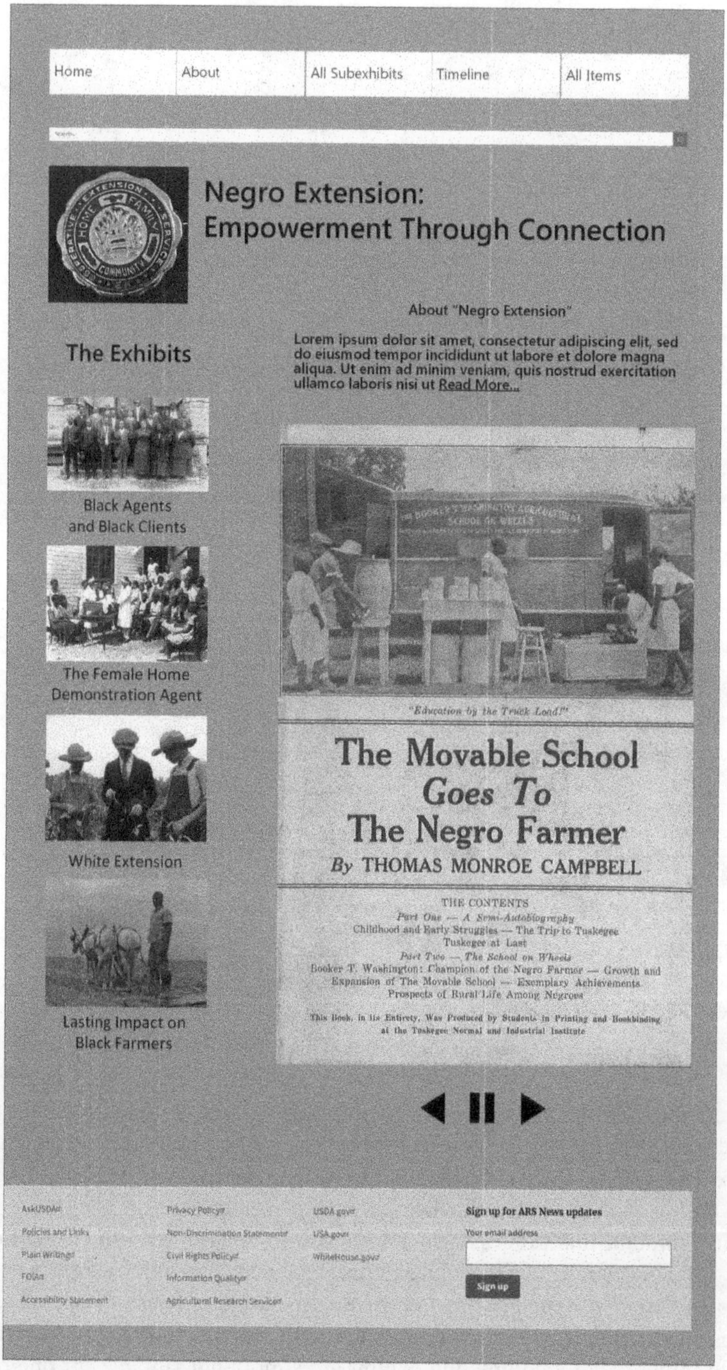

Figure 4.4 Mockup of home page for proposed exhibit on Negro Extension

or another. It is better to know this fact sooner in your exhibit-building process than later.

Exhibit Objects: Arrangement and Selection Criteria

The final section of this chapter will address questions relating to your exhibit's objects: How to display them and how to select them? Perhaps the best observation about the power of exhibit object display was made by Barker,

> Display is always produced by curators, designers, etc. As such, it is necessarily informed by definite aims and assumptions and evokes some larger meaning or deeper reality beyond the individual works in the display. In short, it is a form of representation as well as a mode of presentation.
>
> (1999, p. 13)

This conception of object arrangement and display as an expression of a rhetorical program and, at times, as a creative act itself can be seen in information objects as varied as the European cabinet of curiosities, collage, assemblage, and altered art, the scrapbook, and the Tangible History movement (Rasmussen, 2022; Ulrich et al., 2015).

The most important point to keep in mind is how you place your exhibit objects within a display makes a statement and advances some sort of argument (Mao & Fu, 2021). The nature of this argument as either explicit or implicit, consciously considered or blindly accepted is ultimately up to you. The taxonomy of image–text relationships described by Marsh and White can be useful here for its foundational conception of rhetorical relationships (2003). If multiple discourse objects such as texts and images are placed together, they are advancing an argument which will be shaped by their overtly visual and implicitly intellectual relationships. For example, an image of a specific person or event can be used within an exhibit for several reasons: to simply decorate the text, to provide an illustrated example of the text's meaning, or to somehow contrast with the text to make an aesthetic allusion or to otherwise interpret the text. Within the model, inter-item relationships with an exhibit can be distant, close, or intersectional. Similarly, the team advancing the Tangible History movement posits that their methods can be used to activate three types of rhetorical relationships: contrasting, shifting perspectives, and revealing (Ulrich et al., 2015). The example of Fred Wilson's *Mining the Museum* exhibit analyzed in Chapter 2 is an excellent example of the potential power of object display, albeit within the confines of a physical exhibit. These questions should be engaged directly when you combine different informational objects.

Another issue to consider is the type of display artifact you might want to use for object display, what some in the exhibit world call parerga.

> The display of artefacts always implies an external mediation that influences, and often codifies, the reception of the exhibits. Objects are manipulated,

> restored, appropriated, staged, in short displayed, through various representational strategies that include pedestals, labels, and showcases. These elements, which we could define as parerga, are often ignored because of their utilitarian function.
>
> (Grave et al., 2018, back cover)

Digital parerga such as timelines, image light boxes, and slideshows can greatly increase the engagement factor of an exhibit. The embedded rhetorical arguments that are activated by each tool should be considered carefully, however. The temporal arrangement of timeline items can convey an inevitability to a given sequence of events that can be misleading, for example (Lubar, 2013). Arranging slideshows of a collection of items can convey a conceptual or stylistic relationship between them that you might not intend if you do not configure and deploy this technique with care.

Digital and Physical Exhibits Discussed in This Chapter

Clearing Stones, Sowing Seeds: Photographs from the Travis County Negro Extension Service Collection
Austin History Center & Austin Public Library
https://storymaps.arcgis.com/stories/267a5cb8b6744daab4600c9f9a2ac1a3

Digital Paxton: Digital Collection, Critical Edition, and Teaching Platform
Will Fenton
http://digitalpaxton.org/works/digital-paxton/index.

Women of the Early Harlem Renaissance: African American Women Writers 1900–1922
Amardeep Singh
https://scalar.lehigh.edu/harlemwomen/index

References

Austin History Center & Austin Public Library. (n.d.). *Clearing stones, sowing seeds: Photographs from the Travis County Negro Extension Service Collection*. https://storymaps.arcgis.com/stories/267a5cb8b6744daab4600c9f9a2ac1a3.

Barker, E. (1999). Introduction. In E. Barker (Ed.), *Contemporary cultures of display* (pp. 8–21). New Haven, CT: Yale University Press.

Chong, C., & Smith, D. (2017) Interactive learning units on museum websites. *Journal of Museum Education, 42*(2), 169–178. https://doi.org/10.1080/10598650.2017.1301626.

Clark, A. M., & Sousa, B. J. (2018). The mental health of people doing qualitative research: Getting serious about risks and remedies. *International Journal of Qualitative Methods, 17*(1), 1–3. https://journals.sagepub.com/doi/10.1177/1609406918787244.

Coleman, N. (2020, July 5). Why we're capitalizing Black. *The New York Times*. www.nytimes.com/2020/07/05/insider/capitalized-black.html.

Crosby, E. W. (1983). Limited success against long odds: The Black county agent. *Agricultural History*, *57*(3), 277–288. www.jstor.org/stable/3742454/.

Falk, J., & Dierking, L. (2002). *Lessons without limit: How free-choice learning is transforming education*. Lanham, MD: AltaMira Press.

Gaston, H. K. (2015, February 5). Black history is American history. *The Huffington Post*. www.huffpost.com/entry/black-history-is-american-history_b_6618602.

Gates, Jr., H. L. (2020). *Stony the road: Reconstruction, white supremacy, and the rise of Jim Crow*. London: Penguin Books.

Gazi, A. (2017). Writing text for museums of technology the case of the Industrial Gas Museum in Athens. *Museum Management and Curatorship*, *33*(1), 57–78. https://doi.org/10.1080/09647775.2017.1416310.

Grave, J., Holm, C., Kobi, V., & Van Eck, C. (Eds.). (2018). *The agency of display: Objects, framings and parerga*. Dresden: Sandstein Verlag.

Jones-Branch, C. (2021). *Better living by their own bootstraps: Black women's activism in rural Arkansas, 1914–1965*. Fayetteville, AR: The University of Arkansas Press.

King, L. J. (2020). Black history is not American history: Toward a framework of Black historical consciousness. *Social Education*, *84*(6), 335–341. www.socialstudies.org/social-education/84/6/black-history-not-american-history-toward-framework-black-historical.

Kirchberg, V., & Tröndle, M. (2012). Experiencing exhibitions: A review of studies on visitor experiences in museums. *Curator: The Museum Journal*, *55*(4), 435–452. https://doi.org/10.1111/j.2151-6952.2012.00167.x.

Lin, A. C. H., Fernandez, W. D., & Gregor, S. (2012). Understanding web enjoyment experiences and informal learning: A study in a museum context. *Decision Support Systems*, *53*(4), 846–858. https://doi.org/10.1016/j.dss.2012.05.020.

Lofland, J., & Lofland, L. H. (1995). *Analyzing social settings: A guide to qualitative observation and analysis* (3rd ed.). New York: Wadsworth Publishing Company.

Lubar, S. (2013). Timelines in exhibitions. *Curator: The Museum Journal*, *56*(2), 169–188. https://doi.org/10.1111/cura.12018.

Mao, R., & Fu, Y. (2021). Interweaving multiple contexts for objects in museum exhibitions: A contextual approach. *Museum Management and Curatorship*, 1–22. https://doi.org/10.1080/09647775.2021.1914141.

Marsh, E. (2022a). *A sample of materials discovered during background research for four digital exhibits* [Infographic]. https://emily-marsh.com/Digital_Exhibits_for_Cultural_Institutions/Figure_4.1.jpg.

Marsh, E. (2022b). *Wireframe of home page for proposed exhibit on Negro Extension with slideshow of featured items and list of topic areas* [Infographic]. https://emily-marsh.com/Digital_Exhibits_for_Cultural_Institutions/Figure_4.2.jpg.

Marsh, E. (2022c). *Exhibit proposal with communication plan* [Infographic]. https://emily-marsh.com/Digital_Exhibits_for_Cultural_Institutions/Figure_4.3.jpg.

Marsh, E. (2022d). *Mockup of home page for proposed exhibit on Negro Extension* [Infographic]. https://emily-marsh.com/Digital_Exhibits_for_Cultural_Institutions/Figure_4.4.jpg.

Marsh, E. E., & White, M. D. (2003). A taxonomy of relationships between images and text. *Journal of Documentation*, *59*(6), 647–672. https://doi.org/10.1108/00220410310506303.

Mercier, W. B. (1921). *Extension work among Negroes 1920* (United States Department of Agriculture Department Circular, Number 190). Washington, DC: U.S. Department of Agriculture. https://archive.org/details/extensionworkamo190merc.

Miller, W. L., & Crabtree, B. F. (1992). Primary care research: A multimethod typology and qualitative road map. In B. F. Crabtree & W. L. Miller (Eds.), *Doing qualitative research. Research methods for primary care, volume 3* (pp. 3–30). Newbury Park, CA: SAGE Publications.

National Institute of Food and Agriculture. USDA. (n.d.). *Cooperative extension history*. U.S. Department of Agriculture. www.nifa.usda.gov/about-nifa/how-we-work/extension/cooperative-extension-history.

Paley, L. M. (1941). *The education and responsibilities of Negro home demonstration agents in Texas*. Unpublished Master's Thesis. Kansas State College of Agriculture and Applied Science. https://core.ac.uk/download/pdf/10653109.pdf.

Rasmussen, I. (2022). A homemade history: Documenting the Harlem renaissance in Alexander Gumby's scrapbooks. In S. Helgesson, H. Bodin, & A. M. Alling (Eds.), *Literature and the making of the world: Cosmopolitan texts, vernacular practices* (pp. 173–214). London: Bloomsbury Academic.

Reitstätter, L., Galter, K., & Bakondi, F. (2022). Looking to read: How visitors use exhibit labels in the art museum. *Visitor Studies*, *25*(2), 127–150. https://doi.org/10.1080/10645578.2021.2018251.

Serrell, B. (2015). *Exhibit labels: An interpretive approach* (2nd ed.). Lanham, MD: Rowman & Littlefield.

Serwer, A. (2021). *The cruelty is the point: The past, present, and future of Trump's America*. New York: One World.

Stebbins, R. A. (2015). *Serious leisure: A perspective for our time* (2nd ed.). London: Routledge.

Strauss, A., & Corbin, J. (1994). Grounded theory methodology: An overview. In N. K. Denzin, & Y. S. Lincoln (Eds.), *Handbook of qualitative research* (pp. 273–285). Thousand Oaks, CA: SAGE.

The Ohio State University. (2022). A *brief history of extension*. OSU Extension: College of Food, Agricultural, and Environmental Sciences. https://extension.osu.edu/about/mission-vision-values/osu-extension-brief-history.

Ulrich, L. T., Gaskell, I., Schechner, S. J., Carter, S. A., & van Gerbig, S. (2015). *Tangible things: Making history through objects*. Oxford: Oxford University Press.

U.S. Department of Agriculture. (1951). The home demonstration agent. *Agriculture Information Bulletin, 38*. https://handle.nal.usda.gov/10113/CAT87791369.

Wenger-Trainer, E., & Wenger-Trainer, B. (2015). *Communities of practice a brief introduction*. https://wenger-trayner.com/wp-content/uploads/2015/04/07-Brief-introduction-to-communities-of-practice.pdf.

White, M. D., & Marsh, E. E. (2006). Content analysis: A flexible methodology. *Library Trends*, *55*(1), 22–45. https://doi.org/10.1353/lib.2006.0053.

Winn, J. E. (2008). Documenting racism in an agricultural extension film. *Film & History: An Interdisciplinary Journal of Film and Television Studies*, *38*(1), 33–43. http://doi.org/10.1353/flm.0.0023.

Winn, J. E. (2012). *Documenting racism: African Americans in US Department of Agriculture documentaries, 1921–42*. New York: Continuum. http://dx.doi.org/10.5040/9781628928679.ch-002.

Woodrow Wilson House. (n.d.). *Wilson and race*. www.woodrowwilsonhouse.org/wilson-topics/wilson-and-race/..

5 Looking at These Principles in Action

Five Case Studies

This chapter will cover five extended examples as case studies to demonstrate how the principles covered in earlier chapters can help to drive and shape your creativity to form a finished product. The five exhibits were designed and created by the author for a library and differ in terms of origin and eventual form. The key lessons that will be identified and described in these case studies center on methods that were developed and deployed by the author to analyze content, identify related objects, form unifying and supporting digital structures, and create original explanatory text. Each of these projects presented unique challenges that will be described and analyzed so that other exhibit creators can have examples of methods and strategies to deploy as they go about engaging in their content, whatever it may be.

Now that you have a good understanding of the issues discussed in previous chapters, it would be helpful to go behind the scenes of a few exhibits to understand how they were transformed from a collection of documents, associated objects, explanatory text, big ideas, and small themes into finished projects. This chapter will cover five extended examples as case studies to demonstrate how the principles covered in earlier chapters can help to drive and shape your creativity to form a finished product.

The five exhibits were designed and created by the author for the US National Agricultural Library, and they each differ in terms of origin and eventual form. It seems paradoxical, but the agricultural subject matter of the exhibits and their status as products of an American library are fairly irrelevant within this content. These exhibits can provide lessons for anyone interested in undertaking a comparable project, because the issues discussed are centered much more on process over product. The key lessons that will be identified and described in these case studies center on methods that were developed and deployed by the author to analyze content, identify related objects, form unifying and supporting digital structures, and create original explanatory text. Each of these projects presented unique challenges that will be described and analyzed so that other exhibit creators can have examples of methods and strategies to deploy as they go about engaging in their content, whatever it may be. Offering a narrative of how I created these original strategies, along with the setbacks and failures I experienced along the way, is done in the hope that I can give you the confidence to engage with your

DOI:10.4324/9781003301493-5

project, along with the knowledge that your creative energy can get you to a polished finished product, regardless of your work setting or your exhibit topics.

Each of the following project descriptions contains the exhibit's "big idea" that encapsulates its broad themes and an implicit explanation of why a visitor should be interested in its content (Serrell, 2015). Chapters 2 and 4 of this book address the nature and purpose of an exhibit's big idea with more specificity, for both the end audience and the creative team.

A final note: I had no budget for creating these exhibits. The only organizational resource that was available was my time as a member of the professional library staff. I also maintained all of my regular duties working on interface and interaction design tasks. These observations are offered to demonstrate that it is possible to successfully create an exhibit with a small upfront investment by your organization. Of course, maintaining your exhibit on your organization's server will also require some degree of investment, but that should not pose a large challenge, especially if you already have some sort of web presence and have access to professional information technology staff who are willing to support your project. Organizational buy-in on both technical and managerial levels is a critical factor for any successful exhibit program. If you do not have it, it will be difficult to implement or sustain your work.

Frost on Chickens
(www.nal.usda.gov/exhibits/ipd/frostonchickens/)

Big Idea: The iconic American poet Robert Frost lived and worked as a farmer in Derry, New Hampshire, from 1900 to 1909 and published a dozen articles for two poultry trade journals: *The Eastern Poultryman* and *The Farm-Poultry*.

Small themes: This exhibit uses these articles as a window into Frost's life and poetry, along with the nine themes of chicken farming identified in Frost's articles: poultry farming, housing, backyard chickens, chicken feeding, competitive chicken showing, poultry breeds, egg production, marketing, and poultry trade journals. The home page for the exhibit is pictured in Figure 5.1 (Marsh, 2022a).

This exhibit illustrates a scenario encountered frequently by staff of small cultural heritage organizations. Your institution holds materials that would support a digital exhibit offering relevance and interest to several segments of your audience. Yet there are no members of your staff who are subject matter experts on the specific topic at hand. Furthermore, the likelihood that you can get significant contributions from scholars for an introductory essay, insight into the material, or even a review of the finished product is low. What happens when you have limited experience or expertise with the content of your exhibit?

This is exactly what happened when I was assigned to create an exhibit about Robert Frost's publications in poultry trade journals from the early 1900s. Even though I had no specialized training or expertise in this specific area, I spent a great deal of effort to understand and analyze the poultry articles using the published work of Frost scholars. Although I had no budget from my library for this

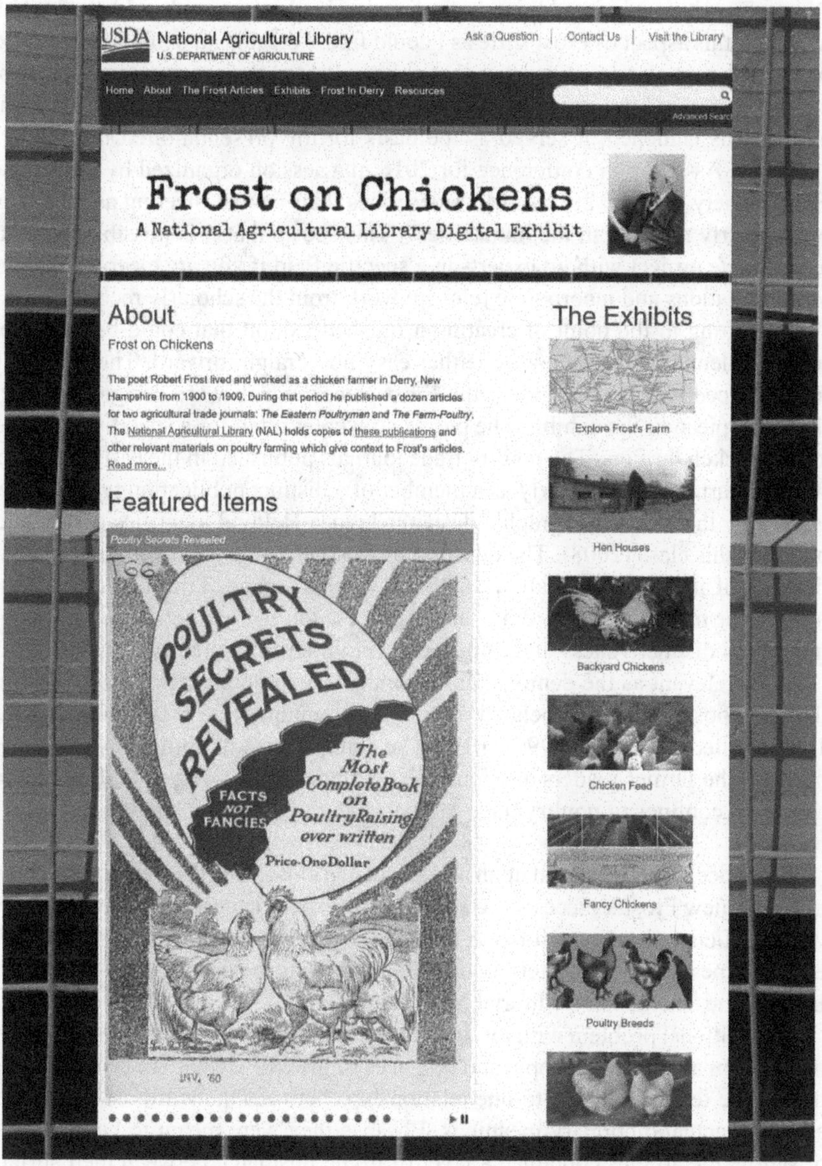

Figure 5.1 Home page of "Frost on Chickens" exhibit about the poet Robert Frost and poultry farming

project, I invested my own funds to build a small personal library of books on Robert Frost's poetry, in addition to finding and reading as much published scholarship on this aspect of Frost's life as I could find. I created an exhibit that contextualized the articles in a structure that acknowledged their significance in terms of Frost's life and the state of poultry farming and science of the time. Once the exhibit was launched, it served as the basis for my presentation at the Modern Language Association conference for 2016 in a session organized by the Robert Frost Society (Marsh, 2016a). MLA describes their annual meeting as "the largest scholarly meeting in the humanities". This shows that it is possible to create a legitimate project without experts in a specific field if you are clear-eyed about your limitations and incorporate relevant work from the scholarly record.

But getting to the point of creating a finished exhibit that could be presented to an academic conference was neither easy nor straightforward. The first challenge I faced was understanding the Frost pieces, which were designed to form the centerpiece of the exhibit. The pieces all were written for a specific audience: small chicken farmers. The poultry trade journals published in the early 1900s for working farmers acted clearly as a member of a distinct publication type. A piece written by the writer and graphic designer Jessica Helfand identifies several elements of this class (2008). The question of whether poultry trade journals rose to the level of an actual publication genre is beyond the scope of this book. One point needs to be made, however. Whether or not these journals demonstrated sufficient inter-class distinctiveness and intra-member similarity to qualify as a true genre is not as relevant as the demonstrable point that their commercial success meant that they possessed an associated discourse community (DC) (Bridwell-Bowles, 1986 as cited in Swales, 1990, 2016). The community was formed by the match between the farmer readers and journalist writers of this material and met in the rhetorical confines of poultry trade journals like the ones which published Frost's pieces.

In essence, I had stumbled upon an artifact of a closed DC that remained opaque to me. I knew Frost's pieces were speaking to a specific audience, but since they were all fictional (except for one biographic profile), I could not decode their essential messages, even after multiple focused readings, despite the assistance of Lathem and Thompson's editorial notes (1963).

An additional problem with the articles lay in their nature as examples of satires of common agricultural people and practices of the early twentieth century. Thus, there were few simple one-to-one relationships between the words of the articles and their actual dictionary meanings. Because they were meant to be humorous or satiric, the articles contained a layer of ironic mismatch between their surface content and the articles' underlying meanings. As explained by Lewis, we often assert,

> "'it's only a joke", but humor is complex, a matter of texts and contexts. As texts, formal jokes and spontaneous witticisms follow grammatical rules, exploit semantic associations, convey affect, thought and disposition. In context—that is, as a shared experience—humor assumes and reveals social

> and psychological relations, cognitive processes, cultural norms and value judgments.
>
> (1989, p. ix)

All of these elements in the Frost pieces combined to form a high wall separating me from an understanding of these discourse artifacts.

After much struggle, I abandoned any sort of literary close reading and instead switched to my past work with reading written text using qualitative methods of analysis (Braun & Clarke, 2006; Miller & Crabtree, 1992; White & Marsh, 2006). The material in Chapter 2 on Reflexive Thematic Analysis and Editing Analysis describes how texts can be analyzed and understood through the kind of systematic creation of themes and categories that qualitative method demands. Using these methods, I was able to break through the barriers presented by Frost's attempts at satire and whimsy and isolate the significance of the texts for the potential audience of the digital exhibit: people interested in what Robert Frost had to write about the poultry trade in twentieth-century New England and people interested in casual chicken farming and its place in a more humanistic context, among other possible use cases.

I ended up with nine themes that acted to organize the 11 articles into a coherent, manageable structure. The themes for the exhibit are Hen Houses, Backyard Chickens, Chicken Feed, Fancy Chickens, Poultry Breeds, Poultry Framing, Egg Production, the Poultry Marketplace, and the Poultry Press. Deciding on these themes was a somewhat difficult task that required much close reading of difficult material, multiple trial-and-error attempts at category building, and many sticky notes. But this work was worth the effort because these categories helped me to organize the exhibit in a way that made the articles sensible and relevant to a modern reader. Identifying these themes also gave me a structure that I could fill with content, from both the Frost pieces themselves and other associated resources.

Each section of the exhibit opens with an introduction that explains the theme briefly and then gives the reader relevant quotations from the Frost articles. These quotations were selected and included in the exhibit to both ensure and demonstrate the validity and reliability of the identified themes, in keeping with the practices of qualitative method and analysis (Freeman et al., 2007). While the casual or uninformed reader might mistake quotations from original sources as mere rhetorical filler or decoration, they are crucial within the qualitative tradition as a means of demonstrating how the researcher's observations and conclusions are grounded in data. So, each of the nine exhibit sections opens with the quotations from Frost's articles that I used as the foundations for each respective theme. Although the number of quotations varied across themes, they were selected to give the reader a sense that the exhibit grew directly and organically out of Frost's work.

These themes also drove my efforts to identify other relevant material that I incorporated into the exhibit to add visual interest. To be clear, there was no roadmap available to me before I started this journey; no magic was involved, either. It required work in the form of significant mental energy to find and read sources with an open mind, the skill to be able to identify points of interest in those sources, and then the willingness to follow those points through searching multiple cultural heritage repositories and web-based content sources.

To be specific, five resources were used to bring the Frost pieces to more vivid life for a modern audience:

1. An assortment of vintage postcards from the Derry, New Hampshire Public Library's Flickr account that included images of people and landmarks that were current when Frost lived on his farm from 1900 to 1909
2. A selection of watercolor paintings of apples from the National Agricultural Library's (NAL's) Pomological Watercolor Collection made from specimens taken from New Hampshire around the time of Frost's residency. These images were included to showcase this popular digital collection and reference the frequent apple imagery in Frost's poetry including *After Apple-Picking* (1915), *The Cow in Apple-Time* (1916), *Good-bye and Keep Cold* (1920), *The Gold Hesperidee* (1921), *New Hampshire* (1923), and *In a Glass of Cider* (1962)
3. Images of the Frost farm, the deed to the property, the final bill of sale, and a vintage map of the farm from 1892 from various repositories
4. Photographs of competitive show chickens used by permission from Tamara Staples. Ms. Staples is a photographer and author of two collections of portraits: *The Magnificent Chicken: Portraits of the Fairest Fowl* (2013) and *The Fairest Fowl: Portraits of Championship Chickens* (2001). I contacted Ms. Staples, and she graciously shared an assortment of photographs that I incorporated into the exhibit
5. Illustrations from Lauren Scheuer, author of *Once Upon a Flock: Life with My Soulful Chickens* (2013). Like Ms. Staples, Ms. Scheuer generously responded to a personal e-mail with several charming images that brought the concept of "backyard chickens" to life

These observations are offered to demonstrate the power of identifying and incorporating visual resources that can amplify and illustrate the themes of a given digital exhibit. Using associated materials also grounds projects of this type to a larger world of cultural heritage materials and demonstrates your knowledge and awareness of the significance of your core materials beyond the confines of your organization. Useful materials can be found within Europeana, the Library of Congress' Prints and Photographs Division, and the National Archives and Records Administration, among countless others, as well as more mundane social media sites such as Flickr, Instagram, and Pinterest. Exhibit creators should spend some time searching for text and image resources that can function to contextualize and illuminate your core exhibit materials. If you find something useful that is protected by copyright, try to reach out to the source's creator. I have found that many authors and photographers are happy to collaborate with your project once you explain it and if you agree to use and attribute their materials in a mutually agreeable way.

This was a very challenging but rewarding project. I learned both the values and the limits of the Omeka platform and how to analyze and present original source materials in ways that did not require a subject matter expert. I found a way to draw upon the published scholarship of true Frost experts, and the value of incorporating associated visual materials relevant to various aspects of Frost's personal life, his poetry, and the world of agriculture in which he lived. I also found ways to incorporate Frost's topics when they overlapped with the work of the exhibit's sponsor: NAL and the US Department of Agriculture (USDA). Finally, it gave me an opportunity to develop a workflow process that I was eager to apply and test on a second digital exhibit.

Apron Strings and Kitchen Sinks: The USDA Bureau of Home Economics (www.nal.usda.gov/exhibits/ipd/apronsandkitchens/)

Big Idea: This exhibit showcases the work related to clothing and kitchen designs of the Bureau of Home Economics, part of the USDA (1923–1962). The Bureau was a pioneering unit for several reasons. It was the first major unit to have been headed by a woman: Louise Stanley, Ph.D. It focused on topics of central concern to middle-class white women, as defined by the cultural norms of the early 20th century: sewing, kitchen design and features, time spent on housework, children's clothing, and food preparation and preservation. Lastly, it took a then-novel approach to its work: It strove to first understand what its primary audience needed within its broad mandate and then shaped its specific programs around those needs.

Small Themes: This exhibit uses these publications as a window into the world of governmental and academic Home Economics of the twentieth century. Figure 5.2 shows the home page of the exhibit (Marsh, 2022b). The five exhibit topic areas are Kitchen and Farmhouse Design Plans, Self-Help Children's Clothing and Standardized Sizing, Sewing and Pattern Design, the USDA Time-Use Studies, and a short history of the Bureau itself. Three of these areas are straightforward and to be expected, but two areas proved to offer some surprises. For a significant period, the Bureau worked to develop standard sizes for children's clothing based on scientific body measurements of large samples of boys and girls. The other surprise was finding publications and artifacts arising from what was named the USDA Time-Use Studies. These inquiries attempted to measure the time taken by white, rural homemakers to fulfill various household tasks in a way to better understand domestic rural life for this population.

Aside from these material and thematic elements, this exhibit was designed to be a more constrained and straightforward project to accomplish two goals: Test the process I developed with the Robert Frost exhibit (for myself) and demonstrate the feasibility of an efficient, sustainable digital exhibit program (for my managers). After learning about the publication of a then-new book by the historian Linda Przybyszewski touching on a defunct USDA organization, I planned a digital exhibit focused on the documented work and publications of this unit: the Bureau of Home Economics (2014). To further limit the scope of the project

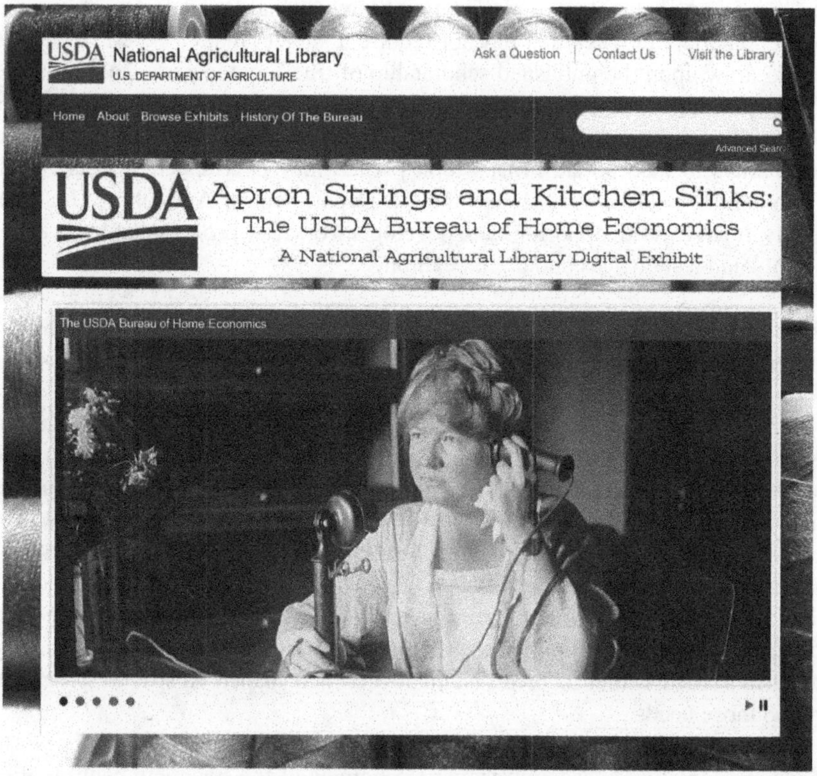

Figure 5.2 Home page of "Apron Strings and Kitchen Sinks" exhibit about the US Department of Agriculture's Bureau of Home Economics

I decided to focus on two themes: the Bureau's work studying and developing the designs of kitchens and women's work clothing. This twin focus was reflected consciously in the title "Apron Strings and Kitchen Sinks".

This exhibit includes associated visual materials which illuminate and enrich the Bureau publications, like those used in the Frost exhibit:

1 Images of vintage clothing patterns developed by the USDA and released to be licensed and sold by private pattern maker found on several social media websites (Vintage Sewing Pattern Wiki, Unsung Sewing Patterns, and Flickr)
2 An embedded video from the National Archives and Records Administration about the Bureau's work designing efficient kitchens designs, *A Step-Saving Kitchen*, along with material from the shooting script of this 1949 USDA instructional film

The essential value of this project, like the Frost exhibit, does not lay in any original analysis or insights but in its creation and presentation of a culturally valid context that revealed the value of the materials to the exhibit visitors. In fact, multiple scholars writing monographs on the history of home economics did reach out to me and used the exhibit materials to enrich their own work, including Danielle Dreilinger (2021). Finally, a link from a story in the *New York Times* to the exhibit further demonstrated the essential value of such a project to showcase library, archival, and museum content to a wider audience to use in their own work, to further their own interests, or simply to learn something new (Ziegelman & Coe, 2016).

George Washington Carver
(www.nal.usda.gov/exhibits/ipd/carver/)

Big Idea: George Washington Carver was an agricultural scientist whose importance arises from his practical work supporting Black farmers and his advocacy for specific crops such as peanuts and sweet potatoes. This exhibit showcases the 38 *Tuskegee Institute Experiment Station Bulletins* held by NAL that were written by George Washington Carver during his tenure as Director. The exhibit also includes a selection of USDA historical publications relevant to Carver's Bulletins. Figure 5.3 displays the exhibit's home page (Marsh, 2022c).

Small Themes: The exhibit has been subdivided into the following topic areas:

1 Crop Development: Bulletins designed to encourage farmers to diversify their lands and grow crops that would provide immediate benefits. These crops included sweet potatoes, black-eyed (cow) peas, corn, alfalfa, tomatoes, cotton, and, of course, peanuts
2 Farm Management: Practical advice for making, saving, and managing money that addressed the real limitations faced by poor, mainly black, farmers of rural Alabama
3 Homemaking Activities: Directions for food preservation, cooking, growing ornamental plants, and using native clay to create color washes for decorating the farmhouse
4 Raising Livestock: Methods for increasing productivity in the poultry yard, livestock feeding using readily available plants such as acorns, and the relationship between overall farm health and livestock production
5 Rural Schools: Ways to use agriculture and gardening to educate children in the science of the natural world
6 Soil Productivity: Instructions for strengthening the then impoverished soils of Alabama's poorest farms

The challenge to describe the bulletins, explain their historical significance, and incorporate relevant images and textual objects was substantial, but relatively straightforward. Several of the images used in the exhibit were Carver's own drawings and illustrations from the bulletins.

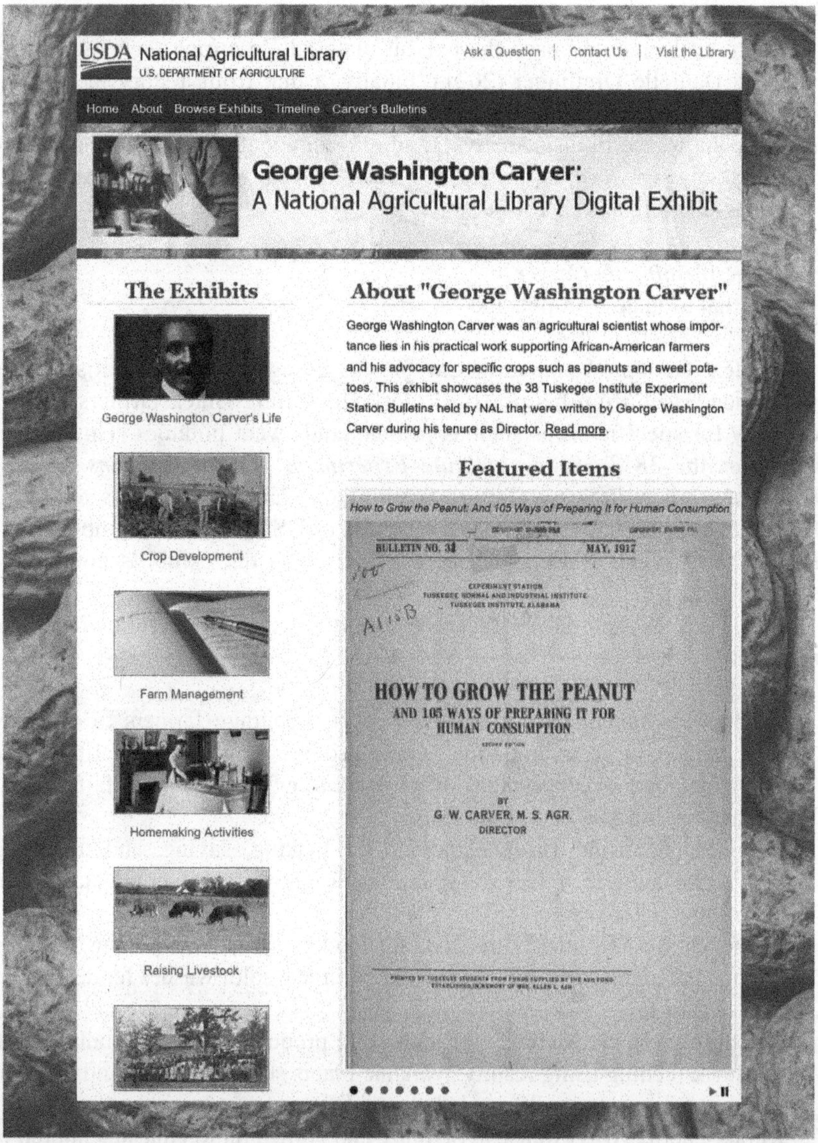

Figure 5.3 Home page of "George Washington Carver" exhibit featuring his technical bulletins

The much more problematic task was to address, or at least consider, a variety of loaded issues including:

- Ways to tactfully acknowledge scholars' divergent conclusions about Carver's ultimate significance as a scientist
- The legacy of racial discrimination experienced by Carver and his home institution, Tuskegee Institute (now University), because of its Black student body, faculty, and administration
- The degree to which Carver's legacy is based on his real scientific achievements in agriculture or a white-dominated society's need to ignore its own racist history by elevating a figure it finds comfortable and "safe"
- Questions about my own institution's commitment to the exhibit. Was it a demonstration of its commitment to racial diversity and equality? Or was it more of a performative gesture that would further contribute to a misleading narrative about Carver as an unthreatening symbol of black agriculture in the United States?

The struggle to engage with these issues in a way that was fair to Carver's legacy, his actual accomplishments, and my organization's needs consumed a fair amount of time and thought. Getting to a point where I could create an exhibit that was simultaneously intellectually sound, practically feasible, and politically savvy was not easy but generated a framework for considering these thorny questions which were addressed both implicitly and explicitly, albeit with some care and tact.

Finally, the exhibit features images from the prominent photographer Frances Benjamin Johnston. They are displayed throughout the exhibit as a means of illustrating Carver and his students at the time he published the bulletins. These photographs of the Tuskegee Institute's faculty and student body were taken by Johnston in the early 1900s. They have been digitized and made available by the Library of Congress' Prints and Photographs Division. A belated *New York Times'* obituary of Johnston contains this passage,

> Johnston's fame today rests largely on the album of photographs she made in 1899 at the Hampton Normal and Agricultural Institute in Virginia (now Hampton University). Established in 1868 to instruct newly freed slaves of the South (and, after 1878, Native Americans), it was coeducational and residential . . . [She did the same for the Tuskegee Institute] in 1902, despite a near-death experience when she and a group of African-American men with whom she was traveling at night were pursued by a white vigilante mob. One of her fellow narrow escapees, George Washington Carver, called her "the pluckiest woman I ever saw".
>
> (Woodward, 2021)

This is an example of how outside images can be used to enliven and humanize a set of (potentially) dry and dated textual documents.

Mailboxes, Mom and Pop Stands, and Markets: Local Foods Then and Now
(www.nal.usda.gov/exhibits/ipd/localfoods/)

Big Idea: The current interest in local foods is reflected in a long-standing focus of the USDA on the best ways to get food from producers to consumers. NAL holds copies of many historical and current materials documenting the ways that food makes its way from the farm to our tables. This exhibit showcases these resources, placed within a larger context of agricultural marketing and purchasing.

Small Themes: The exhibit is divided into three main sections: a review of the "Farm-To-Table" Movement of the early 1900s, a survey of Roadside Stands and Farmers Markets, and a list of current USDA local food initiatives identified by the "Know Your Farmer, Know Your Food" project. There is also an overview of the individual parts of the "local foods" concept and a glossary.

This project arose from my library's leadership and their directive to create an exhibit around the topic of local foods. Once I started with this amorphous "big idea", I worked to find materials and search for specific small themes. The exhibit was then structured around the ideas revealed through this secondary research, especially the 1914–1920 Farm-to-Table Initiative started by the United States Department of Agriculture (Cullen, 2010). The final topical organization of the exhibit is portrayed in Figure 5.4 (Marsh, 2022d). Although difficult and not assured of success, the work done on this exhibit shows that it is possible to create a project that holds interest for the reader and fulfills the needs of an organization even when there is no path laid out ahead of time.

To be specific, aside from the broad subject of "local foods", there was no clear conception of what this exhibit should really address, the materials that should form its core, or what associated concepts it should illustrate. It was only by reading a set of tentatively identified materials using the techniques of Thematic Analysis (Miller & Crabtree, 1992) that I discovered a casual mention of the "farm-to-table" campaigns conducted by postmasters in many cities (Hawbaker & Burmeister, 1918). This was an obvious way to bring relevance to current-day readers and using the now-commonplace, almost clichéd concept of farm-to-table as a small theme, along with associated materials about the postal service, shipping agricultural commodities through the mail, and the then-current state of the roads in rural America.

Some of the associated materials incorporated into the exhibit include:

- Images used after securing direct permission from the National Postal Museum, Smithsonian Institution
- An embedded video of *RFD: To the Country*, a short documentary from the National Postal Museum that relates to the then-current "Farm-to-Table" movement of 1914–1920
- A glossary of terms associated with the local foods construct

Small Agriculture
(www.nal.usda.gov/exhibits/ipd/small/)

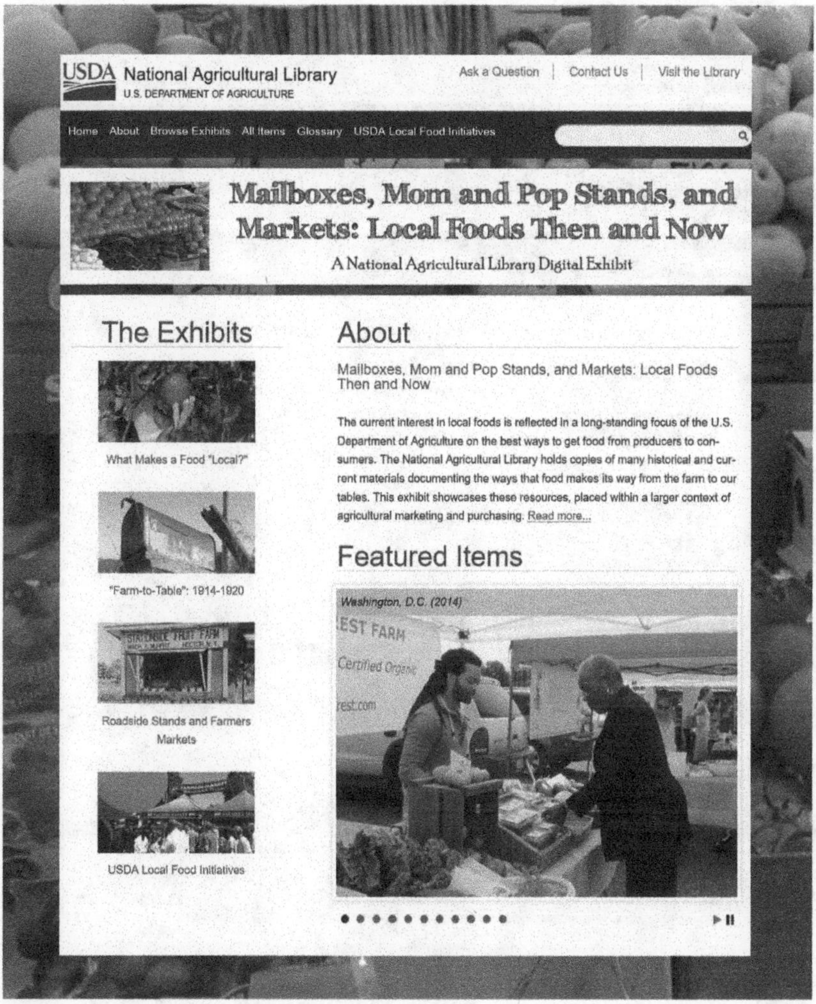

Figure 5.4 Home page of "Mailboxes, Mom and Pop Stands, and Markets: Local Foods Then and Now" exhibit

Big Idea: The US Department of Agriculture has supported small-scale farming and niche agricultural initiatives throughout its lifespan. This exhibit showcases three of these initiatives.

Small Themes:

1 The School Garden: Designed to address various program elements such as the scientific life of the plant, production of food, marketing food products,

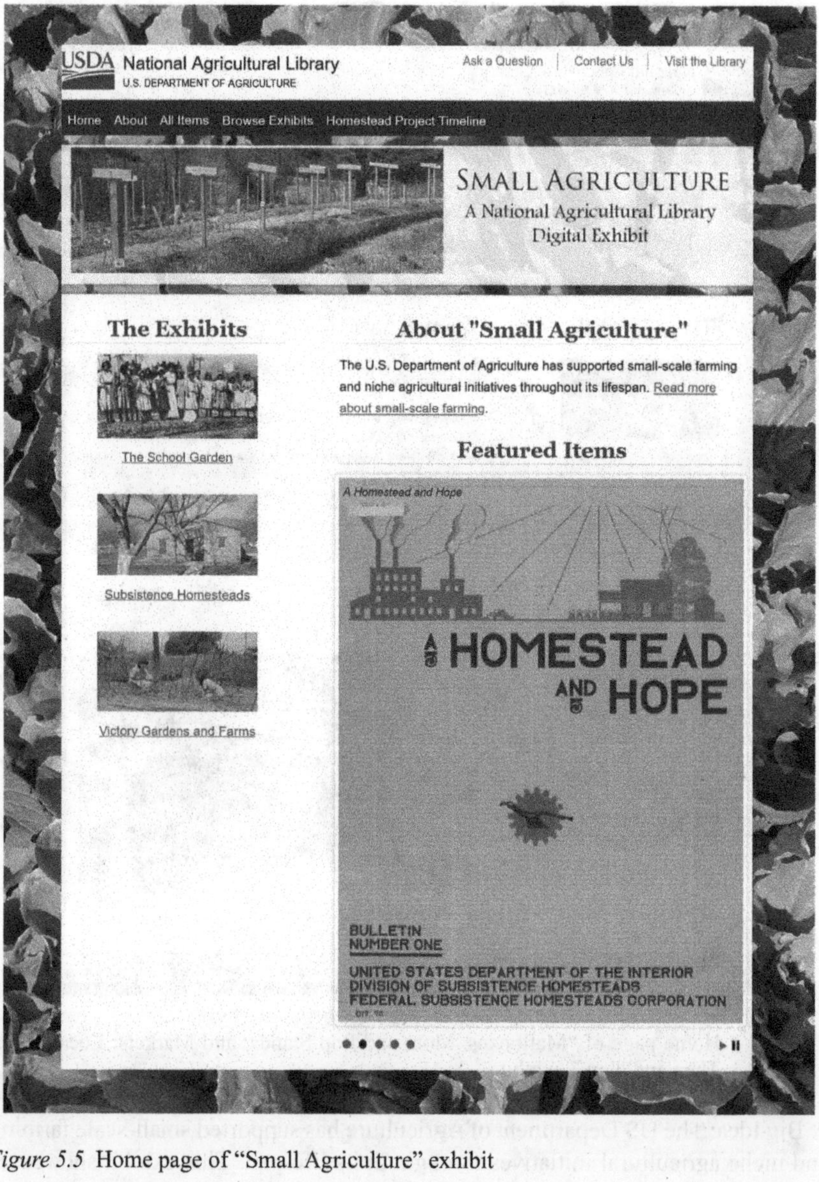

Figure 5.5 Home page of "Small Agriculture" exhibit

engaging with the natural world, being outdoors, and taking responsibility for a specific plot of land

2 Subsistence Homesteads: A federal housing program created in 1933 as a response to the Great Depression that aimed to improve the living conditions of people coming from overcrowded urban centers, while simultaneously giving them a new opportunity to experience small-scale farming and home

ownership. Several images used in this part of the exhibit are photographs taken by Dorothea Lange as part of her work with the Farm Security Administration (FSA)

3 Victory Gardens and Farms: Initiatives carried out to increase the supply and quality of fresh food for the domestic US population during World War II

Finally, the exhibit on small agriculture shows how you can tether several small themes together to form an integrated exhibit united under a larger conceptual umbrella, acting as a big idea (Marsh, 2022e). In this case, subexhibits on school gardens, a historic farming program from the Great Depression, and Victory Gardens and Farms were combined under a single rubric that played off a common idea in American agriculture of bigness to one of smallness.

This exhibit, just like the others, was imagined as part of an organizational information ecosystem for the library (Marsh, 2016b). All the exhibits could act together as a growing "evergreen" content stream that could feed other resources and initiatives of the library. These include social media platforms and their bottomless need for engaging content. Having the exhibits configured with smaller themes and clusters of items also make their content malleable enough to be customized across contexts and timeframes.

Since this chapter is based on the experience of just one person and my perspective, I would encourage the reader to scan the scholarly and professional literature, as well as the digital humanities software community, for accounts of the way others have engaged with this work, such as those found in Cuenca and Kowaleski (2018), Dixon (2016), Hoelscher (2019), Kucsma et al. (2010), Marsh (2017), and Tracy and Hoiem (2017).

In summary, let the materials drive your exhibit in both form and focus. If you have doubts about what direction to take, engaging directly with the textual and visual elements of your collections and those of associated institutions will often reveal paths that will connect you to your reader using a digital exhibit as a point of mutual engagement.

References

Braun, V., & Clarke, V. (2006) Using thematic analysis in psychology. *Qualitative Research in Psychology*, *3*(2), 77–101. https://doi.org/10.1191/1478088706qp063oa.

Bridwell-Bowles, L. (1986, March 12–15). *Designing a comprehensive curriculum for writing with computers*. 37th Annual Conference on College Composition and Communication, New Orleans, LA.

Cuenca, E. L., & Kowaleski, M. (2018). Omeka and other digital platforms for undergraduate research projects on the Middle Ages. *Digital Medievalist*, *11*(1), 1–21. http://doi.org/10.16995/dm.69.

Cullen, R. G. (2010). "Food will win the war": Motor trucks and the farm-to-table postal delivery program, 1917–1918. In T. Lera (Ed.), *The Winton M. Blount postal history symposia: Select papers, 2006–2009. Smithsonian contributions to history and technology* (No. 55, pp. 49–57). Washington, DC: Smithsonian Institution Scholarly Press. https://doi.org/10.5479/si.19486006.55.

Dixon, D. (2016). Imagining the essay as digital assemblage: Collaborative student experiments with writing in Scalar. *Prompt: A Journal of Academic Writing Assignments*, *1*(1). https://doi.org/10.31719/pjaw.v1i1.13.

Dreilinger, D. (2021). *The secret history of home economics: How trailblazing women harnessed the power of home and changed the way we live*. New York: W. W. Norton & Company.

Freeman, M., deMarrais, K., Preissle, J., Roulston, K., & St. Pierre, E. A. (2007). Standards of evidence in qualitative research: An incitement to discourse. *Educational Researcher*, *36*(1), 25–32. https://doi.org/10.3102/0013189X06298009.

Hawbaker, C. C., & Burmeister, C. A. (1918). Marketing berries and cherries by parcel post. *U.S. Department of Agriculture Bulletin*, Number 688. https://archive.org/details/marketingberries688hawb.

Helfand, J. (2008, February 14). Animal magnetism. *Design Observer*. http://designobserver.com/feature/animal-magnetism/6537.

Hoelscher, C. (2019). Constructing history: A student-created public history exhibit using Omeka. *Case Studies on Teaching with Primary Sources*. Case Study #11. https://www2.archivists.org/publications/epubs/Case-Studies-Teaching-With-Primary-Sources.

Kucsma, J., Reiss, K., & Sidman, A. (2010). Using Omeka to build digital collections: The METRO case study. *D-Lib Magazine*, *16*(3/4). www.dlib.org/dlib/march10/kucsma/03kucsma.html.

Lathem, E. C., & Thompson, L. (1963). *Robert Frost: Farm-poultryman*. Hanover, NH: Dartmouth Publications.

Lewis, P. (1989). *Comic effects: Interdisciplinary approaches to humor in literature*. Albany, NY: State University of New York Press.

Marsh, E. (2016a, January 9). *Like a 'fine pullet' at the chicken farm: Robert Frost's poultry paper articles* [Conference presentation]. Austin, TX: Modern Language Association Convention. https://apps.mla.org/conv_listings_details_print?prog_id=A046A&year=2016.

Marsh, E. (2016b, April 15). *If a pdf falls in the forest will anyone see it? Building a library ecosystem for digital materials* [Conference presentation]. Washington, DC: Digital Public Library of America's DPLAFest. https://youtu.be/YQ2TniMc0Dg?t=1551.

Marsh, E. (2017). Chickens, aprons, markets, and cans: How the National Agricultural Library uses Omeka as its content management system for digital exhibits. *Digital Library Perspectives*, *33*(4), 361–377. https://doi.org/10.1108/DLP-03-2017-0009.

Marsh, E. (2022a). *Home page of "Frost on Chickens" exhibit about the poet Robert Frost and poultry farming* [Screenshot]. https://emily-marsh.com/Digital_Exhibits_for_Cultural_Institutions/Figure_5.1.jpg.

Marsh, E. (2022b). *Home page of "Apron Strings and Kitchen Sinks" exhibit about the US Department of Agriculture's Bureau of Home Economics* [Screenshot]. https://emily-marsh.com/Digital_Exhibits_for_Cultural_Institutions/Figure_5.2.jpg.

Marsh, E. (2022c). *Home page of "George Washington Carver" exhibit featuring his technical bulletins* [Screenshot]. https://emily-marsh.com/Digital_Exhibits_for_Cultural_Institutions/Figure_5.3.jpg.

Marsh, E. (2022d). *Home page of "Mailboxes, Mom and Pop Stands, and Markets: Local Foods Then and Now" exhibit* [Screenshot]. https://emily-marsh.com/Digital_Exhibits_for_Cultural_Institutions/Figure_5.4.jpg.

Marsh, E. (2022e). *Home page of "Small Agriculture" exhibit* [Screenshot]. https://emily-marsh.com/Digital_Exhibits_for_Cultural_Institutions/Figure_5.5.jpg.

Miller, W. L., & Crabtree, B. F. (1992). Primary care research: A multimethod typology and qualitative road map. In B. F. Crabtree & W. L. Miller (Eds.), *Doing qualitative research. Research methods for primary care, volume 3* (pp. 3–30). Newbury Park, CA: SAGE Publications.

Przybyszewski, L. (2014). *The lost art of dress: The women who once made America stylish.* New York: Basic Books.

Serrell, B. (2015). *Exhibit labels: An interpretive approach* (2nd ed.). Lanham, MD: Rowman & Littlefield.

Swales, J. M. (1990). *Genre analysis: English in academic and research settings.* Cambridge: Cambridge University Press.

Swales, J. M. (2016). Reflections on the concept of discourse community. *Asp*, *69*, 7–19. https://doi.org/10.4000/asp.4774.

Tracy, D. G., & Hoiem, M. (2017). Teaching digital humanities tools at a distance: A librarian-instructor partnership integrating scalar into a graduate distance course. In D. M. Mueller (Ed.), *At the helm: Leading transformation. The proceedings of the ACRL 2017 conference March 22–25* (pp. 704–713). Chicago, IL: Association of College and Research Libraries. http://hdl.handle.net/2142/95786.

White, M. D., & Marsh, E. E. (2006). Content analysis: A flexible methodology. *Library Trends*, *55*(1), 22–45. https://doi.org/10.1353/lib.2006.0053.

Woodward, R. B. (2021, December 20). Overlooked no more: Frances B. Johnston, photographer who defied genteel norms. *New York Times*, Section B, p. 7.

Ziegelman, J. & Coe, A. (2016, November 24). 'Mock Duck' and other Depression Thanksgiving delights. *New York Times*. https://www.nytimes.com/2016/11/24/opinion/mock-duck-and-other-depression-thanksgiving-delights.html.

6 The Lifecycle of Your Exhibit

Propose, Market, Evaluate, and Retire

Given the range of intellectual, procedural, and technical tasks required for digital exhibit work, it can be difficult to understand them holistically. This chapter will briefly review several key processes and issues of digital exhibits using a temporal framework. It will look at each issue in the lifecycle of a digital exhibit and delineate the major parameters, offer some observations, and propose strategies for addressing them in ways that will increase your project's odds for success. These issues are secondary to the main task of exhibit creation addressed in other chapters but should not be dismissed as trivial or extraneous. Although they are presented within a linear framework here for the sake of clarity, these tasks need to be considered and engaged iteratively because they will eventually involve and affect the entirety of your project.

At the Beginning: Ways to Get Buy-in From Your Organization's Leadership

It is likely that before you can formally start your project, you will need to get approval from the decision makers in your organization. To maximize the odds of approval, you will need to demonstrate how and where your exhibit will fit in the internal structure of your organization just like you need to consider where it fits in the larger external information ecosystem. At times, digital exhibits are perceived as peripheral to an organization's core mission. They can be labeled as trivial or "cute" add-ons to the serious, legitimate work of your library, museum, or archive. As observed by Novara and Novara,

> [A]lthough the topic of exhibits within academic libraries has been investigated to some extent, the focus of previous research has been on "how-to" manuals and descriptions of specific exhibits. A noticeable lack exists in the academic library and archival literature relating to the intellectual and creative process of producing an exhibit and the relationship of exhibits to scholarly research.
>
> (2017, p. 358)

DOI:10.4324/9781003301493-6

Bowen and Roberts make a more explicit point,

> While few academic librarians would label exhibits as a frivolous activity, and while many point out their instructional and promotional value, most librarians do not regard exhibits as an intellectually rigorous activity on a par with producing articles for professional publications. Although considered worthwhile, they are not valued as an essential function, as reference or collection development are, and their creation is not viewed as a fully legitimate scholarly enterprise. Exhibits are the illegitimate children of academic libraries: while we enjoy having them around, they may not quite belong in the family, and we may be uncomfortable about the circumstances surrounding their creation. (1993, p. 407)

Arguing against these prejudicial positions and advocating for your exhibit as something more than a throwaway bit of promotion or a staff member's sideline hobby can be difficult.

There are a variety of reasons that your project might not be approved before it even begins or not supported after it is launched. These reasons might include concerns about centering a project aimed at non-experts (i.e., the general public). If you do not have access to subject matter experts in your exhibit's domain, there may be concerns about the authoritativeness of your exhibit's vision and the original content you have created to express that vision. There may be concerns about the level of technical support needed to launch and maintain an exhibit website. The National Archives' *Digital Engagement Toolkit* argues

> [D]igital exhibitions can deliver relatively poor return on investment in terms of time spent in preparation vs audience attracted and this should be carefully considered. The use of established platforms can reduce development time but these platforms do not necessarily enjoy the significant 'built in' audience of social media and may use unfamiliar controls, design patterns and be inaccessible to users with disabilities. This means they should be used carefully and strategically. (n.d.)

It might be up to you to demonstrate that your project can indeed produce a good return on your investment and deserves a full place at the table of your organization. There are two excellent arguments to support a cogent, politically effective case that may increase the likelihood of your exhibit proposal's acceptance by your organizational leadership.

First, the COVID-19 worldwide pandemic and shutdown provided vivid and unmistakable proof of the value of robust and flexible digital strategies for cultural heritage organizations. This is how a report commissioned by Europeana described this momentous shift:

> Since January 2020 the GLAM sector has, in effect, been thrown into the digital deep end. Organisations reacted, jumped or were forced to shift to digital

> working at a speed of change that would have been unthinkable before. . . . In many ways the first half of 2020 has been a kind of renaissance of digital with GLAM professionals having to step up, shift their thinking and find digital ways to try and maintain an offer to their audiences whilst remaining physically shut.
>
> (Finnis & Kennedy, 2020, p. 11)

This forced renaissance resulted in a variety of digital initiatives that served locked-down audiences hungry for diversion and content. A UNESCO report described the five main classes of digital initiatives carried out by museums during the pandemic: use of previously digitized materials, movement of physical events to digital platforms, increased use of social media, creation of special activities, and creation of academic webinars (2020). Digital exhibits would fit in well with all these activities and would be useful as "evergreen" resources for an organization to use across time and contexts. This new-found perspective is an opportunity for organizations to take advantage of existing digital content, reimagine it in new ways, and connect with existing and new audiences through digital projects such as exhibits.

The digital world is now not just a place for cultural heritage organizations to visit, but to live for good. As observed by King, Smith, Wilson, and Williams,

> [I]t is evident that the COVID crisis has been a pivotal moment for museums and the heritage sector more generally, having accelerated need and heightened the attention for relevant and meaningful digital practice. With this rising atmosphere of change on the horizon, it is important that museums consider such conceptual issues and evaluate audience needs rigorously when developing online offerings to maintain such cultural importance.
>
> (2021, p. 501)

Digital exhibits could be such an online offering.

Second, museums, libraries, archives, and other cultural heritage organizations have invested significant financial and human resources in their digitization programs. An OCLC study from 2017 found that a third of libraries had engaged in digitization of their collections in the three years prior to being surveyed (Morgan & Proffitt, 2017). Overall statistics are hard to find and access, especially for smaller institutions, but there are multiple indicators of an interconnected infrastructure of large-scale GLAM digitization efforts, including books, organizations, and funding sources. While much intellectual effort has been spent on advancing a case for digitization, there is less attention focused on what should happen to material once it is properly selected, digitized, catalogued, and deposited in a search and discovery system. As argued within an article on the Institute of Museum and Library Services' National Digital Platform, "digital library infrastructures must not simply work. They must also manifest the core principles of libraries and archives" (Owens et al., 2018, p. 73). While opinions vary on exactly what these principles are and should be, clearly one of the most central should be an assertion to make materials procedurally and intellectually accessible to users, or as Ranganathan would put it, "books are for use" (1931). Digitizing a printed book and placing its associated digital object in a repository will support one kind of use.

But this is not enough.

> If we truly want to use digitization to help diversify our community, we need to move beyond merely making those digitized products accessible. True integration does not come simply through the presentation of material, but rather from meaningful collaborations across institutions and nations. A clear next step is prioritizing methods to meaningfully involve partners in a dialogue about best practice for implementing these collaborations. Providing a URL to a digitized image is not enough.
>
> (Drew et al., 2017, p. 1790)

But a digital exhibit that incorporates images, documents, and original content in a meaningful structure built with users' needs and interests in mind might be more than just "enough".

A more expansive conception of intellectual access and use is embodied in applied projects such as online exhibits. As argued by Shankweiler and Seguin, library exhibits "enable librarians and curators to showcase unique or underused materials, they provide context for materials which might not otherwise be apparent from a catalog record, and they attract new users" (2018, p. 306). Showcasing and contextualizing digital content in an online exhibit is a good way for GLAM organizations to create novel and accessible ways to ensure that their books are "for use". This is an excellent argument in favor of creating an exhibit using an organization's digital content. The fictional proposal described in Chapter 4 demonstrates how potentially dry, obscure agricultural bulletins published by the US Government could be contextualized and re-imagined within an exhibit structure. This would make them more "usable" for a modern audience demanding new insights that incorporate thoughtful and authentic consideration of diversity and empowerment of previously excluded communities and perspectives.

Marketing Your Exhibit: Connecting Materials, Audiences, and Organizational Goals Through Digital Engagement

The best way to connect your digital exhibit to your users is by grounding your marketing strategy within a holistic model that takes everything into account: your project, your organization's mission, your audience's needs and interests, and the larger cultural heritage landscape. This perspective is echoed in previous chapters where exhibits were conceived as being necessarily grounded in audience needs. If you introduce and incorporate audience needs in the initial stages of your project, you will be better equipped to develop a marketing plan once it is completed and ready to be launched. The example proposal illustrated in Chapter 4 included suggestions for people, events, and outlets like Twitter as relevant resources for a marketing campaign before the exhibit itself was even built. The earlier you start to regard your exhibit as a project with clear goals tied to a clear audience that is clearly delineated and directly addressed, the more prepared you will be to create a formal marketing plan.

There are several good candidates for cultural heritage marketing models. The most obvious are those which see marketing as properly focused on relationships with potential audiences and those that are aimed to increase the social capital of those audiences (Johnson, 2015; Murzyn-Kupisz & Działek, 2013; Osterman, 2012). The Digital Engagement Framework of Visser and Richardson (2013) is especially useful since it actually encompasses the humanistic aims of both the relationship and the social capital-oriented models. As argued by the authors, this view of marketing cultural heritage assets "lets you discover your organisation's digital potential by asking questions about your target audiences, key assets, organisational vision and much more. The Framework allows you to design campaigns and projects that engage and reach out to people" (2013, p. 1). Thus, it is tied closely to the needs of people at both ends of the marketing relationship: staff within the originating organization and the audiences which they are trying to serve through their digital projects. The framework rests upon three core components which are somewhat diffuse and overlapping, but nonetheless are helpful guides to identifying the core significance of your exhibit to both your organization and your audience and how it can be marketed.

1 Long-Term Ambition: what you want your exhibit to achieve in the long term. This should be tied to established organizational aspirations, such as those expressed in mission statements or five-year plans.
2 Short-Term Goals: what you want your exhibit to achieve in the short term. These goals should be cast in terms of SMART objectives. They should be specific, measurable, achievable, relevant, and time-bound (Doran, 1981).
3 Organizational Values: how your exhibit will express and fulfill your larger organization's vision.

These core components are tied to seven elements:

1 General organizational assets: such as your library's collection or staff expertise
2 Content: specific assets used in your exhibit that can be harnessed for marketing purposes
3 Audience(s): who would you like to reach
4 Activities: connecting audiences to assets
5 Digital platforms: channels for reaching audiences including Twitter, TikTok, Flickr, Pinterest, Tumblr, Instagram, and other social media outlets
6 Outreach: methods for reaching new audiences
7 Engagement: methods for further connecting to existing audiences

These approaches to audience engagement and marketing can seem demanding if you consider them in isolation and as essentially separate from the exhibit-building process. But the exhibit proposal described in Chapter 4 shows how you can identify and incorporate all of these elements into your work at the very start. When you engage deeply with your exhibit material to identify the big idea for your exhibit (Serrell, 2015) as well as its smaller themes, you open yourself to all the richness that lies in cultural heritage documentation. Of course, that richness needs to be analyzed and reconceptualized rigorously in order to create an engaging, meaningful exhibit that will connect all of the parties in the communication transaction offered by a digital exhibit. These parties include your audience, your institution and its long- and short-term goals, and your own needs for professional development and creative expression.

Engaging the processes of qualitative inquiry, thematic analysis, and/or other analytic methods of close reading can open your awareness to elements you can use in your marketing plan. The Negro Extension exhibit proposal detailed earlier includes these elements that could be put to direct use:

- Pull quote from a prominent scholar of extension for setting the project's framework
- Sample images
- Twitter suggestions
- Relevant events
- Scholars who would be good candidates for consultation and/or presentation requests

The following image (Figure 6.1) shows two other exhibit proposals which incorporate similar communication plan elements: one for tick control strategies and one for historic efforts to reduce food waste (Marsh, 2022).

The audience analysis processes described in earlier chapters will also reveal relevant communities that would be receptive to your exhibit, as well as their preferred digital platforms. *Ad hoc* marketing campaigns that are hurriedly pulled together after the exhibit is built and launched generally will have less impact than more thoughtful campaigns that grow organically out of your connection to the exhibit material and your organization's vision of itself and its natural audience. Small efforts to collect useful and noteworthy images, quotations, insights, audiences, and outside scholars will pay off with dividends when it becomes time to implement a marketing plan for your exhibit.

One last suggestion is to recast and re-use elements of your finished exhibit in new ways to create alternate channels of engagement. The two frameworks of the Bite, Snack, Meal model of Leslie O'Flahavan (n.d.) and the Skim, Swim, Dive Engagement Framework of Charlotte Sexton (2014) can guide you to create new exhibit content pieces and sections as inspiration for shorter associated content you can use elsewhere by your organization. The foundational idea for both models is a recognition that there are multiple audience needs that can be serviced

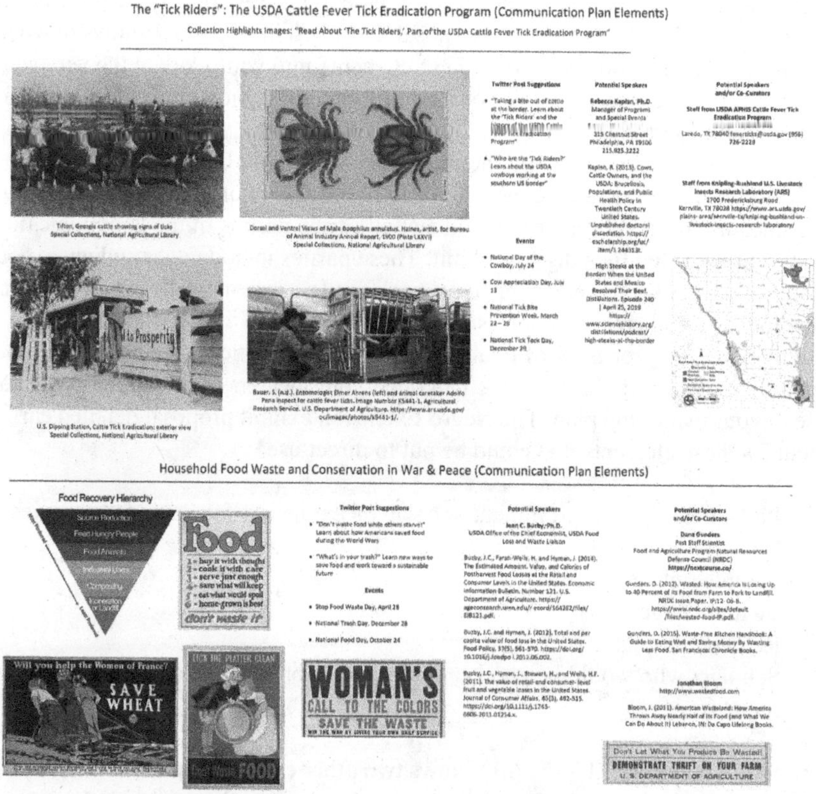

Figure 6.1 Two fictional exhibit communication plans for proposed exhibits on tick control and food waste

by different content approaches. Some audiences will want to engage fully with a completed exhibit, but others will be more open to smaller, shorter pieces of content. This could be in the form of an article focused on one small theme of your exhibit. At the smallest level, a tweet featuring an image could also engage your users and lead them to your exhibit for a fuller content "meal" or "dive". This communication tactic of creating multiple content streams based on a single project presents an effective way to leverage your exhibit and make it harmonize with other aspects of your organization's digital presence. Spinning off content based on components of your exhibit can also demonstrate your exhibit's long-term organizational value. In essence, it becomes a lasting content source feeding a larger information ecosystem to enrich your organization's web presence and social media footprint.

Some notable examples of organizations with rich digital engagement efforts include JSTOR with its *JSTOR Understanding Series* and *JSTOR Daily*, Europeana with its *Story Collection* and *User Galleries*, The British Library's exhibits and blogs, and the National Archives and Records Administration's social media campaigns, online exhibits, and educational collections for students and teachers. Although these large institutions may have financial and human resources unavailable to you, their work can act as an inspirational model for you to reimagine, recast, and reuse your exhibit content in different ways on multiple platforms to better reach audiences with your stories and materials. For example, the University of Delaware's Museum Studies Program (n.d.) maintains an excellent resource for small historical organizations that showcases examples that can be implemented effectively on a smaller scale. Finally, a recent story in the *New York Times* profiles how small museums are using podcasts "recorded in home offices and basements, small museum studios and public radio stations" to "carv[e] out a place in national conversations around art, culture, curation and the museum industry" (Cipolle, 2022).

It might be worthwhile to pursue assistance from organizations designed to support small cultural heritage organizations. Examples include the American Alliance of Museums (www.aam-us.org/), which also maintains several professional development groups including one for small museums and another for audience research and evaluation. The Small Museum Association (www.smallmuseum.org/) is an organization serving small museums in the mid-Atlantic region of the United States. The American Association for State and Local History (https://aaslh.org/) has a community of practice focused on small museums. The Association of Independent Museums (https://aim-museums.co.uk/) supports organizations in the United Kingdom. Some relevant organizations serving the needs of small libraries include the UK-focused Independent Libraries Association (www.independentlibraries.co.uk/), the Association for Small & Rural Libraries (www.arsl.org/), and state-focused organizations.

Evaluation: Demonstrating Value to Users and Organizations

The literature on formal efforts to evaluate physical and digital exhibits tends to focus on those projects built with specific instructional goals in mind, especially when envisioned as educational resources for children. The frameworks described in this literature will be useful if you are working for an organization focused on children or one that is fulfilling an explicit educational mission (Degner et al., 2022; Lin & Gregor, 2006; Packer, 2006; Song et al., 2017). Aside from explicit educational goals, the literature on informal learning also offers a framework that will support evaluation efforts (Brown, 2006; Falk, 2005; Lin et al., 2012; Rogoff et al., 2016; Schugurensky, 2000).

Most exhibits do not have formal instructional objectives as their underlying goals but aim to fulfill less structured goals such as user engagement and collection promotion. There are few available models to consult to measure digital exhibit effectiveness in these circumstances. Sigmond (2019) suggests these six elements as the most common areas of interest for exhibit designers to investigate:

1 Exhibit Imagery: is it effective at attracting interest and evoking a certain mood or mindset in the visitor?

2 Interface usability: is it clear and effective at supporting common user tasks?
3 Exhibit text: is it clear and effective at delivering the intended message?
4 Information structure: is the exhibit laid out in an understandable and cohesive way?
5 Exhibit tone and affect: Is it effective at producing the intended feeling or response from the user?
6 Exhibit relevance: is it clear how the exhibit relates to the user?

Answering these questions will require either a survey or user interviews to be constructed and implemented online for digital exhibits. While these questions may seem simple, they encapsulate complex constructs such as clarity, effectiveness, structure, organization, relevance, and usability. It is beyond the bounds of this book to provide an evaluation model of digital exhibits. Aside from constructing a Likert-based scale for users to rate each of these elements, the best sources for evaluation support are books on exhibit building that include chapters in evaluation such as those written by Hansen (2017), Lord (2014), Roppola (2014), Summers (2018), and Walhimer (2021). On the basis of my experience in both web usability and digital exhibit creation, the standard texts in usability studies would be a good place to start, including those written by Goodwin (2009), Krug (2013), and Rubin and Chisnell (2008). But even a straightforward usability test requires a significant investment in time and effort, so you should proceed only if you have a compelling reason to complete one. Finally, funding agencies may require systematic evaluation efforts to be conducted, so consultation with these organizations would be valuable.

At the End: How to Retire Your Exhibit

There may come a time when you or your organization decide that your exhibit needs to be retired. Aside from simply uninstalling the exhibit and removing it from your site, there are several possibilities for preservation. First, although it is always tempting to store documents (e.g., pdfs) within your chosen exhibit software platform (e.g., Omeka or Scalar), it is recommended to separate your actual content objects from your exhibit and rely on document surrogates such as images, quotations, and links to convey their meaning. Thus, the actual information objects remain in a presumably stable repository and are not dependent on an exhibit platform for their actual existence. This is a useful decision for several reasons, the most important of which is that you will have access to your exhibit's content even if your exhibit is retired or is migrated to another platform.

Another suggestion is to create some sort of static representation of your exhibit in a form that is also outside of your chosen platform. I used to have an outside reviewer request to see my exhibit content in the form of an illustrated text document. Creating this alternate version was, frankly, tedious and required me to systematically copy material from the exhibit site into a Word document. Once the process was completed, however, I had a copy of the exhibit's content that, while lacking most of the experiential artifacts of the exhibit itself, contained its essential meaning and structure. Once you have created this kind of alternate representation, you can use it in several ways. For example, the University of Washington Libraries Special Collections retired an exhibit from 2016 "Just One Look: An Exhibition of Contemporary Book Arts Exploring the Theme of Women and Vision" but make its content available as a pdf document. The University of South Carolina University Libraries (n.d.) has a useful site that contains their retired digital exhibits. The exhibits have been recast as pdfs; so aside from the content, all of the features that make digital exhibits interactive are missing. But there are times when you simply want to preserve content. This site is a model of how to implement that decision.

Aside from replicating and migrating original text, you may have to record the metadata for your items in a spreadsheet or database. But several platforms have the ability to ingest item-level metadata so there is a possibility for reuse. An example is Omeka and its CSV import plugin option. Of course, interactive features such as timelines and sliders will not be able to be easily preserved for re-ingest, so they may have to be redone if you change from one platform to another.

On the opposite side of the continuum, a tool named Conifer is an example of web archiving that claims to preserve all the interactive features of digital exhibits. As its documentation states,

> While most web archive projects automatically create copies of material found on the public web, Conifer is a user-driven platform. Users can create, curate, and share their own collections of web materials. This can even include items that would be only revealed after logging in or performing complicated actions on a web site. . . . On the technical side, Conifer focuses on "high fidelity" web archiving. Items relying on complex scripting, such as embedded videos, fancy navigation, or 3D graphics have a much higher success rate for capture with Conifer than with traditional web archives.
>
> (Rhizome, n.d.)

The Museum of Modern Art has made several exhibits available using Conifer. Examples include a 2008 Flash-based exhibit website "Wunderkammer" and "Henri Matisse: The Cut-Outs" from 2015. Although the user experience on Conifer is not fluid, it is invaluable for allowing users to access exhibits that were built using tools like Adobe's now defunct Flash that are simply not supported any longer by modern web browsers. Using an archiving service like Conifer will keep you from having to include awkward and unfortunate disclaimers such as that shown by one of the Flash-based exhibits from the United States Holocaust Memorial Museum, "as of December 31, 2020, Adobe will end support for the Flash Player browser plugin. Please note that some content in this exhibition will no longer be available".

Conifer is an example of a web archiving service that has become popular with the explosion of digital data on the web needing some sort of conservation, either for access by users or preservation for organizations or both. There are many web archiving services available aside from Conifer, however. A prominent example is Archive-It by the Internet Archive that is used "by over 800 library, university, government, non-profit, and knowledge organizations from around the world" (Internet Archive, 2022). A UK-based service is the UK Web Archive, a collaboration between six government libraries. Just one example of an exhibit archived this way is "Moving Here", by The National Archives.

In summation, Web archiving services offer a partial long-term solution to the perpetual problem of outdated technologies and unfashionable stylistic conventions that can affect digital exhibits over time. They require long-term financial resources, however, and should be researched carefully.

Digital and Physical Exhibits Discussed in This Chapter

Henri Matisse: The Cut-Outs
Karl Buchberg, Jodi Hauptman, and Samantha Friedman
Museum of Modern Art
www.moma.org/calendar/exhibitions/1429
https://conifer.rhizome.org/nyarc/moma-henri-matisse—the-cut-outs/20201209161512$br:chrome:76/www.moma.org/interactives/exhibitions/2014/matisse/

Just One Look: An Exhibition of Contemporary Book Arts Exploring the Theme of Women and Vision
Wendy Huntington, Sarah Kate Moore, and Lauren Dudley
University of Washington Libraries Special Collections
www.lib.washington.edu/specialcollections/collections/exhibits/justonelook/view
www.lib.washington.edu/specialcollections/collections/exhibits/justonelook/at_download/file

Moving Here
The National Archives
https://webarchive.nationalarchives.gov.uk/ukgwa/+/http:/www.movinghere.org.uk/

Propaganda: Explore the Nazis Sophisticated Propaganda Campaigns and their Legacy
United States Holocaust Memorial Museum
www.ushmm.org/propaganda/

Wunderkammer
Sarah Suzuki
Museum of Modern Art
www.moma.org/calendar/exhibitions/272
https://conifer.rhizome.org/nyarc/moma-wunderkammer/20201215001110$br:chrome:76/www.moma.org/interactives/exhibitions/2008/wunderkammer/

References

Bowen, L. G., & Roberts, P. J. (1993). Exhibits: Illegitimate children of academic libraries? *College & Research Libraries*, *54*(5), 407–415. http://hdl.handle.net/2142/41609.

Brown, S. (2006). Do richer media mean better learning? A framework for evaluating learning experiences in museum web site design. *International Journal of Heritage Studies*, *12*(5), 412–426. https://doi.org/10.1080/13527250600821571.

Cipolle, A. V. (2022, April 27). Using podcasts to broaden the reach of smaller museums. *New York Times*. www.nytimes.com/2022/04/27/arts/design/museum-podcasts.html.

Degner, M., Moser, S., & Lewalter, D. (2022). Digital media in institutional informal learning places: A systematic literature review. *Computers and Education Open*, *3*. https://doi.org/10.1016/j.caeo.2021.100068.

Doran, G. T. (1981). There's a S.M.A.R.T. way to write management's goals and objectives. *Management Review*, *70*(11), 35–36.

Drew, J. A., Moreau, C. S., & Stiassny, M. L. J. (2017). Digitization of museum collections holds the potential to enhance researcher diversity. *Nature Ecology & Evolution*, *1*, 1789–1790. https://doi.org/10.1038/s41559-017-0401-6.

Falk, J. H. (2005). Free-choice environmental learning: Framing the discussion. *Environmental Education Research*, *11*(3), 265–280. https://doi.org/10.1080/13504620500081129.

Finnis, J., & Kennedy, A. (2020). *The digital transformation agenda and GLAMs: A quick scan report for Europeana*. Den Haag: Europeana Foundation. https://pro.europeana.eu/files/Europeana_Professional/Publications/Digital%20transformation%20reports/The%20digital%20transformation%20agenda%20and%20GLAMs%20-%20Culture24,%20findings%20and%20outcomes.pdf.

Goodwin, K. (2009). *Designing for the digital age: How to create human-centered products and services*. Hoboken, NJ: Wiley.

Hansen, B. (2017). *Great exhibits!: An exhibit planning and construction handbook for small museums*. Lanham, MD: Rowman & Littlefield Publishers.

Internet Archive. (2022). *Archive-it pro: Overview*. https://archive-it.org/blog/files/2022/05/Archive-It_pro.pdf.

Johnson, C. A. (2015). Social capital and library and information science research: Definitional chaos or coherent research enterprise? *Information Research*, *20*(4), paper 690. http://informationr.net/ir/20-4/paper690.html#.YycgmbTMK00.

King, E., Smith, M. P., Wilson, P. F., & Williams, M. A. (2021). Digital responses of UK museum exhibitions to the COVID-19 crisis, March–June 2020. *Curator: The Museum Journal*, *64*(3), 487–504. https://doi.org/10.1111/cura.12413.

Krug, S. (2013). *Don't make me think, revisited: A common sense approach to web usability* (3rd ed.). Hoboken, NJ: New Riders.

Lin, A. C. H., Fernandez, W. D., & Gregor, S. (2012). Understanding web enjoyment experiences and informal learning: A study in a museum context. *Decision Support Systems*, *53*(4), 846–858. https://doi.org/10.1016/j.dss.2012.05.020.

Lin, A. C. H., & Gregor, S. (2006). Designing websites for learning and enjoyment: A study of museum experiences. *International Review of Research in Open and Distance Learning*, *7*(3), 1–21. www.learntechlib.org/p/49690/.

Lord, B. (2014). *Manual of museum exhibitions* (2nd ed.). Lanham, MD: Rowman & Littlefield Publishers.

Marsh, E. (2022). *Two fictional exhibit communication plans for proposed exhibits on tick control and food waste* [Infographic]. https://emily-marsh.com/Digital_Exhibits_for_Cultural_Institutions/Figure_6.1.jpg.

Morgan, K., & Proffitt, M. (2017). *Advancing the national digital platform: The state of digitization in US public and state libraries*. Dublin, OH: OCLC Online Computer Library Center, Inc. www.oclc.org/content/dam/research/publications/2017/oclcresearch-advancing-the-national-digital-platform-2017.pdf.

Murzyn-Kupisz, M., & Działek, J. (2013). Cultural heritage in building and enhancing social capital, *Journal of Cultural Heritage Management and Sustainable Development*, *3*(1), 35–54. https://doi.org/10.1108/20441261311317392.

National Archives. (n.d.). *Digital engagement toolkit: Platform guides*. www.nationalarchives.gov.uk/archives-sector/projects-and-programmes/plugged-in-powered-up/digital-engagement-toolkit/platform-guides/digital-exhibitions/.

Novara, E. A., & Novara, V. J. (2017). Exhibits as scholarship: Strategies for acceptance, documentation, and evaluation in academic libraries. *The American Archivist*, *80*(2), 355–372. https://doi.org/10.17723/0360-9081-80.2.355.

O'Flahavan, L. (n.d.). The bite, the snack, and the meal: How to feed content-hungry site visitors. *E-Write*. https://ewriteonline.com/bite-snack-and-meal-how-to-feed-content-hungry-site-visitors/.

Osterman, M. (2012). Museums and Twitter: An exploratory qualitative study of how museums use Twitter for audience development and engagement. *Journal of Educational Multimedia and Hypermedia*, *21*(3), 29–43. www.learntechlib.org/primary/p/39141/.

Owens, T., Sands, A. E., Reyonlds, E., Neal, J., Mayeaux, S., & Marx, M. (2018). Digital infrastructures that embody library principles: The IMLS National Digital Platform as a framework for digital library tools and services. In P. D. Fernandez & K. Tilton (Eds.), *Applying library values to emerging technology: Decision-making in the age of open access, maker spaces, and the ever-changing library* (pp. 73–88). ACRL Publications in Librarianship, Number 72. Chicago, IL: Association of College and Research Libraries. www.imls.gov/publications/digital-infrastructures-embody-library-principles-imls-national-digital-platform.

Packer, J. (2006). Learning for fun: The unique contribution of educational leisure experiences. *Curator: The Museum Journal*, *49*(3), 329–344. https://doi.org/10.1111/j.2151-6952.2006.tb00227.x.

Ranganathan, S. R. (1931). *The five laws of library science* (Madras Library Association). London: Edward Goldston Ltd.

Rhizome. (n.d.). *Conifer*. https://conifer.rhizome.org/.

Rogoff, B., Callanan, M., Guitiérrez, K. D., & Erickson, F. (2016). The organization of informal learning. *Review of Research in Education*, *40*(1), 356–401. https://doi.org/10.3102/0091732X16680994.

Roppola, T. (2013). *Designing for the museum visitor experience*. London: Routledge.

Rubin, J., & Chisnell, D. (2008). *Handbook of usability testing: How to plan, design, and conduct effective tests* (2nd ed.). Hoboken, NJ: Wiley.

Schugurensky, D. (2000). *The forms of informal learning: Towards a conceptualization of the field*. NALL Working Paper #19. Centre for the Study of Education and Work, Ontario Institute for Studies in Education, University of Toronto. https://hdl.handle.net/1807/2733.

Serrell, B. (2015). *Exhibit labels: An interpretive approach* (2nd ed.). Lanham, MD: Rowman & Littlefield.

Sexton, C. (2014). Mobile museums: Where things stand. In J. Pagel & K. Donahue (Eds.), *NEMO annual conference, Bucharest, Romania, November 2013 – 'Museums in the digital age, museums and the development of active citizenship'* (pp. 15–19). Berlin: Network of European Museum Organisations.

Shankweiler, J., & Seguin, T. (2018). Lasting experiences: Taking galleries from glass cases to online access repositories. In P. D. Fernandez & K. Tilton (Eds.), *Applying library values to emerging technology: Decision-making in the age of open access, maker spaces, and the ever-changing library* (pp. 305–313). ACRL Publications in Librarianship, Number 72. Chicago, IL: Association of College and Research Libraries.

Sigmond, C. (2019). The many shapes of formative evaluation in exhibition development. *Exhibition*, Spring, 34–41. https://www.name-aam.org/s/09_Exhibition_TheManyShapesofFormativeEvalution.pdf.

Song, L., Golinkoff, R. M., Stuehling, A., Resnick, I., Mahajan, N., Hirsh-Pasek, K., & Thompson, N. (2017). Parents' and experts' awareness of learning opportunities in children's museum exhibits. *Journal of Applied Developmental Psychology*, *49*, 39–45. https://doi.org/10.1016%2Fj.appdev.2017.01.006.

Summers, J. (2018). *Creating exhibits that engage: A manual for museums and historical organizations*. Lanham, MD: Rowman & Littlefield Publishers.

United Nations Educational, Scientific and Cultural Organization (UNESCO). (2020). *Museums around the world in the face of COVID-19*. Paris: Author. https://unesdoc.unesco.org/ark:/48223/pf0000373530.

University of Delaware Museum Studies Program. (n.d.). Digital storytelling. *Sustaining Places*. https://wuffencuckoo.wordpress.com/digital-strategy-and-content/digital-storytelling/.

University of South Carolina University Libraries. (n.d.). *Digital exhibits archive*. https://sc.edu/about/offices_and_divisions/university_libraries/exhibits_events_news/exhibits/digital_exhibits_archive/index.php.

Visser, J., & Richardson, J. (2013). *Digital engagement framework workbook*. https://web.archive.org/web/20191028115719/http://digitalengagementframework.com/portfolio/digital-engagement-framework-workbook/.

Walhimer, M. (2021). *Designing museum experiences*. Lanham, MD: Rowman & Littlefield Publishers.

7 The Nuts and Bolts of Your Exhibit

Metadata and Software Platforms

Many resources on digital exhibits emphasize the more practical and administrative issues that will be covered here to the detriment of the thematic and theoretical issues covered in previous chapters. Although issues such as metadata and software platform selection require sound judgment and informed choices, addressing them will require you to use an entirely different set of decision-making criteria and skills. Working to answer these questions will be unlike the thicket of content-based issues you have to address when you are creating the main structure of your exhibit.

Perhaps the most common question that potential exhibit creators ask is "What software should I use?" It is natural to start here because, just like choosing a restaurant for a meal, it can play an oversized determinative role for almost every other decision you will need to make. For example, selecting a certain restaurant will drive what type of meal you will be able to eat (lunch or dinner?), when you would visit the restaurant (afternoon or evening?) what type of cuisine is prepared (Indian or Italian?), what kind of seating you will get (counter or table?), what type of beverages you will be able to choose (tea or wine?), how much money you will need to pay the check (budget or luxury?), and even what kind of clothes you will wear (jeans or suit?). Just like getting your meal companions to agree on a restaurant, it makes sense to ask what kind of software to use because that can drastically shape the parameters of your entire exhibit. Drucker and Svensson call this type of software for the digital humanities "middleware" since the software packages themselves

> frame arguments, define and delimit what can be said through the structuring principles of [their] design . . . [and] embody rhetorical assumptions at every level of production (from back-end assumptions about what constitutes the smallest unit of discourse, to the front-end modes of presentation and organization of display).
>
> (2016)

In other words, what is considered an "exhibit", or an "object", or a "page of content", might be one thing in Platform A and something just a little bit different in Platform B, *ad infinitum*.

DOI:10.4324/9781003301493-7

Although the choice of software seems like a natural place to want to start any exhibit project, it can present something of a moving target since platforms come, go, and evolve rapidly. This book is a guide to creating an exhibit, not an algorithm for selecting a piece of software. If we stay with our restaurant example, instead of selecting a particular place and letting that will drive every other decision, we should consider some other, perhaps more difficult, deeper questions. Why do we want to go out for a meal in the first place? What kind of food do we want to eat? How long do we want to stay? Do we want to take a walk through a nearby neighborhood afterward? These represent the type of deeper questions that you should ask before you select a particular software platform.

The software you select should meet the demands of your exhibit instead of requiring you to bend to meet the requirements of the software. The task at hand is to design an interface that strikes a balance between attractive content display, audience expectations, and internal organizational requirements. This is a thorny issue with few ready-made answers. Even if your organization leaves you no choice and mandates you to use a particular application, you will still need to find a way to create the best exhibit possible, operating within this limitation. If you do have authorization to make your own selection, the point is to select software that best meets your needs instead of letting the software itself determine what needs can be fulfilled and how they must be addressed. To help structure your response to this question, instead of describing the ins and outs of specific platforms, this chapter will address the two main types of exhibit software (object-oriented vs. information-oriented) and how they address these deeper questions. Likewise, the exhibit software selected will also affect the interface design of your exhibit. The issues of software selection and configuration are intertwined, so these issues will be addressed iteratively, along with an acknowledgment that you may be constrained in your choice by organizational factors out of your control. No software is perfect, however, so it is best to know the relative strengths and weaknesses of the major platforms available, whichever is empowered to make the selection.

Another key question involves metadata. The metadata elements in your exhibit that describe your objects and, potentially, drive your searching and browsing mechanisms, communicate authenticity and authority to uses, and affect audience analytic metrics which are also common issues for concern and discussion. This chapter will cover the issue of metadata for exhibits taking a preeminently brief and practical approach that assumes your users will not require extensive description of your objects within the exhibit itself when they can access it elsewhere, such as from an affiliated search and discovery systems. Descriptive metadata captures essential information about information objects and includes elements such as title, creator name, date and place of publication, and resource type (e.g., book, report, image). This chapter will focus briefly on these basic but crucial elements and explain why and how you should incorporate them into your exhibit itself and how to send users to richer sources of objects and metadata.

Metadata Needs for Digital Exhibits

Since I am not a cataloger or metadata librarian, I approach the question of what metadata is needed for digital exhibit items from the perspective of a potential user. How should exhibit items be modeled through metadata in a way that supports user needs for description, search, and discovery? How much metadata should be displayed for items in exhibits? How much is enough? How much is too much? Gilliland's view of metadata in the Getty Research Institute-published *Introduction to Metadata* sees it as a way to model three essential aspects of cultural heritage information objects: content, context, and structure (2016). The various mechanisms for modeling these object facets vary, but they all have to do so in a way that facilitates user needs and digital system requirements. Fortunately, many of the major software platforms for digital heritage projects support effective metadata display and deployment.

As to what metadata you will need within your exhibit, it really depends on the nature of your users and their needs for precise and detailed object description. Since this book is directed at staff in small organizations with limited resources, I am going to suggest that you be realistic with your metadata expectations. Most information objects in the exhibits I have created were mass-produced US Government reports written for working farmers or the general citizenry. Although well-digitized, the metadata to which I had access was often based on legacy records designed for card catalogs and created decades ago under very different standards than are currently accepted. Since the data were often sparse, I created new descriptive metadata for the exhibit's object records which then linked back to the official records for the digitized objects, often within the Internet Archive. The vision I had for this process followed the Bite, Snack, Meal model of O'Flahavan (n.d.). I provided minimal metadata (the "bite") for items embedded within the exhibit itself but provided a link to a full object record with richer data (the "snack"). In turn, that object record also linked to the official "item of record" (or "meal") for the object as created and maintained by the National Agricultural Library (NAL).

Figure 7.1 illustrates the three elements of this progressively more detailed chain of exhibit item metadata as carried out in an NAL digital exhibit, *Apron Strings and Kitchen Sinks* (Marsh, 2022).

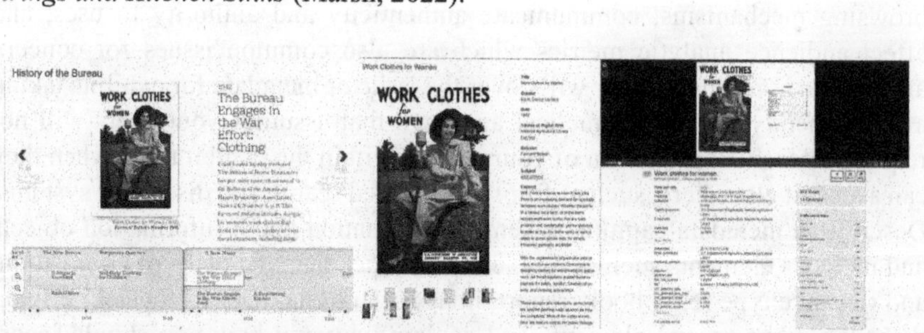

Figure 7.1 Different views of object-level metadata for *Work Clothes for Women* in an exhibit timeline: the "bite", from an item view within an exhibit timeline, the "snack", from the full item record in the exhibit, and from the item's original Internet Archive record, the "meal"

Joshua Wachuta echoes this view of metadata implementation for digital exhibits in a post about the Digital Public Library of America project, *Recollection Wisconsin*.

> The online exhibits at *Recollection Wisconsin* achieve an ideal balance between making rich metadata available for those who want it without interrupting their exhibits' narrative flow. . . . A caption below each object gives its creator, date, and current owner in a concise format that does not distract from the primary exhibit text. Viewers can still access more detailed metadata, however, because each object is hyperlinked to its corresponding database page at the repository that owns the item. The database page provides full catalog metadata including dimensions, physical description, rights, and other information not included in the exhibit captions.
>
> (Wachuta, 2016)

The exhibits I have created follow a similar view of user needs. Readers of exhibit content objects need to have basic information to understand what they are seeing, but not so much that they become distracted from the exhibit narrative. Richer, more detailed item metadata needs to be made easily available, however for those readers who want it, for purposes of more precise identification, to confirm assertions within the main exhibit, or for some other reason.

Metadata schemata and standardized means of knowledge representation raise complex and difficult questions deserving of careful study that lay outside the scope of this book. Perhaps the best guides for metadata in digital exhibits can be found in the software guides for individual exhibit platforms and in the many monographs about metadata for digital libraries and the digital humanities (Bedford, 2021; Drucker, 2021; Gardiner, 2015; Gartner, 2021; Golub & Liu, 2022; Horodyski, 2022; Miller, 2022; Riley, 2017).

The content and structure of your exhibit metadata should also be driven by the user needs of your target communities. These can be determined by your own experience as an information professional, from actual contact with potential audience members when possible, and from a search of the literature on discipline-specific user needs that would be relevant to your exhibit and its intended audience. In contrast to the simple bite-snack-meal model described earlier, Urberg describes the DH project *Six Degrees of Francis Bacon* as containing complex metadata implemented with interacting crosswalks to external sources (2020). She observes

> [F]rom a user perspective, this platform is intended for historians who study early modern Britain. From a metadata perspective, however, this network is an excellent example of how choosing well-developed sets of metadata can make a project interoperable with others.
>
> (p. 216)

Urberg's analysis concludes with a cautionary note about the lack of metadata standards for DH projects overall.

> Metadata internal to a project [such as a digital exhibit] usually grows organically out of specific project needs. It may be harvested from existing data sets . . . but it is more likely created in order to support community needs or to facilitate involvement from a larger group of contributors. Ideally, whatever metadata vocabularies are used, the element sets and schema could be more standardized.
>
> (pp. 222–223)

Until a better plan can be created and implemented systemically across GLAMs, it will be up to individual organizations and exhibit creators to do their best to create, implement, and display object metadata to "support community needs".

Digital Humanities Platform Considerations

Omeka and Scalar are two of the most popular server-side software platforms for digital exhibits, and this section will address them in some depth. The reasons for focusing on these two applications are partially practical and partially theoretical. The practical issues include the author's direct experience with Omeka and Scalar, in addition to their ascendancy within the DH community as the most frequently cited and used tools for a variety of projects, especially for digital exhibits. In fact, it is common to see these two tools compared in reviews almost to the exclusion of all others (Roman, 2018). The theoretical issues arise from their relative orientation as either more object-focused or more user-focused, within the model presented in Chapter 2.

In a related vein, Drucker and Svensson describe the underlying functions of tools like Scalar and Omeka as argument structures and rhetorical assumptions that will influence almost every aspect of any project placed within one of these two platforms (2016). This discussion will build upon this perspective to show how the structures and assumptions of each platform can orient a given digital exhibit toward an emphasis on object representation and presentation or toward user engagement with narratives supported by information objects. A brief description of both platforms will be offered first to ground the analysis and set the conditions for comparison.

Both tools are similar in their mutual expectation that exhibit creators need to perform actions such as:

- Create original object metadata records in the application
- Import records in a variety of formats
- Display items, enriched with metadata
- Associate object records with images or documents
- Create original exhibit text
- Divide exhibits into multiple parts

- Create item collections
- Introduce interactive elements such as image sliders, embedded video, and timelines

It would be foolish to present detailed instructions for completing these tasks for either platform here in this book. Software changes rapidly and web-based sources of instruction are much more likely to be current and provide better, more targeted assistance.

Instead of falling into the trap of "buttonology" (Russell & Hensley, 2017) and trying to demonstrate how to use these platforms, this chapter will offer some analysis into the ways Omeka and Scalar model digital exhibits and fail or succeed to meet administrator and end-user needs. Both Omeka (Corporation for Digital Scholarship, n.d.b.) and Scalar (Alliance for Networking Visual Culture, n.d.c) offer user manuals with more detailed support for the normal tasks of exhibit creation.

Omeka

Omeka is probably the most well-known of all DH tools. It is an open-source application that was created and launched in 2007 by the Center for History and New Media at George Mason University, now the Roy Rosenzweig Center for History and New Media (n.d.a). In 2016, responsibility for the platform was given to an independent organization, the Corporation for Digital Scholarship, formed in part by several past members of the Center. Originally branded by Dan Cohen as "WordPress for exhibits and collections" (2008), Omeka is now described as "a next-generation open source web publishing platform and content management system designed for museums, libraries, historic sites, historical societies, scholars, enthusiasts, and educators" (Corporation for Digital Scholarship, n.d.a.). Despite these aspirational statements, Omeka is generally thought to be a straightforward, easy-to-use platform for digital exhibits. Perhaps the most prominent example of Omeka's potential for extension into something more powerful is Florida's State Library and Archives' Omeka site, *Florida Memory,* which contains over 500,000 objects.

There are three versions of Omeka:

1. Omeka Classic, which is an application that can be self-hosted on a server installed with what is termed a LAMP (Linux, Apache, MySQL, and PHP) software stack. (The following analysis of Omeka will be confined to this version of the application.)
2. Omeka S, which is designed to support multiple exhibits and connect to other resources using semantic data. Omeka S is also a self-hosted option with similar system requirements as Omeka Classic.
3. Omeka.net, which is a hosted service offered through by the Corporation for Digital Scholarship using an annual subscription model. The fees for Omeka.net accounts vary and are based on the number of sites and services you require.

In keeping with Cohen's initial branding of Omeka as a WordPress-like option for DH projects, Omeka does function much in the same way. Like WordPress, the appearance of an Omeka site including CSS-controlled factors such as font types, heading size, background colors, and other aesthetic factors are determined by themes, while other functions are supported by optional plugins. Themes can vary with the features they offer in other ways such as the ways to customize logos and manipulate other aesthetic and functional features. Berlin and Seasons are the two themes offered through the most basic Omeka.net subscription. Since it is logical to conclude they are the most basic of all Omeka themes, they are the best evidence of the rhetorical assumptions underlying Omeka.

Berlin and Seasons are quite similar and vary only in font types and color choices, so this discussion will focus on their similarities. For both themes, the Omeka exhibit administrator is asked to make several selections which will affect the appearance of the project's home page. The specific questions each require a yes or no answer, "Display Featured Item? Display Featured Collection? Display Featured Exhibit? Display Recently Added Items?" These questions reveal important assumptions about the paradigm of the platform and how its developers think their users will configure it. These questions assume a given Omeka project will be made of items that might be regularly updated, that can be designated by the site designer as worthy of being displayed on the home page, based on desired criteria. The project might also contain collections of objects eligible for special display, as well as exhibits, presumably made of items, and somehow relevant to collections.

Even though the abstract possibility of a GLAM exhibit might evoke expansive ideas about creative freedom and endless aesthetic choices, the range of available Omeka themes is usually limited to operating within this narrow range of binary choices. Custom Omeka theming is sometimes described as possible (if not exactly easy) if one has web development skills including facility with PHP, CSS, and HTML, and even easier if one can use tools like Markdown and static web site generators such as Hugo or Jekyll (Graham, 2018). But as soon as the exhibit designer decides to include even basic interactive features as configurable image sliders and timelines, this list can quickly grow to include JavaScript, JSON, and more exotic back-end development tools. This limitation of Omeka and its need for theme customization to accommodate even fairly mundane features of web user engagement was described by Marsh (2017). In addition to themes, Omeka allows for the installation of plugins that can support specialized functions such as image annotation, bulk metadata editing and configuration, and record import and export through APIs (Roy Rosenzweig Center for History and New Media, n.d.b).

It must be pointed out that Omeka customization is supported much more strongly by plugins when it comes to issues of function rather than appearance. Many Omeka sites look and feel eerily similar because the developers decided to focus more energy and ongoing support to the (plugin-driven) functions of digital exhibits and their inner workings of objects, collections, and metadata than to (theme-driven) issues of appearance and means of user engagement. Many sites take on the default platform variables and have one featured item on their home page, along with one featured collection, one featured exhibit, and five recently added items. Although it is possible to create custom Omeka sites that display greater levels of aesthetic sophistication and support for richer user engagement such as *The Story of the Beautiful* and *Wearing Gay History*, this dynamic of valuing function over form and user interactions places Omeka much closer to the object-oriented side of the exhibit orientation continuum. It is not at all difficult to see this characteristic of Omeka as a strength and not a liability, but only if one understands this fact in advance and accepts its inevitable consequences.

Scalar

Scalar is another well-regarded DH platform, created and supported by the Alliance for Networking Visual Culture, University of Southern California. Like Omeka, Scalar is also available as open-source software that can be installed on your organization's server or made available remotely through an account. The Scalar team offers free accounts to anyone who provides "a brief sentence explaining your request. We [also] require that you use an e-mail address affiliated with an academic or cultural heritage institution" (Alliance for Networking Visual Culture, n.d.b.). Unlike Omeka, the versions of the software offered through the self-hosted and remote hosted option are the same, with one important limitation. The remote option limits the exhibit creator to uploading files to the Scalar server that are smaller than two megabytes. Scalar supports the usual DH software tasks of object creation and representation through metadata using various means of visual object surrogates, both embedded within exhibit text and used as illustrations or in arrays that feel more like collections.

There are several main differences between Omeka and Scalar, however. First, Scalar does not rely on the constructs of themes and plugins, so it feels and functions more as a complete, stand-alone DH software application. Another, far more important difference is the degree of freedom afforded by Scalar to exhibit designers and creators to customize how their projects look, feel, and engage with the user. Although it is possible to identify exhibits that are comparably engaging and attractive built with Omeka, it is likely that they do not use either of the "out-of-the-box" themes Berlin or Seasons. The most engaging Omeka exhibits have been subjected to quite a bit of custom theming work (McLeland et al., 2021). In contrast, it is possible to create an exhibit in Scalar that feels quite unique, simply because there are no real "themes" in Scalar. It is left up to the exhibit creator to decide how to organize content in their project, what appears in each content segment, and (within limits) how it will be displayed.

This lack of pre-made organizational structures and openness to creative freedom in Scalar can be seen as either offering a liberating opportunity or presenting an overwhelming burden to different exhibit creators. After working within the Omeka framework of plugins and themes needing customization for almost ten years, I find the more flexible structure of Scalar and its range of visual display options to offer a more supportive conceptual and organizational framework, offering the possibility of richer and more engaging projects. But this openness and lack of standardization can demand a large amount of cognitive and creative overhead from the exhibit builder. Some situations which might lead to Omeka being chosen as the preferred platform include inexperienced exhibit creators needing more structure, staff who are less interested in customization, and organizations which simply do not value rich aesthetic experience or who are in need of a more straightforward, repository-like architecture (Tracy, 2016). Indeed, it is easy to imagine some user communities who would not appreciate the visual rhetoric of Scalar and its capacity to overshadow the more technical aspect of cultural heritage objects behind more interactive features. The next sections of this chapter will explore other points of comparison between these two popular DH platforms.

The "Easiness" of Digital Humanities Tools, Including Omeka and Scalar

Before this comparison can continue, however, it is necessary to address the barriers for entry of these two platforms specifically and DH project tools generally. The Omeka and Scalar development teams make similarly problematic assertions about the difficulty level of their software for administrative end users, that is, the people who build the exhibits, collections, and long-form narratives that are housed within these platforms. Scalar is described as a way to engage in "born-digital, open source, media-rich scholarly publishing that's as easy as blogging" (n.d.b.). Similarly, Omeka is described by the Corporation of Digital Scholarship as "simple to use. Our 'five-minute setup' makes launching an online exhibition as easy as launching a blog. No code knowledge required" (n.d.a). Very strictly speaking, both assertions can be seen as demonstrably true, under certain circumstances. Depending on the way you decide to use either platform, as either self-hosted on a personal or organizational server or through accounts provided by the Corporation of Digital Scholarship (for Omeka) or the Alliance for Networking Visual Culture (for Scalar), it is possible to install or log into both applications simply, with no coding involved. For example, Reclaim Hosting, a major Internet service provider for American academic institutions, allows subscribers to install both Omeka and Scalar with a few clicks after the user provides a few simple pieces of information such as administrator credentials and the domain for the new site (2021a, 2021b). Of course, both applications are open and available from their respective websites or GitHub repositories: https://omeka.org/classic/download/, https://github.com/omeka/Omeka, or https://github.com/anvc/scalar. The options for remote accounts are made available at the respective domains of the platform's originators: www.omeka.net/ or https://scalar.usc.edu/works/.

But logging into a piece of software and expecting to "launch an online exhibition", presumably as a single act, is much like opening a word processing application on a laptop and then expecting a fully formed novel to simply appear on the screen. Software can make many digital projects possible, but it cannot create them. As previous chapters of this book have argued, exhibit creation requires extensive intellectual effort, creativity, trial and error, and tedious data work. In essence, these DH tools are specialized content management systems. Creating the actual content to go into the system to be managed is neither trivial nor easy. Morgan (2018) has catalogued a variety of examples of what she calls "easiness rhetoric" within the documentation of DH tools, including Omeka and Scalar. In the case of DH projects like exhibits, quite a bit of thought and effort is required to create a minimally viable product and none of the work is easy. This critique is not to fault either program so much as it is to observe that the rhetoric of "easy" can set some users up to be surprised and disappointed to find that engaging in DH collection and exhibit work to be much more challenging than they were perhaps led to believe (Long & Leen, 2022; Marsh, 2013; Morgan, 2018).

Omeka's Orientation and Instructional Applications

Direct comparisons of these two platforms are made somewhat difficult by the way that they are described in their respective documentation, aside from ease-of-use assertions. The Scalar development team describes their product as an "authoring and publishing platform that . . . gives authors tools to structure essay- and book-length works in ways that take advantage of the unique capabilities of digital writing, including nested, recursive, and non-linear formats" (Alliance for Networking Visual Culture, n.d.a). The word "exhibit" does not appear in the main description of Scalar, although the first projects listed on the Scalar "showcase" page are indeed digital exhibits. Nevertheless, Scalar is often described more often as a means for authors to create digital versions of long-form literary projects rather than digital exhibits (Ackermans, 2021; Coble et al., 2014; Mihram, & Fletcher, 2019; Wachter, 2021). It is telling that the documentation and the application itself both refer to a single Scalar project as a "book" instead of an exhibit or a project.

In contrast, Omeka is described as "a web publishing platform for sharing digital collections and creating media-rich online exhibits", so its focus on exhibits for information objects as an end goal is straightforward and explicit (Corporation of Digital Scholarship, n.d.a.). Its nature as a display vehicle for objects and content to be used for exhibits is also encoded in its name, described as "a Swahili word meaning to display or layout wares; to speak out; to spread out; to unpack" (Corporation of Digital Scholarship, n.d.b.). At Omeka's ten-year anniversary, its development team observed, "Omeka.net hosts over 45K users and runs nearly 30K sites, and continues to grow" (Brennan, 2018). There is no publicly available data on the number of Scalar projects that have been created, but there is no doubt that it is far less than Omeka's impressive dominance within the DH landscape.

These differences between Omeka and Scalar echo the tension represented by the digital exhibit orientation model described in Chapter 2. Exhibit types can vary between a rhetorical focus on the identification and display of objects versus that of various experiential factors designed to engage with users, including extensive analytic text, interactive features such as timelines, and complex visualizations. It is not a stretch of the imagination to observe that Omeka is closer to the object side of the exhibit continuum with Scalar being oriented more to the needs and interests of users. Indeed, there are many Omeka projects that look and function more as collections than exhibits, including *Florida Memory*, *The Georgetown Slavery Archive*, *The History Harvest*, and the *Lewis & Clark Digital Collections*. Clearly, these resources are provided as a means of object search and discovery, more than complex analysis or argument. Furthermore, many, if not most, of the 30,000 Omeka projects referenced earlier start as student exercises to learn the methods of metadata-driven object representation, and not as full-blown DH projects, *per se*. While both Omeka and Scalar offer free accounts that include exhibit hosting, the Omeka option is much more limited and thus is more appropriate for the beginner who needs to directly engage in the tasks of object representation to learn about their role in librarianship, archives, or general web-based information management.

Learning about the principles of metadata schemata in a classroom-based lecture is one (very useful and valuable) thing but putting those principles into action with real data objects is something else entirely. In this context, options for customizing an exhibit interface and introducing additional analytic tools for the end user to explore would only introduce unneeded complexity and potential distraction from the instructional task at hand. If an instructor uses Omeka to teach metadata implementation and management, its central focus on and support for these tasks is paramount. Many thoughtful pieces on the value of Omeka as a pedagogical device for librarianship and archival studies center on this aspect of Omeka as its primary value and not as a vehicle for creating polished exhibits (Allred, 2017; Cuenca & Kowaleski, 2018; Hoelscher, 2019; Kilroy-Ewbank, 2018; Marsh, 2013; Sibaja, 2017). Let us recall the observation made by the author about her own students' projects, "so far the results of the online exhibits have been mostly disastrous. As a whole, the exhibits are terrible. . . . They have clunky navigation, lack any elegance in design and often are just plain boring" (Marsh, 2013, p. 280). So one needs to be realistic and accept that using exhibit software to teach metadata standards and implementation will not result in polished student exhibits, in all likelihood.

These results might be understandable, if not altogether acceptable, if using the "out-of-the-box" Omeka platform allowed students to develop a sound understanding of the value of metadata, as well as a tentative grasp on its implementation. It is therefore significant that some scholars are beginning to question this central value of Omeka. Maron and Feinberg correctly observe that "Omeka is supposed to enable a novice to easily create information collections that adhere to the conventions espoused by professionals", but in actuality they find that "in terms of actions regarding Dublin Core [its metadata standard], Omeka does not enable its implementation according to established best practices" (2018, pp. 679, 688). This gap between rhetorical claims and actual implementation is somewhat concerning. It means that instructors using Omeka as an educational tool should not rely on it alone to demonstrate good metadata practice relying on the Dublin Core standard.

It should also be pointed that despite Omeka's reputation as being especially strong at metadata support, Scalar also has pre-built support for the Dublin Core standard as well as the International Press Telecommunications Council (IPTC) photo standard, Darwin Core for biological content, the VRA ontology for images, and several other metadata schemata. But the central point remains that the main strength of Omeka lies in its strong support for the tasks required for the object side of digital exhibit orientation. It is possible to enrich Omeka sites with more user-oriented aspects of digital engagement, but it takes some extra design skill and technical effort to do so (Marsh, 2017).

Omeka Versus Scalar

Clearly, both platforms can support good exhibit work that can result in attractive and usable digital projects. If you are directed to use one or the other by your organization and have little say in the choice, you will be well supported by either platform. If I had to choose one application over the other, however, I would select Scalar for the following reasons:

1 As stated earlier, Scalar does not use themes or plugins, so it feels more like an integrated, stand-alone software platform that does not require constant add-ons that sometimes resemble a functional patchwork quilt held together by unstable connections. When you use Scalar, it is not necessary to wonder if an outside volunteer developer created a (well-built, sustained) plugin that will allow you to perform a task. Almost any task that a beginning exhibit creator would need to perform is already well-modeled and supported directly in the interface. Additionally, one installation of Scalar on your or your organization's server can support multiple exhibits which can all be customized so they look and function differently. The classic version of Omeka can support only one exhibit per installation; Omeka S needs to be used for multiple projects.
2 The basic aesthetic options of Scalar allow for more attractive and sophisticated front-end designs than the vast majority of Omeka themes. Scalar assumes that you want to create immersive experiences such as those presented by narrative and data visualizations, enriched by high-resolution images, smooth and intuitive navigation, and flexible presentation options. These elements are offered in highly customizable ways so they can be used in the service of presenting an engrossing narrative. The more traditional layouts of Omeka themes result in exhibit sites that resemble traditional websites more than interactive digital experiences. That may be the better option for some creators and organizations that favor more traditional web delivery systems, however.
3 Scalar assumes that it is just as important to present material to the reader in an interesting and engaging way as it is to act as a content management system adhering to metadata standards and supporting good information management practices. Often Omeka seems to put issues of user experience and aesthetics into a category of lessor importance. The Scalar team seems to recognize more fully that a DH platform needs to perform all these jobs well.

4 Finally, Scalar lets the exhibit creator determine the design of their project with its essential "blank book" architecture that allows for a great deal of customization. This puts a higher burden on the exhibit designer, but the degree of freedom it supports and the resulting projects it can facilitate are well worth it.

Other DH Platforms

There are other tools available that can be used for DH work. They generally fall into one of these categories:

1 Applications created as add-ons for larger repository management platforms. An example is the Spotlight digital exhibit plugin designed to be used with the Blacklight search and discovery interface application (Project Blacklight, n.d.). Both tools require enterprise-level technical infrastructure and programming support and are thus not relevant for most small cultural heritage organizations.
2 Modified instances of traditional CMS like WordPress and Drupal. Both options would also require a fair amount of custom coding and thus do not present realistic choices for resource-limited small GLAM organizations. Even proponents of this method have reconsidered it because it ties a DH-focused mission to a tool type that is essentially a generic CMS that can make its return-on-investment ratio not worth the effort, even for the author of *Drupal for Humanists* (Dombrowski, 2019). Dombrowski also points out that these CMS systems are often sitting atop bloated database-dependent software architecture and are "riddled with security holes" (2022), so spending a great deal of time, effort, and money customizing WordPress or Drupal to try and turn either CMS into a DH system is not advisable.
3 Highly specialized platforms such as ArcGIS StoryMaps that rely on a rhetorical foundation of geographically driven narrative. Unlike other platforms featured in this chapter, StoryMaps requires a subscription purchase that is suited to larger, better-funded institutions (Esri, n.d.). In any event, only a minority of digital exhibits can be recast as geographical narratives, so StoryMaps would not be a usable candidate for many exhibit creators.
4 Products that have arisen out of the minimal computing movement such as Ed (Torrent et al., n.d.), Wax (Nyröp & Gil, 2019), and CollectionBuilder (University of Idaho Library, n.d.). The minimal computing construct was the focus of a recent special issue of *Digital Humanities Quarterly*. Authors in this issue included Alex Gil, generally credited as starting the minimal movement when he posed the provocative question to DH scholars, "what do we need?" (2015). Gil's work is welcome for its acknowledgment that information workers doing DH work face barriers that are real, often systemic, and always resistant to quick interventions. But the central idea behind the movement is essentially that digital projects should use tools that are customized

to meet only the essential needs of a given project using as minimal software architecture as possible (Risam & Gil, 2022). This ethic has, in turn, resulted in the conclusion that a DH project following the minimal computing philosophy should use tools that usually require a fair amount of technical skill in things such as use of the command line, GitHub, HTML, CSS, JavaScript, Markdown, Liquid, Jekyll, Ruby, and/or Rake. Or, in the words of Quinn Dombrowski in the same issue, "minimizing computing maximizes labor" (2022).

Dombrowski's perspective on the true overhead of such "do-it-yourself" DH computing is worth quoting at length:

> To use the most common minimal computing workflow, based on the Jekyll static site generation software, the scholar [or other exhibit creator] would need to install the Ruby programming language, along with a number of Ruby gems using the command line, then install Jekyll. Next, they would need to figure out what changes need to be made to the _config.yml file (without breaking it altogether with a stray space character), and start authoring content in Markdown—potentially while modifying the front matter variables and writing additional Liquid and HTML to use those variables in the templates. Making any layout or design changes involves figuring out where these changes have to go within numerous possible SASS files. Finally, the scholar would need to generate the output HTML using the command line, and determine which errors and warnings need to be addressed in order for the site to function and which can be safely ignored. This workflow is daunting even for the type of digital humanities practitioner who is not in a developer role as such but frequently handles other kinds of web development tasks and basic coding, along with project and program management (e.g., roles commonly found in library digital scholarship centers). . . . Prioritizing minimal computing—whether for environmental, techno-aesthetic, or sustainability reasons—risks leaving behind scholars who lack the technical expertise or ongoing support to manage multiple facets of technical web development.
>
> (2022)

Unless you have extensive skill in do-it-yourself software development, the only way to build digital exhibits using this philosophy and procedural framework would be to hire an outside developer and possibly a designer. Adopting the minimal computing philosophy requires possession of resources and organizational empowerment that have never been available to me or to many professionals working in GLAM organizations.

One can argue truthfully that DH platforms such as Omeka and Scalar are perhaps slightly bloated with unneeded features and might raise preservation and sustainability issues. On the other hand, it is simply unrealistic and somewhat insulting to expect every DH professional to be equally equipped to perform exhibit design, content creation, audience analysis, and information management tasks, and then to demand they build a site from a minimal pre-existing framework using the tools of professional software developers. Until a better GUI-based resource becomes available to the cultural heritage information sector, my recommended exhibit and project platforms are Scalar or Omeka.

Digital and Physical Exhibits Discussed in This Chapter

Apron Strings and Kitchen Sinks
Emily Marsh
National Agricultural Library, US Department of Agriculture
www.nal.usda.gov/exhibits/ipd/apronsandkitchens/

Five Hundred Years of Women's Work: The Lisa Unger Baskin Collection
Michael Daul
Duke University Libraries
https://exhibits.library.duke.edu/exhibits/show/baskin/introduction

Florida Memory
State Library and Archives of Florida
www.floridamemory.com/

The Georgetown Slavery Archive
Georgetown University Working Group on Slavery, Memory, and Reconciliation
http://slaveryarchive.georgetown.edu/

The History Harvest
Department of History, University of Nebraska-Lincoln
https://historyharvest.unl.edu/

Lewis & Clark Digital Collections
Aubrey R. Watzek Library Archives & Special Collections, Lewis & Clark College
http://digitalcollections.lclark.edu/
Recollection Wisconsin Online Exhibits
https://recollectionwisconsin.org/category/online-exhibits

The Story of the Beautiful
Freer Gallery of Art, Arthur M. Sackler Gallery, Smithsonian National Museum of Asian Art, and Wayne State University's Library System
http://peacockroom.wayne.edu/

Wearing Gay History
Eric Nolan Gonzaba, Creator; Amanda Regan, Digital Design Consultant, George Mason University
http://wearinggayhistory.com/

References

Ackermans, H. (2021). Genre-bending on an academic platform: Three creative works on Scalar. In *Proceedings of the 32nd ACM conference on hypertext and social media (HT'21)* (pp. 211–215). New York: Association for Computing Machinery. https://doi.org/10.1145/3465336.3475099.

Alliance for Networking Visual Culture. (n.d.a). *About Scalar*. https://scalar.me/anvc/scalar/features/.

Alliance for Networking Visual Culture. (n.d.b). *Contact*. https://scalar.me/anvc/contact/.

Alliance for Networking Visual Culture. (n.d.c). *Scalar 2 user guide*. https://scalar.usc.edu/works/guide2/index.

Allred, J. (2017). A professor goes overboard with Omeka and DH box. *The Journal of Interactive Technology and Pedagogy*. https://jitp.commons.gc.cuny.edu/a-professor-goes-overboard-with-omeka-and-dh-box/.

Bedford, D. (2021). *Knowledge architectures: Structures and semantics*. London: Routledge.

Brennan, S. (2018). Omeka now public for 10 years. *Omeka News*. https://omeka.org/news/2018/02/20/omeka-now-public-10-years/.

Coble, Z., Potvin, S., & Shirazi, R. (2014). Process as product: Scholarly communication experiments in the digital humanities. *Journal of Librarianship and Scholarly Communication*, *2*(3), eP1137. https://doi.org/10.7710/2162-3309.1137.

Cohen, D. (2008, February 20). *Introducing Omeka*. http://dancohen.org/2008/02/20/introducing-omeka/.

Corporation for Digital Scholarship. (n.d.a). *Omeka Classic*. https://omeka.org/classic/.

Corporation for Digital Scholarship. (n.d.b). *Omeka Classic user manual*. https://omeka.org/classic/docs/.

Cuenca, E. L., & Kowaleski, M. (2018). Omeka and other digital platforms for undergraduate research projects on the middle ages. *Digital Medievalist*, *11*(1), 1–21. http://doi.org/10.16995/dm.69.

Dombrowski, Q. (2019, November 8). *Sorry for all the Drupal: Reflections on the 3rd anniversary of 'Drupal for Humanists'*. https://quinndombrowski.com/blog/2019/11/08/sorry-all-drupal-reflections-3rd-anniversary-drupal-humanists/.

Dombrowski, Q. (2022). Minimizing computing maximizes labor. *Digital Humanities Quarterly*, *16*(2). www.digitalhumanities.org/dhq/vol/16/2/000594/000594.html.

Drucker, J. (2021). *The digital humanities coursebook: An introduction to digital methods for research and scholarship*. London: Routledge.

Drucker, J., & Svensson, P. B. (2016). The why and how of middleware. *Digital Humanities Quarterly*, *10*(2). www.digitalhumanities.org/dhq/vol/10/2/000248/000248.html.

Esri. (n.d.). *ArcGIS StoryMaps overview*. www.esri.com/en-us/arcgis/products/arcgis-storymaps/overview.

Gardiner, E. (2015). *The digital humanities: A primer for students and scholars*. Cambridge: Cambridge University Press.

Gartner, R. (2021). *Metadata in the digital library: Building an integrated strategy with XML*. London: Facet Publications.

Gil, A. (2015, May 21). *The user, the learner and the machines we make*. https://go-dh.github.io/mincomp/thoughts/2015/05/21/user-vs-learner/.

Gilliland, A. J. (2016). Setting the stage. In M. Baca (Ed.), *Introduction to metadata* (3rd ed.). Los Angeles, CA: Getty Research Institute. www.getty.edu/publications/intrometadata/setting-the-stage/.

Golub, K., & Liu, Y.-H. (2022). *Information and knowledge organisation in digital humanities: Global perspectives*. London: Routledge.

Graham, S. (2018, March 9). Using a static site generator to make a nicer Omeka front page. *Electric Archeology*. https://electricarchaeology.ca/2018/03/09/using-a-static-site-generator-to-make-a-nicer-omeka-front-page/.

Hoelscher, C. (2019). Constructing history: A student-created public history exhibit using Omeka. *Case Studies on Teaching with Primary Sources*. Case Study #11. https://www2.archivists.org/publications/epubs/Case-Studies-Teaching-With-Primary-Sources.

Horodyski, J. (2022). *Metadata matters*. Boca Raton, FL: Auerbach Publications.

Kilroy-Ewbank, L. G. (2018). Doing digital art history in a pre-Columbian art survey class: Creating an Omeka exhibition around the Mixtec Codex Zouche-Nuttall. *The Journal of Interactive Technology and Pedagogy, 12*. https://jitp.commons.gc.cuny.edu/doing-digital-art-history-in-a-pre-columbian-art-survey-class-creating-an-omeka-exhibition-around-the-mixtec-codex-zouche-nuttall/.

Long, C., & Leen, D. (2022, July 13). Reflection on the use of Scalar. In *The River-side: Reflections on research collections*. Cork: University College Cork Library. https://blogs.ucc.ie/wordpress/theriverside/2022/07/13/reflection-on-the-use-of-scalar/.

Maron, D., & Feinberg, M. (2018). What does it mean to adopt a metadata standard? A case study of Omeka and the Dublin Core. *Journal of Documentation*, *74*(4), 674–691. https://doi.org/10.1108/JD-06-2017-0095.

Marsh, A. C. (2013). Omeka in the classroom: The challenges of teaching material culture in a digital world. *Literary and Linguistic Computing*, *28*(2), 279–282. https://doi.org/10.1093/llc/fqs068.

Marsh, E. (2017). Chickens, aprons, markets, and cans: How the National Agricultural Library uses Omeka as its content management system for digital exhibits. *Digital Library Perspectives*, *33*(4), 361–377. https://doi.org/10.1108/DLP-03-2017-0009.

Marsh, E. (2022). *Different views of object-level metadata for Work Clothes for Women in an exhibit timeline: The "bite", from an item view within an exhibit timeline, the "snack", from the full item record in the exhibit, and from the item's original Internet Archive record, the "meal"* [Infographic]. https://emily-marsh.com/Digital_Exhibits_for_Cultural_Institutions/Figure_7.1.jpg.

McLeland, C., Chalmers, A., & Bibb, J. (2021). Establishing an Omeka digital exhibits presence: Collaboration and customization. *Library Faculty Presentations & Publications, 95*. https://digitalcommons.unf.edu/library_facpub/95.

Mihram, D., & Fletcher, C. (2019). USC Digital Voltaire: Centering digital humanities in the traditions of library and archival science. *Portal: Libraries and the Academy*, *19*(1), 7–17. https://doi.org/10.1353/pla.2019.0001.

Miller, S. J. (2022). *Metadata for digital collections* (2nd ed.). Chicago, IL: ALA Neal-Schuman.

Morgan, P. C. (2018). The consequences of framing digital humanities tools as easy to use. *College & Undergraduate Libraries*, *25*(3), 211–231. https://doi.org/10.1080/10691316.2018.1480440.

Nyröp, M., & Gil, A. (2019). *Wax*. https://minicomp.github.io/wax/.

O'Flahavan, L. (n.d.). The bite, the snack, and the meal: How to feed content-hungry site visitors. *E-Write*. https://ewriteonline.com/bite-snack-and-meal-how-to-feed-content-hungry-site-visitors/.

Project Blacklight. (n.d.). *Blacklight*. https://projectblacklight.org/.

Reclaim Hosting. (2021a). *Installing Omeka Classic on Reclaim Hosting*. https://support.reclaimhosting.com/hc/en-us/articles/1500005712342-Installing-Omeka-Classic-on-Reclaim-Hosting.

Reclaim Hosting. (2021b). *Installing Scalar*. https://support.reclaimhosting.com/hc/en-us/articles/1500005543242-Installing-Scalar.

Riley, J. (2017). *Understanding metadata: What is metadata, and what is it for? NISO primer series*. Baltimore, MD: National Information Standards Organization. http://groups.niso.org/higherlogic/ws/public/download/17446/Understanding%20Metadata.pdf.

Risam, R., & Gil, A. (2022). Introduction: The questions of minimal computing. *Digital Humanities Quarterly*, *16*(2). www.digitalhumanities.org/dhq/vol/16/2/000646/000646.html.

Roman, G. T. (2018). Scalar and Omeka. *The Journal of the Society of Architectural Historians*, *77*(1), 122–123. https://doi.org/10.1525/jsah.2018.77.1.122.

Roy Rosenzweig Center for History and New Media. (n.d.a). *Omeka*. https://rrchnm.org/portfolio-item/omeka/.

Roy Rosenzweig Center for History and New Media. (n.d.b). *Omeka Classic plugins*. https://omeka.org/classic/plugins/.

Russell, J., & Hensley, M. (2017). Beyond buttonology: Digital humanities, digital pedagogy, and the ACRL framework. *College & Research Libraries News*, *78*(11), 588. https://doi.org/10.5860/crln.78.11.588.

Sibaja, R. (2017). Omeka to ¡Animales! Building a digital repository of research on Argentine soccer. *Journal of Sport History*, *44*(2), 209–224. https://doi.org/10.5406/jsporthistory.44.2.0209.

Torrent, S. A., Catapano, T., Gil, A., & Gillium, J. (n.d.). *Ed*. https://elotroalex.github.io/ed/.

Tracy, D. G. (2016). Assessing digital humanities tools: Use of Scalar at a research university. *portal: Libraries and the* Academy, *16*(1), 163–189. https://doi.org/10.1353/pla.2016.0004.

University of Idaho Library. (n. d.). *CollectionBuilder*. https://collectionbuilder.github.io/.

Urberg, M. (2020). Digital humanities projects and standards: Let's get this conversation started! *Information Services & Use*, *40*(3), 213–224. http://dx.doi.org/10.3233/ISU-200097.

Wachter, C. (2021). Publishing complexity in the digital humanities. *magazén*, *2*(1), 103–118. http://doi.org/10.30687/mag/2724-3923/2021/03/004.

Wachuta, J. (2016, March 25). Metadata on exhibit. *PublicHistory.Media*. https://publichistory.media/2016/03/25/metadata-on-exhibit/.

8 Digital Exhibits, Creativity, & Originality

Why talk about creativity? What tools might cultural knowledge workers such as librarians and archivists have at hand that would fuel the creative effort required for making a digital exhibit? This chapter is focused on process more than product. It asserts that the substantive tasks that go into making an effective exhibit require some degree of creativity. The first question that should be addressed is what is meant by "creativity" generally and in this context? This chapter will open with a brief, selective tour of several of models of creativity relevant to building digital exhibits for cultural heritage organizations. These theories will be applied to better understand and engage with some common creative challenges often encountered within this kind of work. Next, some examples of generic metaphors used in digital and physical exhibits as organizing structures will be analyzed as sources of inspiration. This chapter will look at exhibit work as an inherently creative practice and what that perspective means on both individual and institutional levels. Throughout the chapter points will be illustrated through some notable digital and physical exhibits that can serve as models and sources of inspiration.

What Is Creativity?

In keeping with this book's overall reliance on theory to understand, support, and guide exhibit work and the exhibit creator, this chapter will start with a short review of selected views of creativity as a psychological phenomenon. Robert W. Weisberg's perspective will be useful for this discussion of the role of creativity in exhibit work both for its cogent insights and intellectual clarity (2006, 2020). Weisberg traces the history of creativity research and concludes that much of it relies on definitions that are problematic, if not fundamentally flawed. For example, the common two-factor "standard" definition of creativity includes a requirement of novelty and value (Runco & Jaeger, 2012; Sternberg & Kaufman, 2010). For a given work to be seen as creative, it must be perceived as being both new and displaying value to some entity in some way. The final judge of newness and value can come from a community of peers and/or a critical mass of influential gatekeepers such as critics, museum curators, and gallery owners (in the case of artists), journal editors, publishers, and academics (in the case of most scholars

DOI:10.4324/9781003301493-8

of any field), or the Twittersphere, Instagrammers, and TikTokers (in the case of almost everyone on social media).

Needless to say, the judgments of these various parties are neither infallible nor immune from racism, sexism, heteronormativity, professional insularity, errors of judgment, and changes in fashion and taste. It has always been the case that members of marginalized groups have had to fight long, difficult campaigns to get the barest recognition of the value of their work from standard gatekeepers. Clearly this two-factor definition of creativity is not a valid, reliable metric of anything other than the degree to which a work is held in esteem by a given set of cultural gatekeepers at a specific point in time and in a specific context.

Prominent examples of shifting judgments of value are easy to find in the world of the visual arts, including almost all female artists (Nochlin, 1971), almost all Black American artists (Driskell, 1976), and some notable case studies in critical reappraisal such as that of Betye Saar (Dallow & Matilsky, 2005), the Gee's Bend Quilt creators (Sohan, 2015), Andrew Wyeth (Cateforis, 2014), and, inevitably, Jeff Koons (Diehl, 2014). These simple examples show how critical judgments of creative output, while of enormous interest, legitimacy, and importance, cannot be accepted as neutral assessments of some abstract notion of value. Instead, they are as just as subjective, personal, and open to changing tastes and popularity as the artistic works themselves and should be interrogated accordingly. As argued by Kaufman and Beghetto, "despite our best guesses about what will be considered eminently creative across time, it is often hard to distinguish fashions and fads from permanent contributions" (2009, p. 4).

After discharging the construct of objective value from his consideration of creativity, Weinberg argues that "a creative work [is] one that is *novel* and is *produced intentionally* in response to the situation" (2020, p. 51). Weinberg argues correctly that the addition of intentionality to the definition is necessary to distinguish work that is indeed novel, but otherwise merely bizarre. A truly creative work needs to be both new in some way and the product of conscious intention or, put another way, directed artistic vision. This vision, backed up by conscious artistic intention differentiates entities that are simply odd from works of creativity that harness expressions of strangeness or bizarreness in service of a larger artistic program. It could be argued that entire genres of art are defined specifically by this type of creative oddity including Dadaism, Surrealism, Performance Art, Cubism, Abstract Expressionism, Outsider Art, Conceptual Art, and Minimalism. Of course, what was seen as odd or bizarre at one time can quickly take on the air of the avant-garde, and then the mainstream, and finally, that of the clichéd as time and popular taste change and move on.

While visual artists work to intentionally carry out a personal vision, the creator of a digital exhibit needs to carry out a different type of program. In this case, the "situation" in Weinberg's definition of creativity is to create an intentional environment to display and explain the selected objects of a given cultural heritage organization. Further, a truly creative exhibit within this paradigm would also create an environment that was somehow novel or fresh. I agree with Weinberg's definition and argue that these two goals of freshness and intention are both eminently achievable within the activity of digital exhibit building. I also think that exhibits which fulfill both goals should be seen as deserving of the designation of serious creative work, and thus eligible for the status that entails. Presently many scholars from multiple disciplines have advocated for the academy to accept and recognize various digital projects as being worthy of the status of "scholarship", and thus eligible to support efforts such as tenure and promotion application packages (Cabrera et al., 2018; Day et al., 2013; Weller, 2012).

Some metrics of value for digital exhibits can be seen implicitly within exhibit building guides and the few entities which award recognition for this kind of project. For example, the Katharine Kyes Leab and Daniel J. Leab American Book Prices Current Exhibition Catalogue Awards issue criteria for their digital exhibit awards (Rare Books and Manuscripts Section, Association of College and Research Libraries, n.d.). Their evaluation criteria for digital exhibits are divided into two groups: intellectual content and design. The first element listed under each group is the same: originality. Alas, we return to the problem of subjectivity and gatekeepers. At present the intellectual and professional infrastructure that would support digital scholarship, including exhibits, is still somewhat limited. Thus, there are few gatekeepers who could definitively and authoritatively confer the designation of "originality" and "intention" backed up with the type of power like that conferred upon the peer review process for conference presentations and scholarly publications. But the trendlines certainly look like digital projects and will only increase in popularity and sophistication, so this situation will probably change accordingly.

Creativity for Digital Exhibits: The Three "Cs"

In any event, this short review of Weisberg's definition of creativity leads to a discussion of his associated construct of "inside-the-box" thinking. The most basic explanation of this idea is that new creative insight is based upon existing ideas, "creative thinking is based on *continuity with the past*" (2020, p. 14). New creative ideas are created based on thoughtful application and modification of existing paradigms, methods, and ideas. Using multiple case studies and clear analysis of faulty theories, Weisberg argues forcefully that the idea that true creativity can only be produced by leaps into the unknown made by geniuses is false. He illustrates ways that the same procedures they use to arrive at creative solutions to problems are available to us all. Creative thinking uses the very same processes as every day "common" thinking, simply applied to a novel endpoint.

There are degrees of creativity, however; not every new idea is an expression of genius. The common acts of variation of which we are all capable (e.g., adding spice to a recipe, driving a novel route to a destination) are expressions of "everyday" creativity (Villanova & eCunha, 2020) or "Little-C" creativity (Kaufman & Beghetto, 2009). Creative effort and work that merits inclusion into the "Big-C" or exceptional category is described as "major productions of scientific, technological, social, or artistic importance [such as] Darwin's theory of evolution; the invention of the printing press; Picasso's *Guernica* painting; the development of the double helix model of DNA" (Gilhooly & Gilhooly, 2021, p. 22).

Occupying a liminal space that is neither strictly inside or outside of the box is "Pro-C" creativity, which "represents the developmental and effortful progression beyond Little-C (but that has not yet attained Big-C status)" (Kaufman & Beghetto, 2009, p. 5). As described by Weisberg,

> [T]he next level of creative achievement is "professional creativity" . . . advances made by people in their professional activities. Pro-C products are significant advances, but they do not have the wide-ranging transformative effects on the world that Big-C advances do. A scientist, for example, might design an experiment to test a prediction from an important new theory. Designing that experiment is an act of Pro-C creativity. Creating the significant new theory was Big-C creativity.
>
> (2020, pp. 113–114)

Clearly, creating a digital exhibit falls somewhere in this middle space of Pro-C work. It is neither at the everyday, Little-C level of either a personal hobby or serious leisure (Stebbins, 2020), nor generally comparable to the grand accomplishments associated with Big-C creativity. It needs to be observed, however, that Weisberg argues correctly that many of the component processes and actions that lead to Big-C productions are available to those of us toiling in within the category of Pro-C creative work. Finally, and most importantly, Pro-C work benefits from the training and professional practices of the creators involved in this work. Thus, library and archival exhibits benefit from the professional knowledge of their creators: librarians, archivists, and other information workers. These Pro-C skills include:

- Understanding exhibit users' information needs, behaviors, and interests
- Knowledge of metadata principles that models exhibit materials in a way that connects the material to its intended audiences
- Expertise in current principles of web design and information architecture
- Library and archival research skills
- Judgment of information source quality and reliability
- Experience in the analysis of information and its synthesis into new forms
- Ability to create a focused information project that conveys a singular point of view that is grounded in a thoughtful understanding of the relevant information landscape and potential audiences

For those of us in the information professions, engaging in these types of familiar activities counts as "thinking inside the box".

It would be reasonable to wonder what difference all this makes to exhibit practice. Who cares if exhibit creation is Little-C, Pro-C, Big-C, or no C at all? What will be gained by describing this work as creative in this very specific way? It is important to acknowledge and support the work required by serious digital projects such as exhibits. While not on the order of creativity required by such digital scholarship as thematic research collections (Palmer, 2004; Fenlon, 2017), interactive scholarly work (Meeks & Grossner, 2012), or flat-out narratives (Murray, 1997), exhibits are worthy of attention and should be judged as legitimate creative works. It is worthwhile to consider what kind of creativity is necessary for exhibits. It makes sense to recognize that making a conceptually legitimate, thoughtfully designed exhibit requires a degree of creativity that sits somewhere between the mundane (Little-C) and the divine (Big-C) that sits at the high functioning professional level of Pro-C.

In order to provide support for the creators of digital exhibits, it would be useful to review some of the procedures of creativity that Weisberg identifies as being relevant to Pro-C work. Engaging with these processes in a direct, thoughtful way can greatly ease the burden of finding entry points into a given set of exhibit objects which can serve as organizing themes or display methods that can help to shape your exhibit.

Thinking and Boxes and Metaphors: Inside and Outside

After Weisberg demythologizes creative work as something that occurs inside the box of existing knowledge applied in a new way, he goes on to describe the essential factors of creativity as:

1 The ability to see and apply both "near" and "far" analogies thoughtfully
2 The ability to develop new ideas from past practice
3 The ability to develop and apply insights
4 The ability to use innate talent
5 The ability to use ideas which can arise from unconscious processes
6 The possibility of a complex, non-determinative relationship between creativity and psychopathology

Clearly, the last two factors of unconscious processing and pathology are beyond the scope of this book and will not be addressed, along with the role of innate talent. Weisberg's entire thesis of inside-the-box thinking actually de-emphasizes the importance of grand flashes of insight arising from innate talent.

The first three factors are variations on the construct of cognitive transfer: applying some unit of knowledge (an analogy, an idea, an insight) from one situation to another. Cognitive transfer techniques and artifacts have been described as being "involved in all learning, remembering, problem solving and cognitive activities" (McKeachie, 1987, p. 707). They have been studied extensively by a variety of researchers, especially cognitive psychologists for the value they may have in the learning process. One could argue that the ability to see and apply relevant analogies, apply past experience to current practice, and develop insight are hallmark activities of nearly every type of work requiring some level of expertise. That observation touches upon the central nerve of Weisberg's entire thesis: Creativity depends on the types of thinking used every day, "inside-the-box". Within the context or "box" of library and information studies, digital humanities, and museum studies, these are merely some of the critical abilities that must be used on a regular basis. This means that engaging in the kinds of creative work necessary for digital exhibit design and creation is not only within our grasp but also arguably situated in the metaphorical center of relationships between materials and users, and bringing one to the other.

Our focus will narrow onto the subtopics of analogy and metaphor, their commonality in everyday life, ways to apply metaphor in exhibit work, and some suggestions for fostering creativity, on both individual and organization levels.

Everyday Metaphor

Perhaps the most well-known proponents of the centrality of analogy and metaphor in every day, "inside-the-box" thinking are George Lakoff and Mark Johnson. Their work on the linguistic manifestations of common cognitive patterns led them to conclude "that most of our ordinary conceptual system is metaphorical in nature" (1980, p. 4). So, far from being simply a poetic device, metaphor and analogy often govern how we speak and think about almost everything. The canonical example is "argument as war". If one thinks of an argument in terms of a war, then every act and utterance is framed within that context. Thus, one can "win" or "lose" an argument. Utterances are not simple speech acts but are seen as "attacks". An attack is judged as being "on" or "off" target. People engaged in argument are combatants. This work echoes that of Marvin Minsky and his idea of cognitive frames as governing both human thought and, potentially, computerized implementations of artificial intelligence (1975).

A charming example of this use of metaphor to structure a physical library display lies in the University of Wisconsin Libraries' "Blind Date with a Book Display" shown in Figure 8.1. Created for Valentine's Day and designed by student Syaza Noor Azmi, the display changes the expected framing of a Valentine book from being about love to a Valentine book as being the love object itself. To further the metaphor, the book as love object is shielded from view and described in the first person using intriguing phrases such as "I'm the strong and silent type" and "You may have seen me on a film screen, but I'm better on paper", thereby completing the metaphorical frame by comparing the prospect of a user checking the book out to acceptance of a blind date (University of Wisconsin-Madison Libraries, 2017).

The other two "every day" transfer skills of applying past experience to create new ideas and develop new insights are more difficult to illustrate with examples from existing digital exhibits, simply because there is no easy way to isolate them simply by external examination of the final product. It is difficult or impossible to determine how a creator applied cognitive transfer techniques to build a digital exhibit simply by examining the exhibit itself.

But we can learn a bit more by returning to the literature on creativity and cognitive transfer. In essence, these elements of the transfer process can be seen as two sides of a single coin: identification and application of past experience

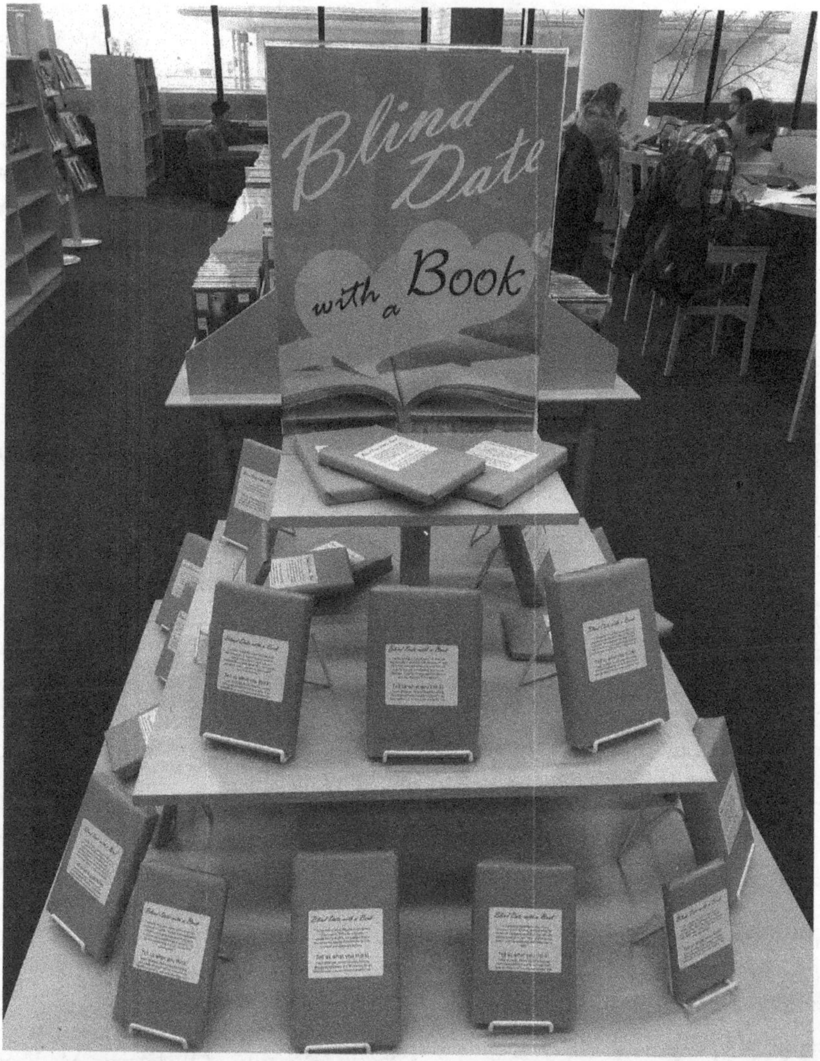

Figure 8.1 *Blind Date with a Book Display in Open Book* by University of Wisconsin-Madison Libraries is used under the Creative Commons Attribution 2.0 Generic License (CC BY 2.0)

through persistent trial and error and a perception of something new in the form of an insight. Lucas and Nordgren make the intriguing point that "emerging research suggests people's lay beliefs may not adequately reflect both routes. We propose that people exhibit an insight bias, such that they undervalue persistence and overvalue insight in the creative process" (2021, p. 6).

The stereotype that creativity is essentially a reactive, straightforward process of merely waiting for an "A-ha!" moment to arrive is termed insight bias.

"Generating ideas via insight feels less effortful and less mentally exhausting than generating ideas via persistence. This more pleasant experience of insight, versus persistence, leads people to think and feel more positively about insight" (Lucas & Nordgren, 2021, p. 6). Indeed, this is a common stereotype that is unfortunately replicated in much of the creativity literature when it places an emphasis on piercing the opaque veil that surrounds the myth of creative genius. The common suggestion to apply "out-of-the-box" thinking to more commonplace, non-artistic situations requiring creativity also models the essential situation within a flawed structure (de Bono, 1970; Gawain, 2008; Gladwell, 2009; Randel, 2010). There is a presumption that creativity requires the innovator to reach outside of the "box" of normal cognitive practice to access the unfamiliar, exotic tools needed to complete the job, all while experiencing an intense flash of insight. Sometimes these authors claim that they are actually helping the reader to reach inside to tap their own "inner" creativity, but often they are really claiming that the reader needs to think and act somehow differently, else why buy their books?

In any event, the important point to take from this work is that creativity is already in abundant use in everyday acts of human thought and speech occurring all around us. This is equally true for information professionals in GLAM and cultural heritage organizations, especially for those staff who aim to serve and interact directly with their user communities. It is up to the thoughtful exhibit maker to identify, select, and apply useful artifacts such as metaphors and cognitive frames to power exhibit structure when appropriate. The following examples illustrate how general and specific organizing structures are used to create well-modeled digital exhibits and associated interactive tools.

Note: It is critical that the exhibit creator deploy these tools with a specific purpose aside from a desire to add "interactivity" or "excitement" to a project or simply because a plugin or tool is available. If your users cannot ascertain the rhetorical purpose behind a given timeline, map, or other organizing or presentation device, then their efforts to interact with your content might instead be perceived as mere clicking, or scrolling, or zooming with little purpose and will be abandoned quickly. Your choices to use a given information device should be made just as carefully and consciously as your content selections.

Organizing Metaphor: Timelines

It should be observed that any exhibit which uses a digital timeline wherein events are mapped onto a linear, left-to-right display is employing the "time is space" metaphor of Western culture analyzed by Lakoff (1993). Time is an abstract concept even though the convention of representing the past as a physical space that can be "behind" us while the future is "ahead" of us is an efficient metaphor that allows simple tools like timelines and planes to illustrate significant events in a given digital exhibit space. A prominent example of a digital resource driven by time as a general and fundamental organizing principle is *The Museum of the World* exhibit, which allows visitors to "discover objects from the British Museum's collection from prehistory to the present using the most advanced WebGL (Web Graphics Library) technology available" (British Museum, n.d.). Museum object records are represented as dots arranged on a two-dimensional, interactive plane mapped by space and time. The Metropolitan Museum's *Heilbrunn Timeline of Art History* offers almost 300 chronologies of art organized by location and time.

Timelines need to be used with care, however. As observed by Lubar,

> The timeline carries with it assumptions about the narrative structure of history, about the primacy of chronological understanding, and about progress. It makes it seem as though history is a path to the present. More to the point, it hides those assumptions remarkably well. Timelines seem natural.
>
> (2013, p. 169)

It is this very familiarity and "naturalness" that offer a seductive answer to the thorny problem of depicting reality accurately. Timelines can organize a potentially tedious or confusing set of events into a coherent, thoughtful structure or can move the visitor along in an artificially linear path to a, perhaps, unjustified conclusion. In order to avoid these problems, Lubar recommends exhibit creators add elements like key decision points to timelines with added exposition, overlapping or linking multiple timelines to show how different events might have been experienced in different ways, and introducing other variables aside from time such as place and topic to enrich a given timeline's perspective and analysis.

A recent review of time as a culturally situated and driven construct cites Lakoff and Johnson's commonly recognized notion of time as grounded in our collective experience as humans moving through space (1980). Thus, to move forward in time means that the very notion of the future, present, and past gets mapped onto a physical location of just ahead, right here, and behind, respectively. Although most scholars accepted this observation as true simply on its face, Callizo-Romero and his colleagues describe several cultural models of time that do not adhere to this blueprint (2020). For example, in the Pormpuraawan languages spoken by members of the Australian Aboriginal community, time flows from the East (the past) to the West (the future). Similarly, for some speakers of the "Aymara, an Amerindian language spoken in the Andean highlands of Western Bolivia, southeastern Peru, and northern Chile", time is experienced differently than the Western model that lies at the heart of Lakoff and Johnson's construct (Núñez & Sweetser, 2006). Thus, if a given person is facing forward, she is actually looking at the past, in a direct refutation of Lakoff and Johnson's assertion of the universality of the time moves forward metaphor. As Núñez and Sweetser observe, "in Aymara, the basic word for FRONT (nayra, 'eye/front/sight') is also a basic expression meaning PAST, and the basic word for BACK (qhipa, 'back/behind') is a basic expression for FUTURE meaning" (2006, 402).

This example was included simply to demonstrate the danger in forgetting that the way you model your exhibit and its information architecture is a product of your creativity and should be acknowledged as such. It should be structured in a way that consciously acknowledges the choices that were made as being driven by a purpose other than convenience, default, fashion, or simple neglect.

The timelines I created for three exhibits were each included to demonstrate different kinds of artifacts and make different kinds of arguments. The mapping of George Washington Carver's life was placed on a timeline to show Carver in a light that strived to be respectful of his full personhood as an artist, scientist, teacher, and member of a continually oppressed community, especially within the world of agriculture and to show images of him in his youth since he is portrayed most often as an elder. A more specifically temporal argument drove the implementation of the timeline for the Bureau of Home Economics in the exhibit *Apron Strings and Kitchen Sinks*. One scholar described this now-defunct American government unit as being essentially "reorganized out of existence", driven in part by its focus on issues labeled as women-centered (food, clothing, textiles, and kitchen and home design) and because of the Bureau's tradition of then-novel female leadership (Rossiter, 1998, p. 284). Noting all the various moves and organizational changes that were spread out over two decades onto a compressed timeline was done to reveal the hidden effects of these seemingly random actions of an anonymous, impartial bureaucracy. Lastly, in an exhibit titled *Small Agriculture*, I wanted to show how the Subsistence Homestead Project of the Depression was always likely to fail given that it never had a stable home within the US Government. It was created by the Department of the Interior but headed by someone from the Department of Agriculture (USDA). Just three years later, the entire program moved over to the USDA, along with its director. And then just one year later, the program was moved to the Federal Public Housing Authority and then, unsurprisingly, was terminated. Again, the timeline was used consciously to map out a compressed display of bureaucratic neglect and eventual decline as a visual argument built with temporal evidence.

Organizing Metaphor: Calendars

Another example of the way that common cognitive frames and analogies can function in the exhibit context is the digital "advent calendar" created by the Royal College of Surgeons of England. The digital calendar presents as a series of doors which the user needs to click in order to "open" to reveal the object records. The site states our

> December digital advent calendar will give you a snapshot of our Library, Archive and Museum collections. Our advent door design was inspired by the old Museum doors that were uncovered during recent renovation work at our historic building in Lincolns' Inn Fields.
>
> (2019)

Just like the construct of a digital "door", the common interaction devices of digital page turners and digital lightboxes act as metaphorical affordances that tap into our common understandings of how book pages and images are displayed and can be manipulated, both in the physical world and metaphorically in digital information resources (Gibson, 1979; Norman, 1988).

The only danger posed by using these types of exhibit features is a risk that they may come to feel dated quickly.

> Metaphors degrade over time. They become stale ('dead') and lose meaning and power. The Computer Workstation is a Desktop metaphor has been around for over twenty years as of this writing. Does anyone consciously think of the computer as a physical desktop any longer?
>
> (Saffer, 2005, p. 20)

In the early days of the Internet, many sites seized upon these types of interaction devices to provide a sense of familiarity to users who perhaps were still uncomfortable with digital information structures. While an article from 2010 might have praised an e-commerce site that used a real-life metaphor of posters on a wall as stand-ins for a navigational schema as "contemporary . . . elegant . . . unconventional yet interesting", this type of one-to-one match between physical objects and their representations on a website now seems primitive and dated (Friedman, 2010).

While some common web tools such as page turners and buttons have been accepted as digital equivalents to their analog counterparts, these types of navigational and architectural devices that rely on metaphor need to be used with care. Since the modern advent calendar is commonly understood as an experiential, recreational artifact for children to use at Christmastime and not a tool for actual time representation, there is little danger that its use will be seen as anything other than charming, albeit in a low-key way. Obviously another kind of exhibit type could conceivably be organized around another temporal system such as the Aztec or Mayan calendars.

Organizing Metaphor: Maps

Many digital exhibits use spatial representations to convey a perspective on their material and to provide a particular experience for their users. Perhaps the most creative aspect of spatial maps as presentation devices is the possibility to introduce time as an intervening rhetorical factor by including maps from different eras. Here are some selected examples of digital exhibits that either include or totally reside within a representation of mapped space. It is to be expected that the majority of map-based exhibits have subjects that are tied to a particular place.

- *The Voices of Grand Canyon* by the Grand Canyon Trust combines maps, oral history, and personal profiles to tell stories of the American Grand Canyon as a "spiritual home to Native peoples whose ancestors farmed along the river, built homes in the cliffs, and hunted along the canyon rims since time immemorial".
- The *Black Liberation 1969 Archive* contains both a timeline and an interactive map to illustrate and document the events which occurred at Swarthmore

College relating to student-led non-violent protests demanding more support for and representation of Black students within the campus hierarchy.

- *Mapping Amazon* uses geospatial information about Amazon and its fulfillment centers to make a sophisticated argument about the company's business model and its relationship to its customers and where they live.
- The *Building History* exhibit from the Illinois Institute of Technology provides a series of entries about its campus, the buildings, as well as its surrounding neighborhood to illustrate this "modernist landmark with 20 buildings designed by Ludwig Mies van der Rohe", overlaid on a map that contains clickable representations of the Institute's buildings (Illinois Institute of Technology Paul V. Galvin Library, n.d.). In addition to space, the map also accounts for time and allows users to scroll through a connected timeline that shows how various campus landmarks appeared, disappeared, and were eventually replaced with new structures.
- *The Mexican Restaurants of New York City* uses maps to tell several stories about Mexican restaurants, food trucks, cuisine, and neighborhoods in New York.
- *Digital Chicago* includes "Sacred Spaces in 360°" a selection of "virtual reality walkthroughs" of local churches that played significant roles in the history of Chicago, Illinois.

Organizing Metaphor: The Period Room

A less generic, more fully developed organizing frame is that of the period room exhibit. Reid defines this as

> a museological device that combines architecture, furnishings, decorative art, and functional objects to represent an interior of a certain time, place, and style. A feature of many museums, the rooms purport to represent domestic settings in authentic and preservationist ways.
>
> (2021)

Duncan provides a sharp warning about this style of display when she writes, "From their inception, art museum period rooms have raised issues of authenticity, authority and audience, and have been the subject of celebration and controversy" (2011, p. 227). The central questions of the selection of furnishings and objects, the ways they are displayed, the physical structure and design of the setting, and, most important, the perspective that is being accepted, modeled, and represented within the metaphor of the room are all highly contested issues within this field.

The special difficulties contained within the period room genre lie in a fundamental dialectic between its outer physical form and its inner, implicit message (Simpson, 2012). As Ivan Gaskell puts it, the "matter-of-fact" physical shell of the museum period room contains a similar level of argument and artifice as any other exhibit format (2018). On the one hand, the period room presents as something fundamentally straightforward and natural to the viewer. Through the period room, the museum seems to say, "here is a setting that shows how people in the past lived". For example, the Daughters of the American Revolution Museum describe its period rooms as matter-of-fact offers to "Explore the American Home! Each of these 31 period rooms looks like you're stepping into a room from the past. You can peek into an 1810s bedroom, 1820s dining room, 1860s parlor, and many more" (National Society Daughters of the American Revolution (NSDAR), 2021). On the other hand, there is little that is straightforward or natural about such a constructed display. Just as René Magritte's painting of a pipe is, in fact, not a pipe, so too are museum period rooms not rooms at all. They are spaces created by human curators and exhibit builders that always adhere to a specific agenda. Of course, the Daughters of the American Revolution Museum's assertions beg the question, "whose past is being portrayed?" Pilgrim argues these exhibits often fail to reveal and explain that agenda to their visitors. "Is the room a fantasy or is it a fairly accurate approximation of the past? Is the point of view historical or aesthetic? What is the room trying to show or prove?" (1978, p. 4). This failure might account for the conveners of a 2014 conference on the period room to observe, "the Period Room is, for some: a signifier for the inauthentic, an outmoded method of display and an example of unfashionable museum interpretation" (The Bowes Museum, 2022).

In contrast, Bryant (2009) makes a cogent case in favor of the genre when he observes that it provides a good framework when situated in the realm of material culture studies, centered on "objects, their properties, and the materials that they are made of, and the ways in which these material facets are central to an understanding of culture and social relations" (Woodward, 2013).

A rich and suggestive variation on the period room is the Metropolitan Museum of Art's exhibit *Before Yesterday We Could Fly: An Afrofuturist Period Room*, curated by Hannah Beachler. The exhibit takes the physical form of a period room.

> In 2021, The Met's newest room considers domestic lives previously omitted from the scope of the Museum's period displays: the home of an African American family based on the historical settlement of Seneca Village, a vibrant, predominantly Black community that flourished in the mid-nineteenth century just a few hundred yards west of The Met's current location. Seneca Village thrived from the 1820s until 1857, when the city used a process of eminent domain to raze the site and create Central Park. This period room imagines a different future for the residents of Seneca Village. Through its furnishings, art, and spatial organization, the installation represents a domestic interior that is only one proposition for what might have been, had the settlement been allowed to thrive into the present and beyond. *Before Yesterday We Could Fly: An Afrofuturist Period Room* pushes the boundaries of what a period room can accomplish.
>
> (Alteveer et al., 2022, pp. 7–8)

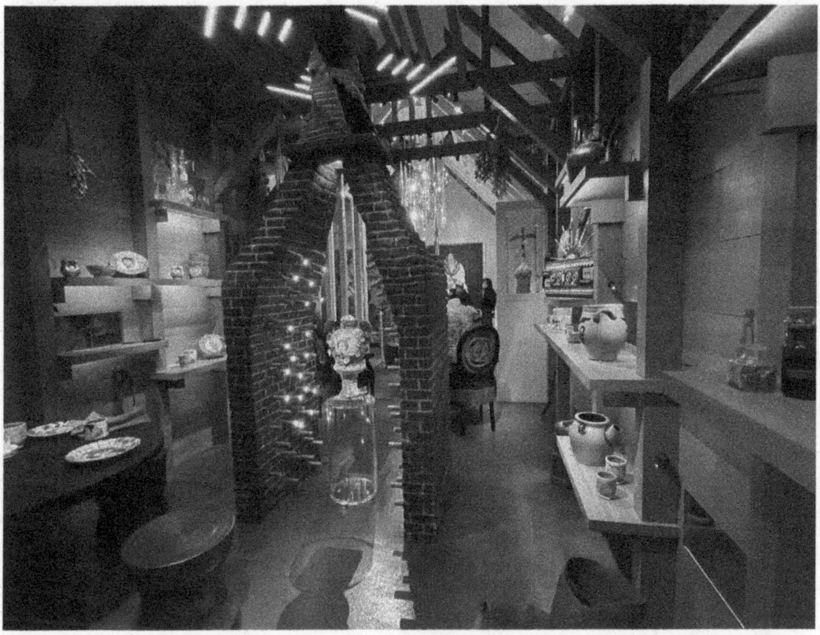

Figure 8.2 Afrofuturist Period Room by Allison Meier is used under the Creative Commons Attribution-ShareAlike 2.0 Generic License (CC BY-SA 2.0)

A photograph of the exhibit appears in Figure 8.2 (Meier, 2022). Other examples of variations on a period room or a cabinet of curiosities (also termed *wunderkammer*) are found in the physical work of contemporary conceptual artists Mark Dion, Martha Glowacki, Allison Moore, and Dan Estabrook, among many others.

These physical works show the power that novel and unexpected ways of understanding, selecting, arranging, and juxtaposing objects can offer the creator of a digital exhibit. Even though they work with object surrogates arranged in a wholly digital context, the processes and potential effects can be similar for the creator of digital exhibits as it is for the artist or curator of physical works. As museum curator Brian Dillon explains his exhibit, *Curiosity: Art and the Pleasures of Knowing*,

> [C]uriosity is the desire to uncover what lies beyond our present understanding of the world. . . . Alongside wonder, which was traditionally considered the origin of philosophy, curiosity is valued because it leads us into new territories. . . . Like the cabinet of curiosities, which mixed science and art, ancient and modern, reality and fiction, this exhibition refuses to choose between knowledge and pleasure. It juxtaposes historical periods and categories of objects to produce an eccentric map of curiosity in its many senses.
>
> (Cabinet Magazine, n.d.)

This new perspective on curiosity and creative object display within assembled settings or imagined rooms offers a promising path forward for digital exhibit design. The important point for this type of exhibit display is to acknowledge explicitly three central points: (1) the metaphor of a period room or curiosity cabinet is just that, a metaphor; (2) it is up to the exhibit creator to understand what arguments are being advanced by the metaphor and its component parts; and (3) communicate those arguments clearly to the visitor in an appealing and engaging way.

In addition to *Before Yesterday We Could Fly: An Afrofuturist Period Room*, the following digital and physical resources illustrate the potential this genre of exhibit design can offer to the creator of digital exhibits.

- *The Story of the Beautiful* is a digital exhibit about the Peacock Room, a creation of the artist James McNeill Whistler. Just like the room itself, the exhibit aims to create an "immersive virtual environment in which users can explore the room, learn about the objects it has contained, and see how the places and faces associated with the room contributed to its history" (Smithsonian Institution & Wayne State University Library System, 2022). By employing the simple metaphor of a digital room wherein visitors can "move" and "interact" with objects, this exhibit shows how cognitive structures can be harnessed and employed in the service of displaying object records, exploring narratives, and providing absorbing visitor experiences.
- Another example of an "immersive" re-created experience is offered by *Seeing Ireland*, a digital exhibit about a landmark exhibit of Irish art held in Paris in 1922, the "*Exposition D'Art Irlandais*". The exhibit allows the user to explore a digital recreation of the physical galleries and the artwork they contained in the century-old event, as well as an accompanying interactive map that displays 1922 Paris and locations relevant to the original exhibit.
- *Raid the Icebox Now* is an update of a 1969 project by Andy Warhol and the Rhode Island School of Design that relies upon a novel means of object selection and placement. "In 1969 Andy Warhol was invited to raid the storage of the RISD Museum. The hope was that he would reveal what was hiding there, attract the attention of disinterested art students, and connect a fairly conservative museum to contemporary-art practices. But Warhol did not create a new narrative that disrupted the canon—instead he laid bare the arbitrary nature of the museum's collection itself. Victorian umbrellas, hatboxes, Windsor chairs, Navajo blankets, noteworthy and second-rate European paintings as well as the apparatuses of museum work, including storage cabinets, packing crates, and a forklift, sat side by side in the gallery, just as they had in storage" (Blythe, 2019). The updated project extended a similar offer to artists to create personal interpretations of similar "rooms" of objects.
- The Minneapolis Institute of Art project, *Living Rooms: The Period Room Initiative* is an attempt to "reinvigorate" the period room "for today's visitors, placing the past in dialogue with the present, while simultaneously

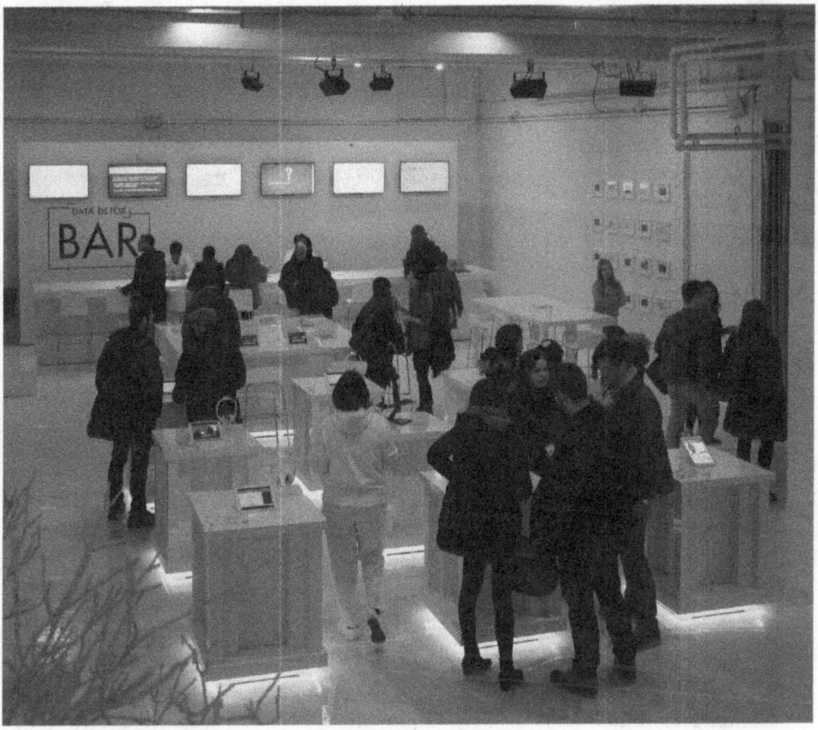

Figure 8.3 *The Glass Room* by Rhododendrites is used under the Creative Commons Attribution-ShareAlike 4.0 International License (CC BY-SA 4.0)

broadening the conversation to include other histories—of marginalized people, of the senses, and even of time itself" (Minneapolis Institute of Art, n.d.).

- *The Glass Room* is described as a pop-up exhibit space by Tactical Tech and Firefox and takes the form of a retail store much like the Apple stores, but with a twist. Instead of offering technical products like phones and computers for sale, it offers opportunities for visitors to better understand how these products function in the modern world in terms of their own personal data and the privacy and security concerns raised by living in such a connected world. A view of the room including its "Data Detox Bar" appears in Figure 8.3 (Rhododendrites, 2016).

Fostering Personal and Professional Creativity in the Exhibit Realm

Teresa M. Amabile's work on creativity and organizational culture as a Professor of the Harvard Business School will be instructive as we move the focus from exhibit form back to the exhibit creator (Amabile, 1998; Amabile et al., 2002, 2004, 2005;

Amabile & Kramer, 2011). Amabile's work is grounded in case studies of real business processes and thus she does not shy away from realistic assessments such as "there can be no doubt: creativity gets killed much more often than it gets supported" (Amabile, 1998, p. 77). She and her colleagues have identified what they think are the key factors that affect how creative work gets either encouraged and nourished or suppressed and punished in different organizational cultures. Although written from a business perspective, Amabile's observations are relevant to the world of cultural heritage organizations and their processes of digital curation and document analysis and the products of those efforts: digital exhibits.

Amabile's perspective of the individual employee engaged in creative work can be seen as containing three spheres of focus: their levels of expertise, creative thinking skills, and motivation, both external and internal. The employee's organization can affect all three of these characteristics to one degree or another, but the most powerful effects come from the ways in which an employee's managers and overall culture affect levels of intrinsic motivation: "passion and interest—a person's internal desire to do something" (Amabile, 1998, p. 79). While increasing extrinsic motivation through money and other material incentives can be helpful and appreciated, those tools alone will not result in increased innovation in the workplace. The best ways to support creative work such as that demanded by exhibit work are interventions aimed at addressing key processes of intrinsic motivation.

1 Challenge: Managers need to know their employees' strengths and weaknesses well enough to match the right person to the right work task, so everyone is challenged in just the right way, at just the right level. Amabile argues that the ability to assign work correctly can make the most positive impact on the level of organizational creativity, innovation, and effectiveness. She observes that it is unfortunate that managers do not engage in the "often difficult and time consuming" work to gather insight into their employees as people and that "perhaps that's why good matches are so rarely made" (1998, p. 81).
2 Freedom: To facilitate the maximum amount of productive creativity from employees, managers need to communicate project goals clearly and grant the maximum amount of freedom over the way in which these goals are achieved. Amabile's research documents how managerial disingenuousness with either the nature of the goals and/or the amount of freedom employees actually have over work processes plays into this dynamic
3 Resources: Managers need to allocate sufficient time to reach the identified goals, along with assigning the right people to the project and allocating a sufficient budget. Clearly, many problems can still occur, from managers misjudging staff abilities, creating artificial or overly tight deadlines, and lack of monetary resources, all of which will negatively impact employee creativity.
4 Work-Group Features: Managers need to create work groups made of people with diverse, yet complementary skills, who are invested in the project, and who will be mutually respectful of differences and supportive of each other. This factor also shows how a poor match between work team members and goals will result in cascading failures.

5 Supervisory Encouragement: High-performing, effective, creative employees respond best to managers who engage them in ways that increase intrinsic motivation. The most effective types of encouragement for these people must communicate to them that their work matters to the organization in a real and meaningful way. Clearly managers can only offer this kind of genuine encouragement if they have a genuine relationship with their employees.

6 Organizational Support: Managers who engage in superficial demonstrations such as generic participation awards or monetary compensation divorced from meaningful connection to the organization will not foster creative innovation from their employees. Instead, Amabile suggests a free flow of information and proactive efforts to prevent organizational politics to fester and exert an outsized effect on creative work.

It is a rare organization that would engage in, or even acknowledge the importance of, all these employee-centered supportive actions. Even given the inherently humanistic orientation of most GLAM institutions, sometimes organizational hierarchies get calcified, bureaucratic bullies get empowered, incompetent sycophants get promoted, and the creativity necessary for a digital exhibit can be seen as a source of threat to managerial order. In my own case, multiple digital exhibits helped to generate three national conference presentations and a peer-reviewed journal article (Marsh, 2016a, 2016b, 2016c, 2017). In some organizations, the kind of creativity encapsulated in an exhibit is not really going to be welcomed, much less supported with the actions advocated by Amabile.

Even if you are given the freedom and agency to create the kind of exhibit you want, what kinds of external supports are available to help you drive and structure your creativity? The following books may help you with various aspects of the creative process and introduce new perspectives that may be illuminating.

Lynda Barry (2019). *Making Comics*. Montreal, Canada: Drawn and Quarterly.

Anne H. Berry, Kareem Collie, Penina Acayo Laker, Lesley-Ann Noel, Jennifer Rittner, and Kelly Walters, Editors (2022). The Black Experience in Design: Identity, Expression, & Reflection. New York: Allworth Press. https://blackexperienceindesign.com/.

Susan Cain (2012) Quiet: The Power of Introverts in a World That Can't Stop Talking. New York: Broadway Books.

Julia Cameron (2016). The Artist's Way: A Spiritual Path to Higher Creativity. New York: TarcherPerigee. https://juliacameronlive.com/books-by-julia/the-artists-way-a-spiritual-path-to-higher-creativity/.

Danny Gregory (2019). How to Draw Without Talent. New York: North Light Books.

Eric Maisel (1995). Fearless Creating: A Step-by-Step Guide to Starting and Completing Your Work of Art. New York: Penguin Putnam.

Silas Munro (2018). W. E. B. Du Bois's Data Portraits: Visualizing Black America. New York: Princeton Architectural Press.

Linda Norris & Rainey Tisdale (2013). Creativity in Museum Practice. London: Routledge.

Kassia St. Clair. (2016). The Secret Lives of Color. New York: Penguin Books.
Eviatar Zerubavel (1999). *The Clockwork Muse*. Cambridge, MA: Harvard University Press.

Practice Recommendations

1 Consciously step out of yourself and your understanding of the exhibit's materials and look at them through the perspective of multiple, specific user types. What kind of person would want to read about these materials? Why? How would they want or need to go about the process of learning about and experiencing them? Why would they prefer your exhibit to another on the same topic? These questions need to be asked and addressed throughout the exhibit creating process.
2 Librarians, archivists, and similar information professionals are already well-situated within the Pro-C "box" of professional understanding of users and information. The knowledge gained through education and professional practice will support you well as you go about creating an engaging and intellectually sound structure for your exhibit materials.
3 Be conscious of and thoughtful about the cognitive frames and metaphors you may be introducing in your exhibit, as both specific linguistic techniques and overall explanatory and organizing structures.
4 Creativity does not follow a linear path. You might have to stop and start your work to regroup and get a new perspective.
5 Simple is better. Using a simple metaphor such as a "room" or a "store" as an overarching organizing principle can act as a powerful core and conceptual driver for your digital exhibit.
6 Do not stop yourself from looking at other exhibits for inspiration and ideas, including physical exhibits. The popular press and media can also present sources of inspiration and can alert you to trends that might relate to your collections and serve as a starting point for an exhibit.
7 Do not let yourself become paralyzed waiting for an "A-ha!" moment of inspiration and insight. Insights generally come when engaged in the difficult work of engagement with the unknown and unclear.
8 Not all GLAM institutional cultures are equal. If you find yourself trying to do this work in a culture that does not understand or support creative work, you might need to reach out to other sources for help with your journey.

Digital and Physical Exhibits Discussed in This Chapter

Apron Strings and Kitchen Sinks
Emily Marsh
National Agricultural Library, US Department of Agriculture
www.nal.usda.gov/exhibits/ipd/apronsandkitchens/

Before Yesterday We Could Fly: An Afrofuturist Period Room
Hannah Beachler

Metropolitan Museum of Art
www.metmuseum.org/exhibitions/listings/2021/afrofuturist-period-room

Black Liberation 1969 Archive
Allison Dorsey, Nabil Kashyap, Alison Roseberry-Polier, John Gagnon, and Maria Mejia
Swarthmore College
https://blacklib1969.swarthmore.edu/

Building History
Adam Strohm and Max King
Illinois Institute of Technology Paul V. Galvin Library
https://buildinghistory.iit.edu/

December Digital Advent Calendar
Royal College of Surgeons of England
https://scp.rcseng.ac.uk/client/en_GB/exhibitions/search/results?qu=%22rcs%3A+DX00004%22&rt=false|||IDENTIFIER|||Resource+Identifier

Digital Chicago
Lake Forest College and The Chicago History Museum
http://digitalchicagohistory.org/

George Washington Carver
Emily Marsh
National Agricultural Library, US Department of Agriculture
www.nal.usda.gov/exhibits/ipd/carver/

The Glass Room
Tactical Tech and Firefox
https://theglassroom.org/

Living Rooms Project
Jennifer Komar Olivarez
Minneapolis Institute of Arts
https://new.artsmia.org/living-rooms/

Mapping Amazon 2.0
Christine Wen
Good Jobs First
https://storymaps.arcgis.com/stories/144d21045a794cf8b7834b0c49fdd0c0

Metropolitan Museum's Heilbrunn Timeline of Art History
Metropolitan Museum of Art
www.metmuseum.org/toah/

The Mexican Restaurants of New York City
Lori A. Flores, Ximena López-Carrillo, and Fernando Amador II
Stony Brook University
https://storymaps.arcgis.com/stories/5d130c3dc16b4a86a5066c36b3b72b16

The Museum of the World
WEIR+WONG
The British Museum
https://britishmuseum.withgoogle.com/

Raid the Icebox Now
Museum of Art, Rhode Island School of Design
https://publications.risdmuseum.org/raid-icebox-now

Seeing Ireland
Billy Shortall and Ciaran O'Neill
Trinity College Dublin
www.seeingireland.ie/

Small Agriculture
Emily Marsh
National Agricultural Library, US Department of Agriculture
www.nal.usda.gov/exhibits/ipd/small/

The Story of the Beautiful
Freer Gallery of Art and Arthur M. Sackler Gallery, the Smithsonian's National Museum of Asian Art, and Wayne State University's Library System
http://peacockroom.wayne.edu/

The Voices of Grand Canyon
Grand Canyon Trust
https://storymaps.arcgis.com/stories/b22a6a09bb2344ff845d9efd3e4152f7

References

Alteveer, I., Beachler, H., & Lawrence, S. (2022). Before yesterday we could fly: Envisioning an Afrofuturist period room at the met. *The Metropolitan Museum of Art Bulletin*, *79*(3). www.metmuseum.org/art/metpublications/Before_Yesterday_We_Could_Fly_An_Afrofuturist_Period_Room.

Amabile, T. M. (1998). How to kill creativity. *Harvard Business Review*, *76*(5), 77–89. https://hbr.org/1998/09/how-to-kill-creativity.

Amabile, T. M., Barsade, S. G., Mueller, J. S., & Staw, B. M. (2005). Affect and creativity at work. *Administrative Science Quarterly*, *50*(3), 367–403. https://doi.org/10.2189/asqu.2005.50.3.367.

Amabile, T. M., Hadley, C. N., & Kramer, S. J. (2002). Creativity under the gun. *Harvard Business Review*, *80*, 52–63. https://hbr.org/2002/08/creativity-under-the-gun.

Amabile, T. M., & Kramer, S. J. (2011). The power of small wins. *Harvard Business Review*, *89*(5), 70–81. https://hbr.org/2011/05/the-power-of-small-wins.

Amabile, T. M., Schatzel, E. A., Moneta, G. B., & Kramer, S. J. (2004). Leader behaviors and the work environment for creativity: Perceived leader support. *The Leadership Quarterly*, *15*(1), 5–32. https://doi.org/10.1016/j.leaqua.2003.12.003.

Blythe, S. G. (2019). All behind the icebox door. *Raid the Icebox Now*. Museum of Art, Rhode Island School of Design. https://publications.risdmuseum.org/raid-icebox-now/all-behind-icebox-door.

British Museum. (n.d.). *About this project*. https://britishmuseum.withgoogle.com/about.

Bryant, J. (2009). Museum period rooms for the twenty-first century: Salvaging ambition. *Museum Management and Curatorship*, *24*(1), 73–84. https://doi.org/10.1080/09647770902731866.

Cabinet Magazine. (n.d.). Exhibition/"curiosity of knowing: Art and the pleasures of knowing." *Cabinet Magazine*. www.cabinetmagazine.org/exhibitions/dillon_curiosityartandthepleasuresofknowing.php.

Cabrera, D., Roy, D., & Chisolm, M. S. (2018). Social media scholarship and alternative metrics for academic promotion and tenure. *Journal of the American College of Radiology*, *15*(1, Part B), 135–161. https://doi.org/10.1016/j.jacr.2017.09.012.

Callizo-Romero, C., Tutnjević, S., Pandza, M., Ouellet, M., Kranjec, A, Ilić, S., Gu, Y., Göksun, T., Chahboun, S., Casasanto, D., & Santiago, J. (2020). Temporal focus and time spatialization across cultures. *Psychonomic Bulletin & Review*, *27*(6), 1247–1258. https://doi.org/10.3758/s13423-020-01760-5.

Cateforis, D. (Ed.). (2014). *Rethinking Andrew Wyeth*. Berkeley, CA: University of California Press.

Cerquetti, M. (2011). Local art museums and visitors: Audience and attendance development. Theoretical requirements and empirical evidence. *ENCATC: Journal of Cultural Management and Policy*, *1*(1), 20–27.

Dallow, J., & Matilsky, B. C. (2005). *Family legacies: The art of Betye, Lezley, and Alison Saar*. Chapel Hill, NC: Ackland Art Museum and The University of North Carolina at Chapel Hill.

Day, M., Delagrange, S. H., Palmquist, M., Pemberton, M. A., & Walker, J. R. (2013). What we really value: Redefining scholarly engagement in tenure and promotion protocols. *College Composition and Communication*, *65*(1), 185–208. www.jstor.org/stable/43490813.

de Bono, E. (1970). *Lateral thinking: Creativity step by step*. New York: HarperCollins Publishers.

Diehl, T. (2014, September 2). After Jeff Koons: A retrospective. *Los Angeles Review of Books*. https://lareviewofbooks.org/article/jeff-koons-retrospective/.

Driskell, D. C. (1976). *Two centuries of Black American art*. Los Angeles, CA/New York: Los Angeles County Museum of Art/Alfred A. Knopf, Inc.

Duncan, S. A. (2011). Introduction. *Visual Resources*, *21*(5), 227–231. https://doi.org/10.1080/01973760500166590.

Fenlon, K. (2017). Thematic research collections: Libraries and the evolution of alternative digital publishing in the humanities. *Library Trends*, *65*(4), 523–539. https://doi.org/10.1353/lib.2017.0016.

Friedman, V. (2010, May 20). Web design trends 2010: Real-life metaphors and CSS3 adaptation. *Smashing Magazine*. www.smashingmagazine.com/2010/05/web-design-trends-2010-real-life-metaphors-and-css3-adaptation/.

Gaskell, I. (2018). Display displayed. In C. van Eck, J. Grave, C. Holm, & V. Kobi (Eds.), *The agency of display: Objects, framings and parerga* (pp. 22–43). Dresden: Sandstein Verlag.

Gawain, S. (2008). *Creative visualization: Use the power of your imagination to create what you want in your life*. Novato, CA: New World Library.

Gibson, J. J. (1979). *The ecological approach to visual perception*. Boston, MA: Houghton Mifflin.

Gilhooly, K. J., & Gilhooly, M. L. M. (2021). Chapter 1—creativity: Introduction. In K. J. Gilhooly & M. L. M. Gilhooly (Eds.), *Aging and creativity* (pp. 1–25). Cambridge, MA: Academic Press. https://doi.org/10.1016/B978-0-12-816401-3.00009-3.

Gladwell, M. (2009). *What the dog saw: And other adventures*. New York: Little, Brown and Company.

Illinois Institute of Technology Paul V. Galvin Library. (n.d.). *Building history*. https://buildinghistory.library.iit.edu/.

Kaufman, J. C., & Beghetto, R. A. (2009). Beyond big and little: The Four C model of creativity. *Review of General Psychology*, *13*(1), 1–12. https://doi.org/10.1037/a0013688.

Lakoff, G. (1993). The contemporary theory of metaphor. In A. Ortony (Ed.), *Metaphor and thought* (2nd ed., pp. 202–251). Cambridge: Cambridge University Press. https://doi.org/10.1017/CBO9781139173865.013.

Lakoff, G., & Johnson, M. (1980). *Metaphors we live by*. Chicago, IL: The University of Chicago Press.

Lubar, S. (2013). Timelines in exhibitions. *Curator: The Museum Journal*, 56(2), 169–188. https://doi.org/10.1111/cura.12018.

Lucas, B. J., & Nordgren, L. F. (2021). Lay people's beliefs about creativity: Evidence for an insight bias. *Trends in Cognitive Sciences*, *26*(1), 6–7.

Marsh, E. (2016a, January 9). *Like a 'fine pullet' at the chicken farm: Robert Frost's poultry paper articles* [Conference presentation]. Austin, TX: Modern Language Association Convention. https://apps.mla.org/conv_listings_details_print?prog_id=A046A&year=2016.

Marsh, E. (2016b, March 8) *Showcasing digital assets* [Conference presentation]. Washington, DC: Computer in Libraries, Library Labs: Research, Innovation, & Imagination. https://conferences.infotoday.com/documents/220/B103_Marsh.pptx.

Marsh, E. (2016c, April 15). *If a pdf falls in the forest will anyone see it? Building a library ecosystem for digital materials* [Conference presentation]. Washington, DC: Digital Public Library of America's DPLAFest. https://youtu.be/YQ2TniMc0Dg?t=1551.

Marsh, E. (2017). Chickens, aprons, markets, and cans: How the National Agricultural Library uses Omeka as its content management system for digital exhibits. *Digital Library Perspectives*, *33*(4), 361–377. https://doi.org/10.1108/DLP-03-2017-0009.

Marsh, E. (2022). *Different views of object-level metadata for Work Clothes for Women in an exhibit timeline: The "bite", from an item view within an exhibit timeline, the "snack", from the full item record in the exhibit, and from the item's original Internet Archive record, the "meal"* [Infographic]. https://emily-marsh.com/Digital_Exhibits_for_Cultural_Institutions/Figure_7.1.jpg.

McKeachie, W. J. (1987). Cognitive skills and their transfer: Discussion. *International Journal of Educational Research*, *11*(6), 707–712. https://doi.org/10.1016/0883-0355(87)90010-3.

Meeks, E., & Grossner, K. (2012). ORBIS: An interactive scholarly work on the Roman world. *Journal of Digital Humanities, 1*(3). http://journalofdigitalhumanities.org/1-3/orbis-an-interactive-scholarly-work-on-the-roman-world-by-elijah-meeks-and-karl-grossner/.

Meier, A. (2022, January 9). *Afrofuturist period room* [Photograph]. www.flickr.com/photos/astrozombie/51937289179/.

Minneapolis Institute of Art. (n.d.). *Living rooms: The period room initiative.* https://new.artsmia.org/living-rooms/.

Minsky, M. (1975). A framework for representing knowledge. In P. H. Winston (Ed.), *The psychology of computer vision* (pp. 211–277). New York: McGraw Hill.

Murray, J. (1997). *Hamlet on the holodeck: The future of narrative in cyberspace.* New York: The Free Press.

National Society Daughters of the American Revolution (NSDAR). (2021). *DAR museum period rooms*. Author. www.dar.org/museum/dar-museum-period-rooms.

Nochlin, L. (1971). Why are there no great women artists? In V. Gornick & B. K. Moran (Eds.), *Woman in sexist society: Studies in power and powerlessness* (pp. 344–366). New York: Basic Books.

Norman, D. A. (1988). *The psychology of everyday things*. New York: Basic Books.

Núñez, R. F., & Sweetser, E. (2006). With the future behind them: Convergent evidence from Aymara language and gesture in the crosslinguistic comparison of spatial construals of time. *Cognitive Science, 30*(3), 401–450. https://doi.org/10.1207/s15516709cog0000_62.

Palmer, C. L. (2004). Thematic research collections. In Schreibman, S., Siemens, R., & Unsworth, J. (Eds.), *A companion to digital humanities*. Hoboken, NJ: Wiley-Blackwell. https://doi.org/10.1002/9780470999875.ch24.

Pilgrim, D. H. (1978). Inherited from the past: The American period room. *The American Art Journal, 10*(1), 4–23. www.jstor.org/stable/1594106.

Randel, J. (2010). *The skinny on creativity: Thinking outside the box.* Westport, CT: Rand Media Company.

Rare Books and Manuscripts Section, Association of College and Research Libraries. (n.d.). *The Katharine Kyes Leab & Daniel J. Leab American book prices current exhibition awards: Guidelines and rules for submissions*. American Library Association. https://rbms.info/committees/exhibition_awards/submission-rules/.

Reid, T. (2021, December 2). Light years: The Met's Afrofuturist period room thinks inside the box. *Artforum Slant*. www.artforum.com/slant/the-met-s-afrofuturist-period-room-thinks-inside-the-box-87375.

Rhododendrites. (2016, December 17). *The glass room* [Photograph]. https://commons.wikimedia.org/wiki/File:The_Glass_Room_(71744).jpg.

Rossiter, M. W. (1998). *Women scientists in America: Before affirmative action, 1940–1972*. Baltimore, MD: Johns Hopkins University Press.

Royal College of Surgeons of England. (2019). *Digital exhibitions*. https://scp.rcseng.ac.uk/client/en_GB/exhibitions.

Runco, M. A., & Jaeger, G. J. (2012). The standard definition of creativity. *Creativity Research Journal, 24*(1), 92–96. https://doi.org/10.1080/10400419.2012.650092.

Saffer, D. (2005). *The role of metaphor in interaction design*. Unpublished master's thesis. Pittsburgh, PA: Carnegie Mellon University.

Simpson, A. L. (2012). Objectifying objects: Omitting ideology in Gustav Stickley Craftsman period rooms. *Shift: Graduate Journal of Visual and Material Culture, 5*. http://shiftjournal.org/wp-content/uploads/2014/11/simpson.pdf.

Smithsonian Institution & Wayne State University Library System. (2022). *About the story of the beautiful*. http://peacockroom.wayne.edu/about.

Sohan, V. K. (2015). "But a quilt is more": Recontextualizing the discourse(s) of the Gee's bend quilts. *College English*, *77*(4), 294–316. www.jstor.org/stable/24240050.

Stebbins, R. A. (2020). *The serious leisure perspective: A synthesis*. London: Palgrave Macmillan.

Sternberg, R. J., & Kaufman, J. C. (2010). Constraints on creativity: Obvious and not so obvious. In J. C. Kaufman & R. J. Sternberg (Eds.), *The Cambridge handbook of creativity* (pp. 467–482). New York: Cambridge University Press.

The Bowes Museum. (2022). *The period room: Museum, material, experience*. www.thebowesmuseum.org.uk/Collection/Research-Scholarship/The-Period-Room-Museum-Material-Experience.

University of Wisconsin-Madison Libraries. (2017, February 7). *Blind date with a book* [Photograph]. https://flickr.com/photos/20245378@N03/40199332782.

Villanova, A., & eCunha, M. P. (2020). Everyday creativity: A systematic literature review. *The Journal of Creative Behavior*, *55*(3), 673–695. https://doi.org/10.1002/jocb.481.

Weisberg, R. W. (2006). Expertise and reason in creative thinking: Evidence from case studies and the laboratory. In J. C. Kaufman & J. Baer (Eds.), *Creativity and reason in cognitive development* (pp. 7–42). New York: Cambridge University Press.

Weisberg, R. W. (2020). *Re-thinking creativity: Inside-the-box thinking as the basis for innovation*. New York: Cambridge University Press.

Weller, M. (2012, April 29). The virtues of blogging as scholarly activity. *Chronicle of Higher Education*. https://www.chronicle.com/article/the-virtues-of-blogging-as-scholarly-activity/.

Woodward, S. (2013). *Material culture. Oxford bibliographies*. Oxford: Oxford University Press. www.oxfordbibliographies.com/view/document/obo-9780199766567/obo-9780199766567-0085.xml.

Bibliography

Ackermans, H. (2021). Genre-bending on an academic platform: Three creative works on Scalar. In *Proceedings of the 32nd ACM conference on hypertext and social media (HT'21)* (pp. 211–215). New York: Association for Computing Machinery. https://doi.org/10.1145/3465336.3475099.

Allen, S. (2004). Designs for learning: Studying science museum exhibits that do more than entertain. *Science Education*, *8*(S1), S17–S33. https://doi.org/10.1002/sce.20016.

Alliance for Networking Visual Culture. (n.d.a). *About Scalar*. https://scalar.me/anvc/scalar/features/.

Alliance for Networking Visual Culture. (n.d.b). *Contact*. https://scalar.me/anvc/contact/.

Alliance for Networking Visual Culture. (n.d.c). *Scalar 2 user guide*. https://scalar.usc.edu/works/guide2/index.

Allred, J. (2017). A professor goes overboard with Omeka and DH box. *The Journal of Interactive Technology and Pedagogy*. https://jitp.commons.gc.cuny.edu/a-professor-goes-overboard-with-omeka-and-dh-box/.

Alteveer, I., Beachler, H., & Lawrence, S. (2022). Before yesterday we could fly: Envisioning an Afrofuturist period room at the met. *The Metropolitan Museum of Art Bulletin*, *79*(3). www.metmuseum.org/art/metpublications/Before_Yesterday_We_Could_Fly_An_Afrofuturist_Period_Room.

Amabile, T. M. (1998). How to kill creativity. *Harvard Business Review*, *76*(5), 77–89. https://hbr.org/1998/09/how-to-kill-creativity.

Amabile, T. M., Barsade, S. G., Mueller, J. S., & Staw, B. M. (2005). Affect and creativity at work. *Administrative Science Quarterly*, *50*(3), 367–403. https://doi.org/10.2189/asqu.2005.50.3.367.

Amabile, T. M., Hadley, C. N., & Kramer, S. J. (2002). Creativity under the gun. *Harvard Business Review*, *80*, 52–63. https://hbr.org/2002/08/creativity-under-the-gun.

Amabile, T. M., & Kramer, S. J. (2011). The power of small wins. *Harvard Business Review*, *89*(5), 70–81. https://hbr.org/2011/05/the-power-of-small-wins.

Amabile, T. M., Schatzel, E. A., Moneta, G. B., & Kramer, S. J. (2004). Leader behaviors and the work environment for creativity: Perceived leader support. *The Leadership Quarterly*, *15*(1), 5–32. https://doi.org/10.1016/j.leaqua.2003.12.003.

Anderson, S. (2019). Visitor and audience research in museums. In K. Drotner, V. Dziekan, R. Parry, & K. C. Schrøder (Eds.), *The Routledge handbook of museums, media, and communication* (pp. 80–95). London: Routledge.

Arya, R. (2021). Cultural appropriation: What it is and why it matters? *Sociology Compass*, *15*(10), e12923. https://doi.org/10.1111/soc4.12923.

Ash, D. B. (2022). *Reculturing museums: Embrace conflict, create change*. London: Routledge.

Audience Agency. (2020). *The Audience Agency digital audience survey*. London: Author. www.theaudienceagency.org/asset/2547.

Augustin, L., Kokoschko, B., Wiesner, M., & Schabacker, M. (2020). Toward a comprehensive definition of the non-user. In *Proceedings of the Design Society: DESIGN Conference* (Vol. 1, pp. 1853–1862). Cambridge: Cambridge University Press. https://doi.org/10.1017/dsd.2020.124.

Ball, M. S., & Smith, G. W. H. (1992). *Analyzing visual data*. Thousand Oaks, CA: SAGE Publishing.

Baltimore Museum of Art. (2022). *Guarding the art: Overview*. https://artbma.org/exhibition/bma-security-officers-take-center-stage-as-guest-curators-of-a-new-exhibition-opening-in-march-2022.

Banks, M. (2018). *Using visual data in qualitative research* (2nd ed.). Thousand Oaks, CA: SAGE Publishing.

Barker, E. (1999). Introduction. In E. Barker (Ed.), *Contemporary cultures of display* (pp. 8–21). New Haven, CT: Yale University Press.

Barsch, P. (2020). Online exhibitions: The curator as director. *OnCurating*, *45*, 59–64. https://on-curating.org/issue-45-reader/online-exhibitions-the-curator-as-director.html#.YnwSF-jMK01.

Baumann, J. (2013, November 22). The Silence=Death poster. *LGBTQ at NYPL*. New York Public Library. www.nypl.org/blog/2013/11/22/silence-equals-death-poster.

Bedford, D. (2021). *Knowledge architectures: Structures and semantics*. London: Routledge.

Berkowitz, R. (2003). *Stayin' alive: The invention of safe sex*. Boulder, CO: Westview Press.

Bitgood, S. (2010). An analysis of visitor circulation: Movement patterns and the general value principle. *Curator*, *49*(4), 463–475. https://doi.org/10.1111/j.2151-6952.2006.tb00237.x.

Blythe, S. G. (2019). All behind the icebox door. *Raid the Icebox Now*. Museum of Art, Rhode Island School of Design. https://publications.risdmuseum.org/raid-icebox-now/all-behind-icebox-door.

Bourdieu, P., & Darbel, A. (1991). *The love of art: European art museums and their public*. Cambridge: Polity Press.

Bowen, L. G., & Roberts, P. J. (1993). Exhibits: Illegitimate children of academic libraries? *College & Research Libraries*, *54*(5), 407–415. http://hdl.handle.net/2142/41609.

Braun, V., & Clarke, V. (2006) Using thematic analysis in psychology. *Qualitative Research in Psychology*, *3*(2), 77–101. https://doi.org/10.1191/1478088706qp063oa.

Brennan, S. (2018). Omeka now public for 10 years. *Omeka News*. https://omeka.org/news/2018/02/20/omeka-now-public-10-years/.

Bridwell-Bowles, L. (1986, March 12–15). *Designing a comprehensive curriculum for writing with computers*. 37th Annual Conference on College Composition and Communication, New Orleans, LA.

British Museum. (n.d.). *About this project*. https://britishmuseum.withgoogle.com/about.

Brown, D. M. (2007). *Communicating design: Developing web site documentation for design and planning*. Indianapolis, IN: New Riders Publishing.

Brown, S. (2006). Do richer media mean better learning? A framework for evaluating learning experiences in museum web site design. *International Journal of Heritage Studies*, *12*(5), 412–426. https://doi.org/10.1080/13527250600821571.

Bryant, J. (2009). Museum period rooms for the twenty-first century: Salvaging ambition. *Museum Management and Curatorship*, *24*(1), 73–84. https://doi.org/10.1080/09647770902731866.

Cabinet Magazine. (n.d.). Exhibition/"curiosity of knowing: Art and the pleasures of knowing." *Cabinet Magazine*. www.cabinetmagazine.org/exhibitions/dillon_curiosityartandthepleasuresofknowing.php.

Cabrera, D., Roy, D., & Chisolm, M. S. (2018). Social media scholarship and alternative metrics for academic promotion and tenure. *Journal of the American College of Radiology*, *15*(1, Part B), 135–161. https://doi.org/10.1016/j.jacr.2017.09.012.

Callizo-Romero, C., Tutnjević, S., Pandza, M., Ouellet, M., Kranjec, A, Ilić, S., Gu, Y., Göksun, T., Chahboun, S., Casasanto, D., & Santiago, J. (2020). Temporal focus and time spatialization across cultures. *Psychonomic Bulletin & Review*, *27*(6), 1247–1258. https://doi.org/10.3758/s13423-020-01760-5.

CARLI Created Content Committee. (2020). *Guidelines for the promotion of digital collections: Best practices for promotion and marketing*. Champaign, IL: Consortium of Academic and Research Libraries in Illinois (CARLI). www.carli.illinois.edu/sites/files/digital_collections/documentation/guidelines_for_promotion.pdf.

Carliner, S. (2003). Modeling information for three dimensional space: Lessons learned from museum exhibit design. *Technical Communication*, *50*(4), 554–570.

Caro, S. (2016). *Digitizing your collection: Public library success stories*. Chicago, IL: American Library Association.

Case, D. O., & Given, L. M. (2016). *Looking for information: A survey of research on information seeking, needs, and behavior* (4th ed.). Bingley: Emerald Publishing Limited.

Casey, M. (2015). *Content strategy toolkit: The methods, guidelines, and templates for getting content right*. Indianapolis, IN: New Riders Publishing.

Cateforis, D. (Ed.). (2014). *Rethinking Andrew Wyeth*. Berkeley, CA: University of California Press.

Cerquetti, M. (2011). Local art museums and visitors: Audience and attendance development. Theoretical requirements and empirical evidence. *ENCATC: Journal of Cultural Management and Policy*, *1*(1), 20–27.

Cerquetti, M. (2016). More is better! Current issues and challenges for museum audience development: A literature review. *ENCATC: Journal of Cultural Management and Policy*, *6*(1), 30–43.

Cerquetti, M., & Ferrara, C. (2018). Marketing research for cultural heritage conservation and sustainability: Lessons from the field. *Sustainability*, *10*(3), 774. https://doi.org/10.3390/su10030774.

Chang, H. (2021). Presentist history for pluralist science. *Journal for General Philosophy of Science*, *52*. https://doi.org/10.1007/s10838-020-09512-8.

Chatman, E. A. (1987). The information world of low-skilled workers. *Library and Information Science Research*, *9*(4), 265–283.

Chatman, E. A. (1996). The impoverished life-world of outsiders. *Journal of the American Society for Information Science*, *47*(3), 193–206. https://doi.org/10.1002/(SICI)1097-4571(199603)47:3%3C193::AID-ASI3%3E3.0.CO;2-T.

Chatman, E. A. (1999). A theory of life in the round. *Journal of the American Society for Information Science*, *50*(3), 207–217. https://doi.org/10.1002/(SICI)1097-4571(1999)50:3%3C207::AID-ASI3%3E3.0.CO;2-8.

Chong, C., & Smith, D. (2017) Interactive learning units on museum websites. *Journal of Museum Education*, *42*(2), 169–178. https://doi.org/10.1080/10598650.2017.1301626.

Cipolle, A. V. (2022, April 27). Using podcasts to broaden the reach of smaller museums. *New York Times*. www.nytimes.com/2022/04/27/arts/design/museum-podcasts.html.

Clark, A. M., & Sousa, B. J. (2018). The mental health of people doing qualitative research: Getting serious about risks and remedies. *International Journal of Qualitative Methods, 17*(1), 1–3. https://journals.sagepub.com/doi/10.1177/1609406918787244.

Clarke, V., & Braun, V. (2013). Teaching thematic analysis. *The Psychologist, 26*, 120–123.

Coble, Z., Potvin, S., & Shirazi, R. (2014). Process as product: Scholarly communication experiments in the digital humanities. *Journal of Librarianship and Scholarly Communication, 2*(3), eP1137. https://doi.org/10.7710/2162-3309.1137.

Cohen, D. (2008, February 20). *Introducing Omeka*. http://dancohen.org/2008/02/20/introducing-omeka/.

Coleman, N. (2020, July 5). Why we're capitalizing Black. *The New York Times*. www.nytimes.com/2020/07/05/insider/capitalized-black.html.

Cooper, A. (2004). *The inmates are running the asylum: Why high tech products drive us crazy and how to restore the sanity*. Indianapolis, IN: Sams.

Corporation for Digital Scholarship. (n.d.a.). *Omeka Classic*. https://omeka.org/classic/.

Corporation for Digital Scholarship. (n.d.b). *Omeka Classic user manual*. https://omeka.org/classic/docs/.

Corporation for Digital Scholarship. (n.d.c). *Project*. https://omeka.org/about/project/.

Corrin, L. (2010). Mining the museum: An installation confronting history. *Curator: The Museum Journal, 36*, 302–313. http://dx.doi.org/10.1111/j.2151-6952.1993.tb00804.x.

Council on Library and Information Resources. (n.d.). *Digitizing hidden special collections and archives: Amplifying unheard voices*. www.clir.org/hiddencollections/.

Cox, A. (2011). *Visualizing data at the New York Times*. www.slideshare.net/openjournalism/amanda-cox-visualizing-data-at-the-new-york-times.

Crane, D. (1972). *Invisible colleges: Diffusion of knowledge in scientific communities*. Chicago, IL: University of Chicago Press.

Creative Commons. (2019). *Creative Commons for educators and librarians*. Chicago: ALA Editions.

Crosby, E. W. (1983). Limited success against long odds: The Black county agent. *Agricultural History, 57*(3), 277–288. www.jstor.org/stable/3742454/.

Cuenca, E. L., & Kowaleski, M. (2018). Omeka and other digital platforms for undergraduate research projects on the Middle Ages. *Digital Medievalist, 11*(1), 1–21. http://doi.org/10.16995/dm.69.

Cullen, R. G. (2010). "Food will win the war": Motor trucks and the farm-to-table postal delivery program, 1917–1918. In T. Lera (Ed.), *The Winton M. Blount postal history symposia: Select papers, 2006–2009. Smithsonian contributions to history and technology* (No. 55, pp. 49–57). Washington, DC: Smithsonian Institution Scholarly Press. https://doi.org/10.5479/si.19486006.55.

Dallow, J., & Matilsky, B. C. (2005). *Family legacies: The art of Betye, Lezley, and Alison Saar*. Chapel Hill, NC: Ackland Art Museum and The University of North Carolina at Chapel Hill.

Dandar, D., Clifton-Ross, J., Dale, A., & Croft, R. (2020). Showcasing institutional research: Curating library exhibits to support scholarly communication. *Journal of Librarianship and Scholarly Communication, 8*, eP2335. https://doi.org/10.7710/2162-3309.2335.

Dawson, E. (2014a) Equity in informal science education: Developing an access and equity framework for science museums and science centres. *Studies in Science Education, 50*(2), 209–247. https://doi.org/10.1080/03057267.2014.957558

Dawson, E. (2014b). "Not designed for us": How science museums and science centers socially exclude low-income, minority ethnic groups. *Science Education*, *98*(6), 981–1008. https://doi.org/10.1002/sce.21133.

Dawson, E. (2019). *Equity, exclusion and everyday science learning: The experiences of minoritized groups*. London: Routledge.

Dawson, E., & Jensen, E. (2011). Towards a 'contextual turn' in visitor studies: Evaluating visitor segmentation and identity-related motivations. *Visitor Studies*, *14*(2), 127–140. http://dx.doi.org/10.1080/10645578.2011.608001.

Day, M., Delagrange, S. H., Palmquist, M., Pemberton, M. A., & Walker, J. R. (2013). What we really value: Redefining scholarly engagement in tenure and promotion protocols. *College Composition and Communication*, *65*(1), 185–208. www.jstor.org/stable/43490813.

de Bono, E. (1970). *Lateral thinking: Creativity step by step*. New York: HarperCollins Publishers.

Degner, M., Moser, S., & Lewalter, D. (2022). Digital media in institutional informal learning places: A systematic literature review. *Computers and Education Open*, *3*. https://doi.org/10.1016/j.caeo.2021.100068.

Denzin, N. K., & Lincoln, Y. S. (Eds.). (2017). *The SAGE handbook of qualitative research* (5th ed.). Thousand Oaks, CA: SAGE Publishing.

Derclaye, E. (Ed.). (2011). *Copyright and cultural heritage: Preservation and access to works in a digital world*. Cheltenham: Edward Elgar Publishing.

Després, C. (1991). The meaning of home: Literature review and directions for future research and theoretical development. *Journal of Architectural and Planning Research*, *8*(2), 96–115. www.jstor.org/stable/43029026.

Diehl, T. (2014, September 2). After Jeff Koons: A retrospective. *Los Angeles Review of Books*. https://lareviewofbooks.org/article/jeff-koons-retrospective/.

Dixon, D. (2016). Imagining the essay as digital assemblage: Collaborative student experiments with writing in Scalar. *Prompt: A Journal of Academic Writing Assignments*, *1*(1). https://doi.org/10.31719/pjaw.v1i1.13.

Dombrowski, Q. (2019, November 8). *Sorry for all the Drupal: Reflections on the 3rd anniversary of 'Drupal for Humanists'*. https://quinndombrowski.com/blog/2019/11/08/sorry-all-drupal-reflections-3rd-anniversary-drupal-humanists/.

Dombrowski, Q. (2022). Minimizing computing maximizes labor. *Digital Humanities Quarterly*, *16*(2). www.digitalhumanities.org/dhq/vol/16/2/000594/000594.html.

Doran, G. T. (1981). There's a S.M.A.R.T. way to write management's goals and objectives. *Management Review*, *70*(11), 35–36.

Dorner, D. G., Li Liew, C., & Ping Yeo, Y. (2007). A textured sculpture: The information needs of users of digitised New Zealand cultural heritage resources. *Online Information Review*, *31*(2), 166–184. https://doi.org/10.1108/14684520710747211.

Dreilinger, D. (2021). *The secret history of home economics: How trailblazing women harnessed the power of home and changed the way we live*. New York: W. W. Norton & Company.

Drew, J. A., Moreau, C. S., & Stiassny, M. L. J. (2017). Digitization of museum collections holds the potential to enhance researcher diversity. *Nature Ecology & Evolution*, *1*, 1789–1790. https://doi.org/10.1038/s41559-017-0401-6.

Driskell, D. C. (1976). *Two centuries of Black American art*. Los Angeles, CA/New York: Los Angeles County Museum of Art/Alfred A. Knopf, Inc.

Droitcour, B. (2018, May 1). Subcultural treasures. *Art in America*. www.artnews.com/art-in-america/features/subcultural-treasures-63510/.

Drucker, J. (2021). *The digital humanities coursebook: An introduction to digital methods for research and scholarship*. London: Routledge.

Drucker, J., & Svensson, P. B. (2016). The why and how of middleware. *Digital Humanities Quarterly*, *10*(2). www.digitalhumanities.org/dhq/vol/10/2/000248/000248.html.

Duncan, S. A. (2011). Introduction. *Visual Resources*, *21*(5), 227–231. https://doi.org/10.1080/01973760500166590.

Earhart, A. E., & Taylor, T. L. (2016). Pedagogies of race: Digital humanities in the age of Ferguson. In M. K. Gold & L. F. Klein (Eds.), *Debates in the digital humanities 2016* (pp. 251–264). Minneapolis, MN: University of Minnesota Press. https://doi.org/10.5749/j.ctt1cn6thb.24.

Easthope, H. (2010). A place called home. *Housing, Theory and Society*, *21*(3), 128–138. https://doi.org/10.1080/14036090410021360.

Elkington, S., & Stebbins, R. A. (2014). *The serious leisure perspective: An introduction*. London: Routledge.

Esri. (n.d.). *ArcGIS StoryMaps overview*. www.esri.com/en-us/arcgis/products/arcgis-storymaps/overview.

Everett, M., & Barrett, M. S. (2009) Investigating sustained visitor/museum relationships: Employing narrative research in the field of museum visitor studies. *Visitor Studies*, *12*(1), 2–15. https://doi.org/10.1080/10645570902769084.

Falk, J. H. (2005). Free-choice environmental learning: Framing the discussion. *Environmental Education Research*, *11*(3), 265–280. https://doi.org/10.1080/13504620500081129.

Falk, J. H. (2009). *Identity and the museum visitor experience*. London: Routledge.

Falk, J. H. (2013). Understanding museum visitors' motivations and learning. In I. E. Lundgaard & J. T. Jensen (Eds.), *Museums: Social learning spaces and knowledge producing processes* (pp. 106–127). København V and Hovedstaden: Kulturstyrelsen.

Falk, J. H., & Dierking, L. D. (1992). *The museum experience*. Washington, DC: Howells House.

Falk, J. H., & Dierking, L. D. (2000). *Learning from museums: Visitor experiences and the making of meaning*. Lanham, MD: Rowman & Littlefield.

Falk, J. H., & Dierking, L. D. (2002). *Lessons without limit: How free-choice learning is transforming education*. Lanham, MD: AltaMira Press.

Falk, J. H., & Dierking, L. D. (2004). The contextual model of learning. In G. Anderson (Ed.), *Reinventing the museum: Historical and contemporary perspectives on the paradigm shift* (pp. 139–142). Walnut Creek, CA: AltaMira Press.

Feinstein, N. W., & Meshoulam, D. (2014). Science for what public? Addressing equity in American science museums and science centers. *Journal of Research in Science Teaching*, *51*(3), 368–394. https://doi.org/10.1002/tea.21130.

Fenlon, K. (2017). Thematic research collections: Libraries and the evolution of alternative digital publishing in the humanities. *Library Trends*, *65*(4), 523–539. https://doi.org/10.1353/lib.2017.0016.

Ferguson, B. W. (1996). Exhibition rhetorics: Material speech and utter sense. In R. Greenburg, B. W. Ferguson, & S. Nairine (Eds.), *Thinking about exhibitions* (pp. 126–136). London: Routledge.

Fidel, R. (1994). User-centered indexing. *Journal of the American Society for Information Science*, *45*(8), 572–576. https://doi.org/10.1002/(SICI)1097-4571(199409)45:8%3C572::AID-ASI11%3E3.0.CO;2-X.

Finnis, J., & Kennedy, A. (2020). *The digital transformation agenda and GLAMs: A quick scan report for Europeana*. Den Haag: Europeana Foundation. https://pro.europeana.eu/files/Europeana_Professional/Publications/Digital%20transformation%20reports/

The%20digital%20transformation%20agenda%20and%20GLAMs%20-%20Culture24,%20findings%20and%20outcomes.pdf.

Fludernik, M. (2009). *An introduction to narratology*. London: Routledge.

Fouracre, D. (2015). Making an exhibition of ourselves? Academic libraries and exhibitions today. *The Journal of Academic Librarianship*, *41*, 377–385. http://dx.doi.org/10.1016/j.acalib.2015.05.008.

Fox, L. (2007) *Conceptualising home: Theories, laws and policies*. London: Hart.

Freeman, M., deMarrais, K., Preissle, J., Roulston, K., & St. Pierre, E. A. (2007). Standards of evidence in qualitative research: An incitement to discourse. *Educational Researcher*, *36*(1), 25–32. https://doi.org/10.3102/0013189X06298009.

Frey, B. B. (2018). Member check. In *The SAGE encyclopedia of educational research, measurement, and evaluation*. Thousand Oaks, CA: SAGE Publications. https://dx.doi.org/10.4135/9781506326139.n426.

Friedman, V. (2010, May 20). Web design trends 2010: Real-life metaphors and CSS3 adaptation. *Smashing Magazine*. www.smashingmagazine.com/2010/05/web-design-trends-2010-real-life-metaphors-and-css3-adaptation/.

Gardens, Libraries and Museums of the University of Oxford. (n.d.). *Statement on inclusion*. www.glam.ox.ac.uk/statement-on-inclusion.

Gardiner, E. (2015). *The digital humanities: A primer for students and scholars*. Cambridge: Cambridge University Press.

Gartner, R. (2021). *Metadata in the digital library: Building an integrated strategy with XML*. London: Facet Publications.

Gaskell, I. (2018). Display displayed. In J. Grave, C. Holm, V. Kobi, & C. van Eck (Eds.), *The agency of display: Objects, framings and parerga* (pp. 22–42). Dresden: Sandstein Verlag.

Gaston, H. K. (2015, February 5). Black history is American history. *The Huffington Post*. www.huffpost.com/entry/black-history-is-american-history_b_6618602.

Gates, Jr., H. L. (2020). *Stony the road: Reconstruction, white supremacy, and the rise of Jim Crow*. London: Penguin Books.

Gawain, S. (2008). *Creative visualization: Use the power of your imagination to create what you want in your life*. Novato, CA: New World Library.

Gazi, A. (2017). Writing text for museums of technology the case of the Industrial Gas Museum in Athens. *Museum Management and Curatorship*, *33*(1), 57–78. https://doi.org/10.1080/09647775.2017.1416310.

Gertner, R. K. (2019). The impact of cultural appropriation on destination image, tourism, and hospitality. *Thunderbird International Business Review*, *61*(6), 873–877. https://doi.org/10.1002/tie.22068.

Getty Research Institute. (2017). *Art & Architecture Thesaurus® online*. Los Angeles, CA: The Getty. www.getty.edu/research/tools/vocabularies/aat/index.html.

Giannini, T., & Bowen, J. P. (2022). Museums and digital culture: From reality to digitality in the age of COVID-19. *Heritage*, *5*, 192–214. https://doi.org/10.3390/heritage5010011.

Gibson, J. J. (1979). *The ecological approach to visual perception*. Boston, MA: Houghton Mifflin.

Gil, A. (2015, May 21). *The user, the learner and the machines we make*. https://go-dh.github.io/mincomp/thoughts/2015/05/21/user-vs-learner/.

Gilhooly, K. J., & Gilhooly, M. L. M. (2021). Chapter 1—creativity: Introduction. In K. J. Gilhooly & M. L. M. Gilhooly (Eds.), *Aging and creativity* (pp. 1–25). Cambridge, MA: Academic Press. https://doi.org/10.1016/B978-0-12-816401-3.00009-3.

Gilliland, A. J. (2016). Setting the stage. In M. Baca (Ed.), *Introduction to metadata* (3rd ed.). Los Angeles, CA: Getty Research Institute. www.getty.edu/publications/intrometadata/setting-the-stage/.
Gladwell, M. (2009). *What the dog saw: And other adventures*. New York: Little, Brown and Company.
Golub, K., & Liu, Y.-H. (2022). *Information and knowledge organisation in digital humanities: Global perspectives*. London: Routledge.
Goodwin, K. (2009). *Designing for the digital age: How to create human-centered products and services*. Hoboken, NJ: Wiley.
Graham, S. (2018, March 9). Using a static site generator to make a nicer Omeka front page. *Electric Archeology*. https://electricarchaeology.ca/2018/03/09/using-a-static-site-generator-to-make-a-nicer-omeka-front-page/.
Grave, J., Holm, C., Kobi, V., & Van Eck, C. (Eds). (2018). *The agency of display: Objects, framings and parerga*. Dresden, Germany: Sandstein Verlag.
Greenblatt, S. (1991). Resonance and wonder. In I. Karp & S. D. Lavine (Eds.), *Exhibiting cultures: The poetics and politics of museum display* (pp. 42–56). Washington, DC: Smithsonian Institution.
Halvorson, K. (2011). Understanding the discipline of web content strategy. *Bulletin of the American Society for Information Science and Technology*, *37*(2), 23–25. https://doi.org/10.1002/bult.2011.1720370208.
Halvorson, K., & Rach, M. (2012). *Content strategy for the web* (2nd ed.). Indianapolis, IN: New Riders Publishing.
Hane, C., & Atherton, M. (2017). *Designing connected content: Plan and model digital products for today and tomorrow*. Indianapolis, IN: New Riders Publishing.
Hanks, L. H., Hale, J., & MacLeod, S. (2012). Introduction: Museum making. The place of narrative. In L. H. Hanks, J. Hale, & S. MacLeod (Eds.), *Museum making: Narratives, architectures, exhibitions* (pp. xix–xxiii). London: Routledge.
Hannah-Jones, N., Roper, C., Silverman, I., & Silverstein, J. (Eds.). (2021). *The 1619 project: A new origin story*. New York: One World.
Hansen, B. (2017). *Great exhibits!: An exhibit planning and construction handbook for small museums*. Lanham, MD: Rowman & Littlefield Publishers.
Hartwich, M. (2016). *Mushroom in the Hills of Adelaide* [Photograph]. https://commons.wikimedia.org/wiki/File:Mushroom_in_the_Hills_of_Adelaide.jpg.
Hawbaker, C. C., & Burmeister, C. A. (1918). Marketing berries and cherries by parcel post. *U.S. Department of Agriculture Bulletin*, Number 688. https://archive.org/details/marketingberries688hawb.
Helfand, J. (2008, February 14). Animal magnetism. *Design Observer*. http://designobserver.com/feature/animal-magnetism/6537.
Hinchman, K. A., & Moore, D. W. (2013). Close reading: A cautionary interpretation. *Journal of Adolescent & Adult Literacy*, *56*(6), 441–450. https://doi.org/10.1002/JAAL.163.
Hoelscher, C. (2019). Constructing history: A student-created public history exhibit using Omeka. *Case Studies on Teaching with Primary Sources*. Case Study #11. https://www2.archivists.org/publications/epubs/Case-Studies-Teaching-With-Primary-Sources.
Hohmann, J. (2013) *The right to housing: Law, concepts, possibilities*. London: Hart.
Hooper-Greenhill, E. (2006). Studying visitors. In S. McDonald (Ed.), *A companion to museum studies* (pp. 362–376). Malden, MA: Blackwell Publishing.
Horodyski, J. (2022). *Metadata matters*. Boca Raton, FL: Auerbach Publications.
Illinois Institute of Technology Paul V. Galvin Library. (n.d.). *Building history*. https://buildinghistory.library.iit.edu/.

Internet Archive. (2022). *Archive-It Pro: Overview*. https://archive-it.org/blog/files/2022/05/Archive-It_pro.pdf.

Iser, W. (1972). The reading process: A phenomenological approach. *New Literary History*, *3*(2), 279–299. www.jstor.org/stable/468316.

Iser, W. (1978). *The act of reading: A theory of aesthetic response*. Baltimore, MD: Johns Hopkins University Press.

Johnson, B. S. (1973). *Aren't you rather young to be writing your memoirs?* London: Hutchinson.

Johnson, C. A. (2015). Social capital and library and information science research: Definitional chaos or coherent research enterprise? *Information Research*, *20*(4), paper 690. http://informationr.net/ir/20-4/paper690.html#.YycgmbTMK00.

Jones-Branch, C. (2021). *Better living by their own bootstraps: Black women's activism in rural Arkansas, 1914–1965*. Fayetteville, AR: The University of Arkansas Press.

Kaufman, J. C., & Beghetto, R. A. (2009). Beyond big and little: The Four C model of creativity. *Review of General Psychology*, *13*(1), 1–12. https://doi.org/10.1037/a0013688.

Kelly, E. J. (2018). Use of Louisiana's digital cultural heritage by wikipedians. *Journal of Web Librarianship*, *12*(2), 85–106. https://doi.org/10.1080/19322909.2017.1391733.

www.tandfonline.com/doi/full/10.1080/0142159X.2020.1755030.

Kilroy-Ewbank, L. G. (2018). Doing digital art history in a pre-Columbian art survey class: Creating an Omeka exhibition around the Mixtec Codex Zouche-Nuttall. *The Journal of Interactive Technology and Pedagogy*, *12*. https://jitp.commons.gc.cuny.edu/doing-digital-art-history-in-a-pre-columbian-art-survey-class-creating-an-omeka-exhibition-around-the-mixtec-codex-zouche-nuttall/.

King, E., Smith, M. P., Wilson, P. F., & Williams, M. A. (2021). Digital responses of UK museum exhibitions to the COVID-19 crisis, March–June 2020. *Curator: The Museum Journal*, *64*(3), 487–504. https://doi.org/10.1111/cura.12413.

King, L. J. (2020). Black history is not American history: Toward a framework of Black historical consciousness. *Social Education*, *84*(6), 335–341. www.socialstudies.org/social-education/84/6/black-history-not-american-history-toward-framework-black-historical.

Kirchberg, V., & Tröndle, M. (2012). Experiencing exhibitions: A review of studies on visitor experiences in museums. *Curator: The Museum Journal*, *55*(4), 435–452. https://doi.org/10.1111/j.2151-6952.2012.00167.x.

Knight Foundation. (2020). *Digital readiness and innovation in museums: A baseline national survey*. Miami: Knight Foundation. https://knightfoundation.org/wp-content/uploads/2020/10/Digital-Readiness-and-Innovation-in-Museums-Report.pdf.

Kowalski, M. (2017). Breaking down silo walls: Successful collaboration across library departments. *Library Leadership & Management*, *31*(2), 1–15.

Krug, S. (2013). *Don't make me think, revisited: A common sense approach to web usability* (3rd ed.). Hoboken, NJ: New Riders.

Kucsma, J., Reiss, K., & Sidman, A. (2010). Using Omeka to build digital collections: The METRO case study. *D-Lib Magazine*, *16*(3/4). www.dlib.org/dlib/march10/kucsma/03kucsma.html.

Lacher-Feldman, J. L. (2013). *Exhibits in archives and special collections libraries*. Chicago, IL: Society of American Archivists.

Lakoff, G. (1993). The contemporary theory of metaphor. In A. Ortony (Ed.), *Metaphor and thought* (2nd ed., pp. 202–251). Cambridge: Cambridge University Press. https://doi.org/10.1017/CBO9781139173865.013.

Lakoff, G., & Johnson, M. (1980). *Metaphors we live by*. Chicago, IL: The University of Chicago Press.

Latham, K. F. (2013). Numinous experiences with museum objects. *Visitor Studies*, *16*(1), 3–20. https://doi.org/10.1080/10645578.2013.767728.

Lathem, E. C., & Thompson, L. (1963). *Robert Frost: Farm-poultryman*. Hanover, NH: Dartmouth Publications.

Lepore, J. (2002). Historical writing and the revival of narrative. *Nieman Reports: The Nieman Foundation for Journalism at Harvard University*, *56*(1), 51–53. https://niemanreports.org/wp-content/uploads/2014/04/02spring.pdf.

Lewis, P. (1989). *Comic effects: Interdisciplinary approaches to humor in literature*. Albany, NY: State University of New York Press.

Lin, A. C. H., Fernandez, W. D., & Gregor, S. (2012). Understanding web enjoyment experiences and informal learning: A study in a museum context. *Decision Support Systems*, *53*(4), 846–858. https://doi.org/10.1016/j.dss.2012.05.020.

Lin, A. C. H., & Gregor, S. (2006). Designing websites for learning and enjoyment: A study of museum experiences. *International Review of Research in Open and Distance Learning*, *7*(3), 1–21. www.learntechlib.org/p/49690/.

Lofland, J., & Lofland, L. H. (1995). *Analyzing social settings: A guide to qualitative observation and analysis* (3rd ed.). New York: Wadsworth Publishing Company.

Long, C., & Leen, D. (2022, July 13). Reflection on the use of Scalar. In *The River-side: Reflections on research collections*. Cork: University College Cork Library. https://blogs.ucc.ie/wordpress/theriverside/2022/07/13/reflection-on-the-use-of-scalar/.

Lord, B. (2014). *Manual of museum exhibitions* (2nd ed.). Lanham, MD: Rowman & Littlefield Publishers.

Lubar, S. (2013). Timelines in exhibitions. *Curator: The Museum Journal*, *56*(2), 169–188. https://doi.org/10.1111/cura.12018.

Lucas, B. J., & Nordgren, L. F. (2021). Lay people's beliefs about creativity: Evidence for an insight bias. *Trends in Cognitive Sciences*, *26*(1), 6–7.

MacDonald, C. M. (2016). User experience librarians: User advocates, user researchers, usability evaluators, or all of the above? *Proceedings of the Association for Information Science and Technology*, *52*(1), 1–10. https://doi.org/10.1002/pra2.2015.145052010055.

Madrid, M. M. (2013). A study of digital curator competences: A survey of experts. *The International Information & Library Review*, *45*(3–4), 149–156. https://doi.org/10.1016/j.iilr.2013.09.001.

Mallett, S. (2004). Understanding home: A critical review of the literature. *The Sociological Review*, *52*(1), 62–89. https://doi.org/10.1111/j.1467-954X.2004.00442.x.

Mao, R., & Fu, Y. (2021). Interweaving multiple contexts for objects in museum exhibitions: A contextual approach. *Museum Management and Curatorship*, 1–22. https://doi.org/10.1080/09647775.2021.1914141.

Marini, F. (2019). Exhibitions in special collections, rare book libraries and archives: Questions to ask ourselves. *Alexandria: The Journal of National and International Library and Information Issues*, *29*(1/2), 8–29. https://doi.org/10.1177%2F0955749019876122.

Maron, D., & Feinberg, M. (2018). What does it mean to adopt a metadata standard? A case study of Omeka and the Dublin Core. *Journal of Documentation*, *74*(4), 674–691. https://doi.org/10.1108/JD-06-2017-0095.

Marsh, A. C. (2013). Omeka in the classroom: The challenges of teaching material culture in a digital world. *Literary and Linguistic Computing*, *28*(2), 279–282. https://doi.org/10.1093/llc/fqs068.

Marsh, E. (n.d.). *Subsistence homesteads. Stories from the collection*. National Agricultural Library. https://www.nal.usda.gov/collections/stories/subsistence-homesteads.

Marsh, E. (2016a, January 9). *Like a 'fine pullet' at the chicken farm: Robert Frost's poultry paper articles* [Conference presentation]. Austin, TX: Modern Language Association Convention. https://apps.mla.org/conv_listings_details_print?prog_id=A046A&year=2016.

Marsh, E. (2016b, March 8) *Showcasing digital assets* [Conference presentation]. Washington, DC: Computer in Libraries, Library Labs: Research, Innovation, & Imagination. https://conferences.infotoday.com/documents/220/B103_Marsh.pptx.

Marsh, E. (2016c, April 15). *If a pdf falls in the forest will anyone see it? Building a library ecosystem for digital materials* [Conference presentation]. Washington, DC: Digital Public Library of America's DPLAFest. https://youtu.be/YQ2TniMc0Dg?t=1551.

Marsh, E. (2017). Chickens, aprons, markets, and cans: How the National Agricultural Library uses Omeka as its content management system for digital exhibits. *Digital Library Perspectives*, *33*(4), 361–377. https://doi.org/10.1108/DLP-03-2017-0009.

Marsh, E. (2022a). *Display of different types of information resources, ordered by their degree of interpretation and amount of analytical predetermination: Thematic essays, thematic research collections and critical editions, digital exhibits, curated collections, and search and discovery systems* [Infographic]. https://emily-marsh.com/Digital_Exhibits_for_Cultural_Institutions/Figure_1.1.jpg.

Marsh, E. (2022b). Digital exhibit orientation and functions [Infographic]. https://emily-marsh.com/Digital_Exhibits_for_Cultural_Institutions/Figure_2.2.jpg.

Marsh, E. (2022c). *Data librarian persona for a scientific data repository* [Infographic]. https://emily-marsh.com/Digital_Exhibits_for_Cultural_Institutions/Figure_3.1.jpg.

Marsh, E. (2022d). *A sample of materials discovered during background research for four digital exhibits* [Infographic]. https://emily-marsh.com/Digital_Exhibits_for_Cultural_Institutions/Figure_4.1.jpg.

Marsh, E. (2022e). *Wireframe of home page for proposed exhibit on Negro Extension with slideshow of featured items and list of topic areas* [Infographic]. https://emily-marsh.com/Digital_Exhibits_for_Cultural_Institutions/Figure_4.2.jpg.

Marsh, E. (2022f). *Exhibit proposal with communication plan* [Infographic]. https://emily-marsh.com/Digital_Exhibits_for_Cultural_Institutions/Figure_4.3.jpg.

Marsh, E. (2022g). *Home page of "Frost on Chickens" exhibit about the poet Robert Frost and poultry farming* [Screenshot]. https://emily-marsh.com/Digital_Exhibits_for_Cultural_Institutions/Figure_5.1.jpg.

Marsh, E. (2022h). *Home page of "Apron Strings and Kitchen Sinks" exhibit about the US Department of Agriculture's Bureau of Home Economics* [Screenshot]. https://emily-marsh.com/Digital_Exhibits_for_Cultural_Institutions/Figure_5.2.jpg.

Marsh, E. (2022i). *Home page of "George Washington Carver" exhibit featuring his technical bulletins* [Screenshot]. https://emily-marsh.com/Digital_Exhibits_for_Cultural_Institutions/Figure_5.3.jpg.

Marsh, E. (2022j). *Home page of "Mailboxes, Mom and Pop Stands, and Markets: Local Foods Then and Now" exhibit* [Screenshot]. https://emily-marsh.com/Digital_Exhibits_for_Cultural_Institutions/Figure_5.4.jpg.

Marsh, E. (2022k). *Home page of "Small Agriculture" exhibit* [Screenshot]. https://emily-marsh.com/Digital_Exhibits_for_Cultural_Institutions/Figure_5.5.jpg.

Marsh, E. (2022l). *Two fictional exhibit communication plans for proposed exhibits on tick control and food waste* [Infographic]. https://emily-marsh.com/Digital_Exhibits_for_Cultural_Institutions/Figure_6.1.jpg.

Marsh, E. (2022m). *Different views of object-level metadata for Work Clothes for Women in an exhibit timeline: The "bite", from an item view within an exhibit timeline, the "snack", from the full item record in the exhibit, and from the item's original Internet Archive record, the "meal"* [Infographic]. https://emily-marsh.com/Digital_Exhibits_for_Cultural_Institutions/Figure_7.1.jpg.

Marsh, E. E., & White, M. D. (2003). A taxonomy of relationships between images and text. *Journal of Documentation, 59*(6), 647–672. https://doi.org/10.1108/00220410310506303.

Martinez, S., Hand, M. S., Da Pra, M., Pollack, S., Ralston, K., Smith, T., Vogel, S., Clark, S., Lohr, L., Low, S., & Newman, C. (2010). *Local food systems: Concepts, impacts, and issues*. Economic Research Report (ERR) Number 97. https://handle.nal.usda.gov/10113/60454.

Maryland Historical Society. (1992–1993). *Mining the museum: 'Metalwork, 1793–1880.'* [Photograph]. Baltimore, MD: Maryland Center for History and Culture. www.mdhistory.org/resources/mining-the-museum-metalwork-1793-1880/.

Masters, K. (1991, June 2). They went that away. *Washington Post*. www.washingtonpost.com/archive/lifestyle/style/1991/06/02/they-went-thataway/842e3f38-cda4-4b2d-811f-bd315b32f3b5/.

McKeachie, W. J. (1987). Cognitive skills and their transfer: Discussion. *International Journal of Educational Research, 11*(6), 707–712. https://doi.org/10.1016/0883-0355(87)90010-3.

McKechnie, L. E. F., Julien, H., & Oliphant, T. (2008). Communicating research findings to library and information science practitioners: A study of ISIC papers from 1996 to 2000. *Information Research, 13*(4), Paper 375. http://informationr.net/ir/13-4/paper375.html.

McLeland, C., Chalmers, A., & Bibb, J. (2021). Establishing an Omeka digital exhibits presence: Collaboration and customization. *Library Faculty Presentations & Publications, 95*. https://digitalcommons.unf.edu/library_facpub/95.

Meeks, E., & Grossner, K. (2012). ORBIS: An interactive scholarly work on the Roman world. *Journal of Digital Humanities, 1*(3). http://journalofdigitalhumanities.org/1-3/orbis-an-interactive-scholarly-work-on-the-roman-world-by-elijah-meeks-and-karl-grossner/.

Meier, A. (2022, January 9). *Afrofuturist period room* [Photograph]. www.flickr.com/photos/astrozombie/51937289179/.

Mihram, D., & Fletcher, C. (2019). USC Digital Voltaire: Centering digital humanities in the traditions of library and archival science. *Portal: Libraries and the Academy, 19*(1), 7–17. https://doi.org/10.1353/pla.2019.0001.

Miller, S. J. (2022). *Metadata for digital collections* (2nd ed.). Chicago, IL: ALA Neal-Schuman.

Miller, W. L., & Crabtree, B. F. (1992). Primary care research: A multimethod typology and qualitative road map. In B. F. Crabtree & W. L. Miller (Eds.), *Doing qualitative research. Research methods for primary care, volume 3* (pp. 3–30). Newbury Park, CA: SAGE Publications.

Minneapolis Institute of Art. (n.d.). *Living rooms: The period room initiative*. https://new.artsmia.org/living-rooms/.

Minsky, M. (1975). A framework for representing knowledge. In P. H. Winston (Ed.), *The psychology of computer vision* (pp. 211–277). New York: McGraw Hill.

Monson, J. D. (2017). *Getting started with digital collections: Scaling to fit your organization*. Chicago, IL: American Library Association.

Morgan, K., & Proffitt, M. (2017). *Advancing the national digital platform: The state of digitization in US public and state libraries*. Dublin, OH: OCLC Online Computer

Library Center, Inc. www.oclc.org/content/dam/research/publications/2017/oclcresearch-advancing-the-national-digital-platform-2017.pdf.

Morgan, P. C. (2018). The consequences of framing digital humanities tools as easy to use. *College & Undergraduate Libraries*, *25*(3), 211–231. https://doi.org/10.1080/10691316.2018.1480440.

Morris Hargreaves McIntyre. (n.d.a). *Culture segments*. www.culturehive.co.uk/wp-content/uploads/2013/05/CultureSegments2.pdf.

Morris Hargreaves McIntyre. (n.d.b). *Culture segments in action: Grayson Perry at the British Museum*. www.culturehive.co.uk/wp-content/uploads/2020/10/GraysonPerry-case-study-FINAL1-1.pdf.

Murray, J. (1997). *Hamlet on the holodeck: The future of narrative in cyberspace*. New York: The Free Press.

Murzyn-Kupisz, M., & Działek, J. (2013). Cultural heritage in building and enhancing social capital, *Journal of Cultural Heritage Management and Sustainable Development*, *3*(1), 35–54. https://doi.org/10.1108/20441261311317392.

Myburgh, S., & Tammaro, A. M. (2013). *Exploring education for digital librarians: Meaning, modes and models*. Oxford: Chandos Publishing.

National Archives. (n.d.). *Digital engagement toolkit: Platform guides*. www.nationalarchives.gov.uk/archives-sector/projects-and-programmes/plugged-in-powered-up/digital-engagement-toolkit/platform-guides/digital-exhibitions/.

National Institute of Food and Agriculture. USDA. (n.d.). *Cooperative extension history*. U.S. Department of Agriculture. www.nifa.usda.gov/about-nifa/how-we-work/extension/cooperative-extension-history.

National Park Service. Harper's Ferry Center. U.S. Department of the Interior. (2011, October 21). *Museum and visitor center exhibit planning, design, and fabrication process: Summary description*. www.nps.gov/subjects/hfc/upload/EX-PD-Prod-Charts-R.pdf.

National Society Daughters of the American Revolution (NSDAR). (2021). *DAR museum period rooms*. Author. www.dar.org/museum/dar-museum-period-rooms.

Newkirk, P. (2020, April 6). How David C. Driskell shaped the story of Black art in America. *ARTnews*. www.artnews.com/art-news/retrospective/david-c-driskell-shaped-black-art-pamela-newkirk-archives-1202683191/.

Ngai, C. S.-B., & Singh, R. G. (2017). Move structure and communication style of leaders' messages in corporate discourse: A cross-cultural perspective. *Discourse & Communication*, *11*(3), 276–295. https://doi.org/10.1177/1750481317697860.

Nochlin, L. (1971). Why are there no great women artists? In V. Gornick & B. K. Moran (Eds.), *Woman in sexist society: Studies in power and powerlessness* (pp. 344–366). New York: Basic Books.

Norman, D. A. (1988). *The psychology of everyday things*. New York: Basic Books.

Norris, T. B., & Suomela, T. (2017). Information in the ecosystem: Against the "information ecosystem." *First Monday*, *22*(9). https://firstmonday.org/ojs/index.php/fm/article/download/6847/6530.

Northern Ireland Assembly Research and Information Service. (2018, September 12). Measuring museum success: How and why? *Research Matters. Northern Ireland Assembly*. www.assemblyresearchmatters.org/2018/09/12/measuring-museum-success-how-and-why/.

Novara, E. A., & Novara, V. J. (2017). Exhibits as scholarship: Strategies for acceptance, documentation, and evaluation in academic libraries. *The American Archivist*, *80*(2), 355–372. https://doi.org/10.17723/0360-9081-80.2.355.

Núñez, R. F., & Sweetser, E. (2006). With the future behind them: Convergent evidence from Aymara language and gesture in the crosslinguistic comparison of spatial construals of time. *Cognitive Science*, *30*(3), 401–450. https://doi.org/10.1207/s15516709cog0000_62.

Nyröp, M., & Gil, A. (2019). *Wax*. https://minicomp.github.io/wax/.

O'Flahavan, L. (n.d.). The bite, the snack, and the meal: How to feed content-hungry site visitors. *E-Write*. https://ewriteonline.com/bite-snack-and-meal-how-to-feed-content-hungry-site-visitors/.

Osterman, M. (2012). Museums and Twitter: An exploratory qualitative study of how museums use Twitter for audience development and engagement. *Journal of Educational Multimedia and Hypermedia*, *21*(3), 29–43. www.learntechlib.org/primary/p/39141/.

Owens, T., Sands, A. E., Reyonlds, E., Neal, J., Mayeaux, S., & Marx, M. (2018). Digital infrastructures that embody library principles: The IMLS National Digital Platform as a framework for digital library tools and services. In P. D. Fernandez & K. Tilton (Eds.), *Applying library values to emerging technology: Decision-making in the age of open access, maker spaces, and the ever-changing library* (pp. 73–88). ACRL Publications in Librarianship, Number 72. Chicago, IL: Association of College and Research Libraries. www.imls.gov/publications/digital-infrastructures-embody-library-principles-imls-national-digital-platform.

Packer, J. (2006). Learning for fun: The unique contribution of educational leisure experiences. *Curator: The Museum Journal*, *49*(3), 329–344. https://doi.org/10.1111/j.2151-6952.2006.tb00227.x.

Paley, L. M. (1941). *The education and responsibilities of Negro home demonstration agents in Texas*. Unpublished Master's Thesis. Kansas State College of Agriculture and Applied Science. https://core.ac.uk/download/pdf/10653109.pdf.

Pallud, J., & Straub, D. W. (2014). Effective website design for experience-influenced environments: The case of high culture museums. *Information & Management*, *51*(3), 359–373. https://doi.org/10.1016/j.im.2014.02.010.

Palmer, C. L. (2004). Thematic research collections. In Schreibman, S., Siemens, R., & Unsworth, J. (Eds.), *A companion to digital humanities*. Hoboken, NJ: Wiley-Blackwell. https://doi.org/10.1002/9780470999875.ch24.

Pappa, D., & Makropoulos, C. (2021). Novel ways of discovering, capturing and experiencing cultural heritage: A review of current state-of-the-art, challenges and future directions. In D. Turcanu-Carutiu (Ed.), *Heritage*. London: IntechOpen Limited. https://doi.org/10.5772/intechopen.99170.

Patton, M. Q. (1999). Enhancing the quality and credibility of qualitative analysis. *HSR: Health Services Research*, *34*(5 Pt 2), 1189–1208. www.ncbi.nlm.nih.gov/pmc/articles/PMC1089059/pdf/hsresearch00022-0112.pdf.

Pauwels, L., & Mannay, D. (2019). *The SAGE handbook of visual research methods* (2nd ed.). Thousand Oaks, CA: SAGE Publishing.

Peacock, D., & Brownbill, J. (2007). Audiences, visitors, users: Reconceptualising users of museum on-line content and services. In J. Trant & D. Bearman (Eds.), *Museums and The web 2007: Selected papers from an international conference* (pp. 223–240). Toronto, ON: Archives & Museum Informatics. www.archimuse.com/mw2007/papers/peacock/peacock.html.

Pearce, S. M. (1994). Thinking about things. In S. M. Pearce (Ed.), *Interpreting objects and collections* (pp. 125–132). London: Routledge.

Peng, R., Chen, J., & Wu, W. (2021). Mapping innovation research in organizations: A bibliometric analysis. *Frontiers in Psychology*, *12*, 750960. https://doi.org/10.3389/fpsyg.2021.750960.

Pilgrim, D. H. (1978). Inherited from the past: The American period room. *The American Art Journal*, *10*(1), 4–23. www.jstor.org/stable/1594106.

Pink, S. (2012). *Advances in visual methodology*. Thousand Oaks, CA: SAGE Publishing.

Poirier, R., & Richardson, M. (Eds.). (1995). *Robert Frost: Collected poems, prose, and plays*. New York: The Library of America.

Porsdam, H. (Ed.). (2016). *Copyrighting creativity: Creative values, cultural heritage institutions and systems of intellectual property*. London: Routledge.

Posner, M. (2013). No half measures: Overcoming common challenges to doing digital humanities in the library. *Journal of Library Administration*, *53*(1), 43–52. https://doi.org/10.1080/01930826.2013.756694.

Powell, R. R., Baker, L. M., & Mika, J. J. (2002). Library and information science practitioners and research. *Library & Information Science Research*, *24*(1), 49–72. https://doi.org/10.1016/S0740-8188(01)00104-9.

Price, K. M. (2009). Edition, project, database, archive, thematic research collection: What's in a name? *Digital Humanities Quarterly*, *3*(3). www.digitalhumanities.org/dhq/vol/3/3/000053/000053.html.

Priestner, A., & Borg, M. (Eds.). (2016). *User experience in libraries: Applying ethnography and human-center design*. London: Routledge.

Prior, P. (2003, March). *Are communities of practice really an alternative to discourse communities?* [Conference presentation]. Meeting of the American Association of Applied Linguistics (AAAL): The Diversity of Applied Linguistics, Arlington, VA.

Project Blacklight. (n.d.). *Blacklight*. https://projectblacklight.org/.

Przybyszewski, L. (2014). *The lost art of dress: The women who once made America stylish*. New York: Basic Books.

Rafiee, A., Spooren, W., & Sanders, J. (2018). Culture and discourse structure: A comparative study of Dutch and Iranian news texts. *Discourse & Communication*, *12*(1), 58–79. https://doi.org/10.1177/1750481317735626.

Randel, J. (2010). *The skinny on creativity: Thinking outside the box*. Westport, CT: Rand Media Company.

Ranganathan, S. R. (1931). *The five laws of library science* (Madras Library Association). London: Edward Goldston Ltd.

Rare Books and Manuscripts Section, Association of College and Research Libraries. (n.d.). *The Katharine Kyes Leab & Daniel J. Leab American book prices current exhibition awards: Guidelines and rules for submissions*. American Library Association. https://rbms.info/committees/exhibition_awards/submission-rules/.

Rasmussen, I. (2022). A homemade history: Documenting the Harlem renaissance in Alexander Gumby's scrapbooks. In S. Helgesson, H. Bodin, & A. M. Alling (Eds.), *Literature and the making of the world: Cosmopolitan texts, vernacular practices* (pp. 173–214). London: Bloomsbury Academic.

Ravelli, L. J. (2006). *Museum texts: Communication frameworks*. London: Routledge.

Reclaim Hosting. (2021a). *Installing Omeka Classic on Reclaim Hosting*. https://support.reclaimhosting.com/hc/en-us/articles/1500005712342-Installing-Omeka-Classic-on-Reclaim-Hosting.

Reclaim Hosting. (2021b). *Installing Scalar*. https://support.reclaimhosting.com/hc/en-us/articles/1500005543242-Installing-Scalar.

Regan, S. (1998). Reader-response criticism and reception theory. In S. Eliot & W. R. Owens (Eds.), *A handbook to literary research* (pp. 139–149). London: Routledge.

Reid, T. (2021, December 2). Light years: The Met's Afrofuturist period room thinks inside the box. *Artforum Slant*. www.artforum.com/slant/the-met-s-afrofuturist-period-room-thinks-inside-the-box-87375.

Reitstätter, L., Galter, K., & Bakondi, F. (2022). Looking to read: How visitors use exhibit labels in the art museum. *Visitor Studies*. https://doi.org/10.1080/10645578.2021.2018251.

Rhizome. (n.d.). *Conifer*. https://conifer.rhizome.org/.

Rhododendrites. (2016, December 17). *The glass room* [Photograph]. https://commons.wikimedia.org/wiki/File:The_Glass_Room_(71744).jpg.

Richardson, M. (Ed.). (2014). *Robert Frost in context*. Oxford: Oxford University Press.

Riley, J. (2017). *Understanding metadata: What is metadata, and what is it for? NISO primer series*. Baltimore, MD: National Information Standards Organization. http://groups.niso.org/higherlogic/ws/public/download/17446/Understanding%20Metadata.pdf.

Risam, R., & Gil, A. (2022). Introduction: The questions of minimal computing. *Digital Humanities Quarterly*, *16*(2). www.digitalhumanities.org/dhq/vol/16/2/000646/000646.html.

Roberts, L. C. (1997). *From knowledge to narrative: Educators and the changing museum*. Washington, DC: Smithsonian Institution Press.

Rogoff, B., Callanan, M., Guitiérrez, K. D., & Erickson, F. (2016). The organization of informal learning. *Review of Research in Education*, *40*(1), 356–401. https://doi.org/10.3102/0091732X16680994.

Roman, G. T. (2018). Scalar and Omeka. *The Journal of the Society of Architectural Historians*, *77*(1), 122–123. https://doi.org/10.1525/jsah.2018.77.1.122.

Roppola, T. (2013). *Designing for the museum visitor experience*. London: Routledge.

Rosch, E., & Mervis, C. G. (1975). Family resemblances: Studies in the internal structure of categories. *Cognitive Psychology*, *7*(4), 573–605. https://doi.org/10.1016/0010-0285(75)90024-9.

Rossiter, M. W. (1998). *Women scientists in America: Before affirmative action, 1940–1972*. Baltimore, MD: Johns Hopkins University Press.

Rounds, J. (2006). Doing identity work in museums. *Curator: The Museum Journal*, *49*(2), 133–150. https://doi.org/10.1111/j.2151-6952.2006.tb00208.x.

Roy Rosenzweig Center for History and New Media. (n.d.a). *Omeka*. https://rrchnm.org/portfolio-item/omeka/

Roy Rosenzweig Center for History and New Media. (n.d.b). *Omeka Classic plugins*. https://omeka.org/classic/plugins/.

Royal College of Surgeons of England. (2019). *Digital exhibitions*. https://scp.rcseng.ac.uk/client/en_GB/exhibitions.

Rubin, J., & Chisnell, D. (2008). *Handbook of usability testing: How to plan, design, and conduct effective tests* (2nd ed.). Hoboken, NJ: Wiley.

Runco, M. A., & Jaeger, G. J. (2012). The standard definition of creativity. *Creativity Research Journal*, *24*(1), 92–96. https://doi.org/10.1080/10400419.2012.650092.

Russell, J., & Hensley, M. (2017). Beyond buttonology: Digital humanities, digital pedagogy, and the ACRL framework. *College & Research Libraries News*, *78*(11), 588. https://doi.org/10.5860/crln.78.11.588.

Ruthven, I. (2021). Resonance and the experience of relevance. *Journal of the American Society of Information Science and Technology*, *72*(5), 554–569. https://doi.org/10.1002/asi.24424.

Saffer, D. (2005). *The role of metaphor in interaction design*. Unpublished master's thesis. Carnegie Mellon University.

Saracevic, T. (1975). Relevance: A review of and a framework for the thinking on the notion in information science. *Journal of the American Society for Information Science, 26*(6), 321–343. https://doi.org/10.1002/asi.4630260604.

Schugurensky, D. (2000). *The forms of informal learning: Towards a conceptualization of the field.* NALL Working Paper #19. Centre for the Study of Education and Work, Ontario Institute for Studies in Education, University of Toronto. https://hdl.handle.net/1807/2733.

Serrell, B. (2015). *Exhibit labels: An interpretive approach* (2nd ed.). Lanham, MD: Rowman & Littlefield.

Serwer, A. (2021). *The cruelty is the point: The past, present, and future of Trump's America.* New York: One World.

Sexton, C. (2014). Mobile museums: Where things stand. In J. Pagel & K. Donahue (Eds.), *NEMO annual conference, Bucharest, Romania, November 2013 – 'Museums in the digital age, museums and the development of active citizenship'* (pp. 15–19). Berlin: Network of European Museum Organisations.

Shaked, N. (2008). Phantom sightings: Art after the Chicano movement. *American Quarterly, 60*(4), 1057–1072. www.jstor.org/stable/40068561.

Shankweiler, J., & Seguin, T. (2018). Lasting experiences: Taking galleries from glass cases to online access repositories. In P. D. Fernandez & K. Tilton (Eds.), *Applying library values to emerging technology: Decision-making in the age of open access, maker spaces, and the ever-changing library* (pp. 305–313). ACRL Publications in Librarianship, Number 72. Chicago, IL: Association of College and Research Libraries.

Shannon, C. E., & Weaver, W. (1949). *The mathematical theory of communication.* Champaign, IL: University of Illinois Press.

Sibaja, R. (2017). Omeka to ¡Animales! Building a digital repository of research on Argentine soccer. *Journal of Sport History, 44*(2), 209–224. https://doi.org/10.5406/jsporthistory.44.2.0209.

Sigmond, C. (2019). The many shapes of formative evaluation in exhibition development. *Exhibition*, Spring, 34–41. https://www.name-aam.org/s/09_Exhibition_TheManyShapesofFormativeEvalution.pdf.

Simpson, A. L. (2012). Objectifying objects: Omitting ideology in Gustav Stickley Craftsman period rooms. *Shift: Graduate Journal of Visual and Material Culture, 5.* http://shiftjournal.org/wp-content/uploads/2014/11/simpson.pdf.

Sitzia, E. (2016). Narrative theories and learning in contemporary art museums: A theoretical exploration. *Stedelijk Studies, 4*(Spring). https://stedelijkstudies.com/journal/narrative-theories-learning-contemporary-art-museums-theoretical-exploration/.

Skov, M. (2013). Hobby-related information-seeking behaviour of highly dedicated online museum visitors. *Information Research, 18*(4). http://informationr.net/ir/18-4/paper597.html#.YnMUTdrMK00.

Skov, M., & Ingwersen, P. (2008). Exploring information seeking behaviour in a digital museum context. In P. Borlund & J. W. Schneider (Eds.), *IIiX'08: Proceedings of the second international symposium on information interaction in context* (pp. 110–115). New York: Association for Computing Machinery. https://doi.org/10.1145/1414694.1414719.

Smith, B. (1993, March 5). At the Whitney, a biennial with a social conscience. *New York Times*, Section C, Page 1. www.nytimes.com/1993/03/05/arts/at-the-whitney-a-biennial-with-a-social-conscience.html.

Smith, R. (2018, November 1). A long overdue light on Black models of early modernism. *New York Times*, Section C, Page 15. www.nytimes.com/2018/11/01/arts/design/black-models-olympia-columbia-university.html.

Smithsonian Institution. (n.d). *Museum on main street: Exhibition planning guide*. Washington, DC: Smithsonian Institution. https://museumonmainstreet.org/sites/default/files/exhibition_planning_guide_sk_final.pdf.

Smithsonian Institution Office of Policy and Analysis. (2002). *Exhibitions and their audiences: Actual and potential*. Washington, DC: Smithsonian Institution. www.si.edu/content/opanda/docs/rpts2002/02.09.exhibitaudience.final.pdf.

Smithsonian Institution & Wayne State University Library System. (2022). *About the story of the beautiful*. http://peacockroom.wayne.edu/about.

Soergel, D. (1994). Indexing and retrieval performance: The logical evidence. *Journal of the American Society for Information Science*, *45*(8), 589–599. https://doi.org/10.1002/(SICI)1097-4571(199409)45:8%3C589::AID-ASI14%3E3.0.CO;2-E.

Sohan, V. K. (2015). "But a quilt is more": Recontextualizing the discourse(s) of the Gee's bend quilts. *College English*, *77*(4), 294–316. www.jstor.org/stable/24240050.

Song, L., Golinkoff, R. M., Stuehling, A., Resnick, I., Mahajan, N., Hirsh-Pasek, K., & Thompson, N. (2017). Parents' and experts' awareness of learning opportunities in children's museum exhibits. *Journal of Applied Developmental Psychology*, *49*, 39–45. https://doi.org/10.1016%2Fj.appdev.2017.01.006.

Sonnenwald, D. H. (1999). Evolving perspectives of human information behavior: Contexts, situations, social networks and information horizons. In T. Wilson & D. Allen (Eds.), *Exploring the contexts of information behavior: Proceedings of the second international conference in information needs* (pp. 176–190). London: Taylor Graham.

Sonnenwald, D. H., Wildemuth, B. S., & Harmon, G. L. (2001). A research method to investigate information seeking using the concept of information horizons: An example from a study of lower socio-economic students' information seeking behavior. *The New Review of Information Behavior Research*, *2*, 65–86. http://hdl.handle.net/10150/105932.

Stamburg, S. (2021, February 22). Happy birthday to the Phillips Collection, America's first museum of modern art. *NPR*. www.npr.org/2021/02/22/965371115/happy-birthday-to-the-phillips-collection-americas-first-museum-of-modern-art.

Starr, L. (2020, September 24). Laying the foundation for storytelling: Tips for digital transformation & sustainability. *Pass It Down Blog*. www.passitdown.com/blog-posts/laying-the-foundation-for-storytelling-tips-for-digital-transformation-sustainability.

Stebbins, R. A. (2015). *Serious leisure: A perspective for our time* (2nd ed.). London: Routledge.

Stebbins, R. A. (2020). *The serious leisure perspective: A synthesis*. London: Palgrave Macmillan.

Sternberg, R. J., & Kaufman, J. C. (2010). Constraints on creativity: Obvious and not so obvious. In J. C. Kaufman & R. J. Sternberg (Eds.), *The Cambridge handbook of creativity* (pp. 467–482). New York: Cambridge University Press.

Strauss, A., & Corbin, J. (1994). Grounded theory methodology: An overview. In N. K. Denzin, & Y. S. Lincoln (Eds.), *Handbook of qualitative research* (pp. 273–285). Thousand Oaks, CA: SAGE.

Stylianou-Lambert, T. (2010). Re-conceptualizing museum audiences: Power, activity, responsibility. *Visitor Studies*, *13*(2), 130–144. https://doi.org/10.1080/10645578.2010.509693.

Summers, J. (2018). *Creating exhibits that engage: A manual for museums and historical organizations*. Lanham, MD: Rowman & Littlefield Publishers.

Swales, J. M. (1988). Discourse communities, genres and English as an international language. *World Englishes*, *7*(2), 211–220. https://doi.org/10.1111/j.1467-971X.1988.tb00232.x.

Swales, J. M. (1990). *Genre analysis: English in academic and research settings*. Cambridge: Cambridge University Press.

Swales, J. M. (2016). Reflections on the concept of discourse community. *Asp*, *69*, 7–19. https://doi.org/10.4000/asp.4774.

Tate Modern. (2017). *Exhibition guide: The sound of a nation*. London: Tate Modern. www.tate.org.uk/art/sound-of-a-nation.

Tenement Museum. (n.d.). *Reclaiming black spaces*. New York: Tenement Museum. www.tenement.org/reclaiming-black-spaces/.

Terry, G., & Hayfield, N. (2021). *Essentials of thematic analysis*. Washington, DC: American Psychological Association.

The Bowes Museum. (2022). *The period room: Museum, material, experience*. www.thebowesmuseum.org.uk/Collection/Research-Scholarship/The-Period-Room-Museum-Material-Experience.

The Ohio State University. (2022). A *brief history of extension*. OSU Extension: College of Food, Agricultural, and Environmental Sciences. https://extension.osu.edu/about/mission-vision-values/osu-extension-brief-history.

Torrent, S. A., Catapano, T., Gil, A., & Gillium, J. (n.d.). *Ed*. https://elotroalex.github.io/ed/.

Toxey, A. P., & McMillan, P. C. (2009). *Exhibit design and development workbook*. Austin, TX: Texas Historical Commission. www.thc.texas.gov/public/upload/publications/2015%20LR%20Museum%20Services%20Exhibit%20Development%20Workbook%20with%20Introduction.pdf.

Tracy, D. G. (2016). Assessing digital humanities tools: Use of Scalar at a research university. *portal: Libraries and the* Academy, *16*(1), 163–189. https://doi.org/10.1353/pla.2016.0004.

Tracy, D. G., & Hoiem, M. (2017). Teaching digital humanities tools at a distance: A librarian-instructor partnership integrating scalar into a graduate distance course. In D. M. Mueller (Ed.), *At the helm: Leading transformation. The proceedings of the ACRL 2017 conference March 22–25* (pp. 704–713). Chicago, IL: Association of College and Research Libraries. http://hdl.handle.net/2142/95786.

Tzortzi, K. (2014) Movement in museums: Mediating between museum intent and visitor experience. *Museum Management and Curatorship*, *29*(4), 327–348. https://doi.org/10.1080/09647775.2014.939844.

Ulrich, L. T., Gaskell, I., Schechner, S. J., Carter, S. A., & van Gerbig, S. (2015). *Tangible things: Making history through objects*. Oxford: Oxford University Press.

Underwood, T. (2017). A genealogy of distant reading. *Digital Humanities Quarterly*, *11*(2). www.digitalhumanities.org/dhq/vol/11/2/000317/000317.html.

United Nations Educational, Scientific and Cultural Organization (UNESCO). (2020). *Museums around the world in the face of COVID-19*. Paris: Author. https://unesdoc.unesco.org/ark:/48223/pf0000373530.

University of Delaware Museum Studies Program. (n.d.). Digital storytelling. *Sustaining Places*. https://wuffencuckoo.wordpress.com/digital-strategy-and-content/digital-storytelling/.

University of Idaho Library. (n.d.). *CollectionBuilder*. https://collectionbuilder.github.io/.

University of South Carolina University Libraries. (n.d.). *Digital exhibits archive*. https://sc.edu/about/offices_and_divisions/university_libraries/exhibits_events_news/exhibits/digital_exhibits_archive/index.php.

University of Wisconsin-Madison Libraries. (2017, February 7). *Blind date with a book* [Photograph]. https://flickr.com/photos/20245378@N03/40199332782.

Urberg, M. (2020). Digital humanities projects and standards: Let's get this conversation started! *Information Services & Use*, *40*(3), 213–224. http://dx.doi.org/10.3233/ISU-200097.

U.S. Department of Agriculture. (1951). The home demonstration agent. *Agriculture Information Bulletin*, *38*. https://handle.nal.usda.gov/10113/CAT87791369.

Veirum, N. E., & Christensen, M. F. (2011). If it's not on the net it doesn't exist. *Museum Management and Curatorship*, *26*(1), 3–9. https://doi.org/10.1080/09647775.2011.540123.

Vickery, B. (1959). Subject analysis for information retrieval systems. In National Research Council (Ed.), *Proceedings of the international conference on scientific information: Two volumes* (pp. 855–865). Washington, DC: The National Academies Press. https://doi.org/10.17226/10866.

Villanova, A., & eCunha, M. P. (2020). Everyday creativity: A systematic literature review. *The Journal of Creative Behavior*, *55*(3), 673–695. https://doi.org/10.1002/jocb.481.

Visser, J. (2014). Strategies for a heritage revival in the digital age. In L. Egberts & K. Bosma (Eds.), *Companion to European heritage revivals*. New York: Springer.

Visser, J., & Richardson, J. (2013). *Digital engagement framework workbook*. https://web.archive.org/web/20191028115719/http://digitalengagementframework.com/portfolio/digital-engagement-framework-workbook/.

Wachter, C. (2021). Publishing complexity in the digital humanities. *magazén*, *2*(1), 103–118. http://doi.org/10.30687/mag/2724-3923/2021/03/004.

Wachuta, J. (2016, March 25). Metadata on exhibit. *PublicHistory.Media*. https://publichistory.media/2016/03/25/metadata-on-exhibit/.

Walhimer, M. (2021). *Designing museum experiences*. Lanham, MD: Rowman & Littlefield Publishers.

Walsh, D., Hall, M. M., Clough, P., & Foster, J. (2018). Characterising online museum users: A study of the National Museums Liverpool museum website. *International Journal of Digital Libraries*, *21*, 75–87. https://doi.org/10.1007/s00799-018-0248-8.

Weill, S. E. (1999). From being about something to being for somebody: The ongoing transformation of the American museum. *Daedalus*, *128*(3), 229–258. www.jstor.org/stable/20027573.

Weisberg, R. W. (2006). Expertise and reason in creative thinking: Evidence from case studies and the laboratory. In J. C. Kaufman & J. Baer (Eds.), *Creativity and reason in cognitive development* (pp. 7–42). New York: Cambridge University Press.

Weisberg, R. W. (2020). *Re-thinking creativity: Inside-the-box thinking as the basis for innovation*. New York: Cambridge University Press.

Weller, M. (2012, April 29). The virtues of blogging as scholarly activity. *Chronicle of Higher Education*. https://www.chronicle.com/article/the-virtues-of-blogging-as-scholarly-activity/.

Wenger-Trainer, E., & Wenger-Trainer, B. (2015). *Communities of practice a brief introduction*. https://wenger-trayner.com/wp-content/uploads/2015/04/07-Brief-introduction-to-communities-of-practice.pdf.

White, M. D., & Marsh, E. E. (2006). Content analysis: A flexible methodology. *Library Trends*, *55*(1), 22–45. https://doi.org/10.1353/lib.2006.0053.

Wilson, F., & Halle, H. (1993). Mining the museum. *Grand Street*, *44*, 151–172. https://doi.org/10.2307/25007622.

Winn, J. E. (2008). Documenting racism in an agricultural extension film. *Film & History: An Interdisciplinary Journal of Film and Television Studies*, *38*(1), 33–43. http://doi.org/10.1353/flm.0.0023.

Winn, J. E. (2012). *Documenting racism: African Americans in US Department of Agriculture documentaries, 1921–42* (pp. 13–35). New York: Continuum. http://library.oapen.org/handle/20.500.12657/25787.

Wittgenstein, L. (1953). *Philosophical investigations* (G. E. M. Anscombe, Trans.). Oxford: Basil Blackwell.

Ziegelman, J. & Coe, A. (2016, November 24). 'Mock Duck' and other Depression Thanksgiving delights. *New York Times*. https://www.nytimes.com/2016/11/24/opinion/mock-duck-and-other-depression-thanksgiving-delights.html.

Index